States of Marriage

NEW AFRICAN HISTORIES SERIES

SERIES EDITORS: JEAN ALLMAN, ALLEN ISAACMAN, AND DEREK R. PETERSON

Books in this series are published with support from the Ohio University National Resource Center for African Studies.

David William Cohen and E. S. Atieno Odhiambo, *The Risks of Knowledge: Investigations into the Death of the Hon. Minister John Robert Ouko in Kenya, 1990*

Belinda Bozzoli, *Theatres of Struggle and the End of Apartheid*

Gary Kynoch, *We Are Fighting the World: A History of the Marashea Gangs in South Africa, 1947–1999*

Stephanie Newell, *The Forger's Tale: The Search for Odeziaku*

Jacob A. Tropp, *Natures of Colonial Change: Environmental Relations in the Making of the Transkei*

Jan Bender Shetler, *Imagining Serengeti: A History of Landscape Memory in Tanzania from Earliest Times to the Present*

Cheikh Anta Babou, *Fighting the Greater Jihad: Amadu Bamba and the Founding of the Muridiyya in Senegal, 1853–1913*

Marc Epprecht, *Heterosexual Africa? The History of an Idea from the Age of Exploration to the Age of AIDS*

Marissa J. Moorman, *Intonations: A Social History of Music and Nation in Luanda, Angola, from 1945 to Recent Times*

Karen E. Flint, *Healing Traditions: African Medicine, Cultural Exchange, and Competition in South Africa, 1820–1948*

Derek R. Peterson and Giacomo Macola, editors, *Recasting the Past: History Writing and Political Work in Modern Africa*

Moses E. Ochonu, *Colonial Meltdown: Northern Nigeria in the Great Depression*

Emily S. Burrill, Richard L. Roberts, and Elizabeth Thornberry, editors, *Domestic Violence and the Law in Colonial and Postcolonial Africa*

Daniel R. Magaziner, *The Law and the Prophets: Black Consciousness in South Africa, 1968–1977*

Emily Lynn Osborn, *Our New Husbands Are Here: Households, Gender, and Politics in a West African State from the Slave Trade to Colonial Rule*

Robert Trent Vinson, *The Americans Are Coming! Dreams of African American Liberation in Segregationist South Africa*

James R. Brennan, *Taifa: Making Nation and Race in Urban Tanzania*

Benjamin N. Lawrance and Richard L. Roberts, editors, *Trafficking in Slavery's Wake: Law and the Experience of Women and Children*

David M. Gordon, *Invisible Agents: Spirits in a Central African History*

Allen F. Isaacman and Barbara S. Isaacman, *Dams, Displacement, and the Delusion of Development: Cahora Bassa and Its Legacies in Mozambique, 1965–2007*

Stephanie Newell, *The Power to Name: A History of Anonymity in Colonial West Africa*

Gibril R. Cole, *The Krio of West Africa: Islam, Culture, Creolization, and Colonialism in the Nineteenth Century*

Matthew M. Heaton, *Black Skin, White Coats: Nigerian Psychiatrists, Decolonization, and the Globalization of Psychiatry*

Meredith Terretta, *Nation of Outlaws, State of Violence: Nationalism, Grassfields Tradition, and State Building in Cameroon*

Paolo Israel, *In Step with the Times: Mapiko Masquerades of Mozambique*

Michelle R. Moyd, *Violent Intermediaries: African Soldiers, Conquest, and Everyday Colonialism in German East Africa*

Abosede A. George, *Making Modern Girls: A History of Girlhood, Labor, and Social Development in Colonial Lagos*

Alicia C. Decker, *In Idi Amin's Shadow: Women, Gender, and Militarism in Uganda*

Rachel Jean-Baptiste, *Conjugal Rights: Marriage, Sexuality, and Urban Life in Colonial Libreville, Gabon*

Shobana Shankar, *Who Shall Enter Paradise? Christian Origins in Muslim Northern Nigeria, ca. 1890–1975*

Emily S. Burrill, *States of Marriage: Gender, Justice, and Rights in Colonial Mali*

States of Marriage

Gender, Justice, and Rights in Colonial Mali

❧

Emily S. Burrill

OHIO UNIVERSITY PRESS ❧ ATHENS

Ohio University Press, Athens, Ohio 45701
ohioswallow.com
© 2015 by Ohio University Press
All rights reserved

Printed in the United States of America
Ohio University Press books are printed on acid-free paper ∞ ™

25 24 23 22 21 20 19 18 17 16 15   5 4 3 2 1

Library of Congress Cataloging-in-Publication Data

Burrill, Emily, author.
 States of marriage : gender, justice, and rights in colonial Mali / Emily S. Burrill.
   pages cm. — (New African histories)
 Includes bibliographical references and index.
 ISBN 978-0-8214-2144-4 (hc : alk. paper) — ISBN 978-0-8214-2145-1 (pb : alk.
paper) — ISBN 978-0-8214-4514-3 (pdf)
 1. Marriage—Mali—History—20th century. 2. Marriage—Political aspects—
Mali—History—20th century. 3. Marriage law—Mali—History—20th century.
4. Women's rights—Mali—History—20th century. 5. Mali—Social conditions—
20th century. 6. Mali—Colonial influence. I. Title. II. Series: New African
histories series.
 HQ1001.B87 2015
 306.8109662309'04—dc23
                                                        2015007751

*For beloved family, friends, and interlocutors
especially Erik, Rhys, and Judy
and the people of Sikasso, Mali*

Contents

Illustrations

Acknowledgments

THIS BOOK WOULD NOT HAVE BEEN POSSIBLE without the assistance and support of many individuals and organizations. I conducted the initial research for this project with assistance from the Stanford University Department of History, Fulbright Institute of International Education, a Graduate Research Opportunity grant from the School of Humanities and Social Sciences at Stanford University, and the Joseph A. Skinner Fellowship in History from Mount Holyoke College. Bamanankan language study in the United States was funded by Foreign Language and Area Studies fellowships from the United States Department of Education. The Andrew W. Mellon Foundation funded the early writing stages of this book. Follow-up research was made possible by the Center for Global Initiatives and the College of Arts and Sciences at the University of North Carolina at Chapel Hill.

I am indebted to the many women and men of Sikasso and Bamako, Mali, who helped me with the various stages of research on this project. First and foremost, I owe a tremendous debt of gratitude to Oumou Sidibé, historian, teacher, research assistant, translator, collaborator, and steadfast friend. Without Oumou's assistance and companionship in Bamako, Sikasso, and most recently in Chapel Hill, much of the oral research for this book would not have been possible. At this writing, our relationship has spanned continents, years, and major life events. She is integral to this project in many ways. I also thank Ali Ongoïba, Director of the National Archives of Mali, and archivists Alyadjidi (Alia) Almouctar Baby and Timothée Saye. Alia and Timothée are both adept archivists, and I thank them for their professional assistance and friendship throughout my months of research in Mali's national archives. In Senegal, I thank former Director of Archives Saliou M'Baye, whose graciousness and unparalleled stewardship of African history made research in the National Archives of Senegal a joy. Father Ivan Page at the White Fathers Archives in Rome, Italy, was gracious and helpful. I also thank the staff at the Centre des

Archives d'Outre Mer in Aix-en-Provence for their assistance in a late stage of research on this project.

In Sikasso, I am deeply grateful to the Prefect and the Assistant Prefect at the Sikasso Prefecture for their goodwill and for allowing me to photograph countless unclassified archival holdings. Madame Coumba Traoré Coulibaly, Secretary-General of Sikasso *cercle*, and Madame Fatoumata Traoré, administrative assistant to the Prefect, were generous with their time, their resources, and their own personal histories, and I thank them for this. I thank Father Emilio Escudero at the Center for Research on Senufo Culture for his generosity and interest in my project. The Daow family in Sikasso served as a surrogate family, making research much smoother and more enjoyable. Many women and men of the Sikasso district offered their time and personal histories to this project. I thank them all, especially Yaya Dow (now deceased) of Kaboïla, Fatoumata Traoré of Sikasso, Abdoulaye and Mariam Traoré of Sikasso, Fousseyni Traoré and family and Adama Traoré and family of Madubugu. I owe special thanks for companionship and assistance to Melissa Kreek, Ingrid Monson, Jennifer Heibult Sawchuk, Neda Sobhani, and Joan van Wassenhove in Sikasso.

I have had the good fortune of learning from many model scholars. Eugenia (Fi) Herbert provided the first example years ago at Mount Holyoke College, and she continues to be a mentor and an inspiration. Robert Gordon, Walter Hawthorne, Patrick Hutton, Lee McIsaac, Peter Seybolt, Sean Stilwell, and Jue-fei Wang provided guidance and support at a crucial moment in my education and professional development at the University of Vermont. Without them, I would not have pursued a doctoral degree in history at Stanford University. I owe the largest academic and intellectual debt to Richard Roberts. Richard's research serves as an important foundation for my scholarship, and without his groundwork I would not be able to pursue the questions raised in this book. Richard is a healthy model for balancing professional, intellectual, and personal life, and he is a firm but empathetic critic and teacher. I look forward to continuing our conversations on law, gender, and Mali in the years to come. I have also learned a tremendous amount from Estelle Freedman, particularly about the writing process and the political implications of the work we do as scholars. I thank Estelle for her wisdom and perennial clearheadedness. I also thank Sean Hanretta for his advice and keen insights along the way. Thanks to Joel Beinin, David Gutelius, and Liisa Malkki for critical support during my time at Stanford.

I have also had the good fortune to work as an assistant professor at two excellent universities. The University of Kentucky is one of the most collegial places a scholar could imagine. Thank you to the members of the U.K. History Department, who welcomed me and supported me in the very early stages of my career, and thanks to the members of the U.K. Department of Gender and Women's Studies for including me in so much of their intellectual and academic work. Special thanks to Srimati Basu, Kate Black, Kathi Kern, Erin Koch, Sarah Lyon, Lien-Hang Nguyen, and Lucinda Ramberg, for enriching my life in Lexington in so many ways. In Chapel Hill, I warmly thank all of my colleagues in the Department of Women's and Gender Studies at the University of North Carolina, especially Jane Burns, Barbara Harris, Silvia Tomaskova, and Ariana Vigil. Colleagues in the African Studies Center, The Department of African, African-American, and Diaspora Studies, and the Department of History at the University of North Carolina at Chapel Hill have supported me in various essential ways through this process. My students at UNC have enhanced this project in more ways than they can likely imagine, especially the students in "Women and the Law in Africa and the Middle East" and "Gender and Imperialism." I completed much of the final writing of this project while teaching these courses, and I can see the imprint of the classroom in the pages that follow.

This book is enhanced by friends who have read it, talked about it, and provided critical interventions at various stages along the way. For this, I thank Jeremy Berndt, Barbara Cooper, Brandon County, Isaie Dougnon, Gigi Dillon, Abosede George, Rachel Jean-Baptiste, Bruce Hall, Benjamin Lawrance, Christopher Lee, Christian Lentz, Adriane Lentz-Smith, Lisa Lindsay, Emily O'Barr, Ghislaine Lydon, Annie Lyerly, Gregory Mann, Kathryn Mathers, Malissa McLeod, Paula Michaels, Ingrid Monson, Emily Osborn, Brian Peterson, Rachel Petrocelli, Marie Rodet, Sima Rombe-Shulman, Gabe Rosenberg, Brett Shadle, Pamela Scully, Sarah Shields, Liz Thornberry, Brett Whalen, Bruce Whitehouse, and Kari Zimmerman. Dorothy Hodgson provided critical support and substantive feedback at a later stage of my writing process. Lucinda Ramberg's insightful mind and generous friendship improved the quality of this book and my experience writing it. Gillian Berchowitz is a humane and professional editor, for which I am eternally grateful. Thanks to the two outside reviewers of this manuscript for their interventions, and thanks to Jean Allman, Allen Isaacman, and Derek R. Peterson for welcoming and ushering this book into the New African Histories series at Ohio University Press. Don Pirius made the two maps in this book, for which I am grateful. The evidence and arguments set forward in chapter 5 draw from my 2007 article, "Disputing Wife Abuse: Tribunal Narratives of the Corporal Punishment of Wives in Colonial

Sikasso, 1930s," and I thank the journal Cahiers d'Études Africaines for allowing this material to appear in its current book form. On the cover of the book is a photograph by Alexandra Huddleston. The first time that I saw "The Signing of the Marriage Contract," I knew that I wanted it to be the cover of my book. The photograph, taken in Bamako, Mali, in 2004, captures the crowded reality of marriage, as well as its various obligations to family, community, and, of course, the state. I thank Alexandra for permission to use the image here as a window onto my book.

On a personal level, I thank my parents, Kenneth and Susan Burrill, for their constant support of my research in West Africa and their interest in my work. My sisters, Sarah Burrill-Manco and Jessica Burrill, as well as their families, have provided important diversions along the way. Franklin and Eleanor have helped and hindered my writing process in perfect feline form. My extended family, especially Joan and Terry Rose, and Jan and Andy Anderson, championed my writing process in the last critical stages. Erik Anderson is a true partner and makes my life better in every way. I have enjoyed watching his curiosity and interest in Malian history and culture grow over the course of our relationship and the writing of this book. He helped me deliver the goods in so many ways, for which I am endlessly grateful. Our son, Rhys, was born as I completed the writing process. Rhys pushed this project forward as only a child—soon to be born or just born—can do. This book is for both of them.

Judith Dickey was my most constant companion over the past eighteen years. Our common interest in West African history and culture brought us together years ago and served as a consistent theme throughout a long and rich friendship. Judy was my sounding board and my confidante, from study abroad in Dakar when we were college students, to the very last days of the completion of this book. Judy did not live to see this book in its final form, yet she was an essential part of my life throughout its development. I dedicate this book to her memory.

Introduction

States of Marriage in Colonial West Africa

Societal change is not ordered by decree.

—*Amadou Toumani Touré, former president of the
Republic of Mali, 1 September 2009*

IN JULY 2009, THE NATIONAL ASSEMBLY of the Republic of Mali passed a new Personal Status and Family Code. This new code revised the one that was ratified in 1962 following colonial independence from France.[1] The 2009 code significantly reformed the age of consent, provided for equal inheritance rights for both men and women, and offered the possibility of no-fault divorce. It also removed the word "obedience" from a woman's obligations in marriage, and defined marriage as a secular act. Almost immediately, Muslim organizations and politicians protested the new code, arguing that it privileged secularism and reflected the interests of an educated elite whose interests resided with the international community and with Western feminists rather than the people of Mali. The international media described the efforts toward political reform and subsequent backlash as "the women's rights bill and issue."[2] Malian critics of the reform included President Touré's political adversaries and the leaders of Mali's High Islamic Council and the National Union of Muslim Women's Associations. These groups suggested that the new marriage code provided evidence that the democratically elected—and Muslim—president was on the path to forming a political dictatorship that would ignore the interests of the Muslim majority. Protests and demonstrations erupted in the capital and in some Malian cities throughout the summer of 2009.

1

Under public pressure, the president declined to sign the reform and sent the code back to Parliament as a failed bill, stating that "societal change could not be ordered by decree." A revised bill returned to President Touré's desk in December 2011, and included provisions that challenged Mali's commitment to international standards outlined in the Convention on the Elimination of All Forms of Discrimination Against Women (CEDAW) and the Protocol to the African Charter on Human and People's Rights on the Rights of Women in Africa. The Malian Marriage and Personal Status Code of 2011 was one of the last pieces of legislation signed by President Touré before he was overthrown in a coup d'état in March 2012.

These twenty-first-century debates over family authority, marriage, politics, and legal jurisdiction are not new in Mali. Recent conflicts over marriage law reform in Mali are a reminder of twentieth-century colonial-era debates about marriage and its meanings in society and politics. This is not to argue for a timeless quality to the meanings of marriage in Mali, but rather to highlight the enduring centrality of marriage to social and political struggles. Marriage is tied to localized interpretations of authority and access to wealth in goods and wealth in people. Under ideal conditions, institutions such as marriage and the social expectations, gendered obligations, and privileges therein operate according to shared understandings of value and meaning. In practice, however, meanings and expectations of marriage are contested. Grievances and transformations in the domains of marriage are evidence of larger societal and political shifts, and are therefore fertile ground for historical and sociocultural inquiry.

States of Marriage is based on the premise that throughout the colonial period, the institution of marriage played a central role in how empires defined their colonial subjects as gendered persons with particular rights and privileges. It is a modern history of ideological debates, as well as legal and sociopolitical practices. Marriage binds individuals to each other, just as it binds married persons to larger social, religious, and political communities. Marriage serves to create order based on conjugality and gender within households, effectively shaping the obligations, privileges, and claims that women and men can expect of each other before a governing body. Recently, a number of works in various fields of history have taken up the issue of marriage, tracing political debates over the myriad shapes that legal or acceptable marriage might take. Who is entitled (or expected) to participate in marriage? How does marriage shape communities? Nancy Cott's scholarship, for example, shows us how marriage in the United States has been a public institution based on Christian ethics since the founding of the republic, and is thus regarded as a pillar of the state. Legal and institutional definitions of marriage, according to Christian tradition and English common law, inform public sphere definitions and expectations of gender through US history. Cott also tells us that access to state-recognized marriage has been closely aligned with shifts in civil and human rights: the struggle of slaves to have their marriages recognized by the state, the fight for interracial marriage rights, and the current battle for gay rights to marry in the United States are in lockstep, historically, with other civil rights struggles by these minority groups.[3] Suzanne Desan reveals the ways in which women upended unequal relationships in property rights and forged marriages and families in a way that reflected libertarian values and revolutionary ideals in revolutionary France before the Napoleonic Code of 1804.[4] Rochona Majumdar's work shows how arranged marriages in nineteenth- and twentieth-century Bengal are essentially modern, not because they were contracted between individuals who signaled consent, but rather because of the ways in which the marriages were tied to other modern practices of economy, value-based exchange, and cultural commodification.[I cite these seemingly disparate works on marriage in the United States, revolutionary France, and modern Bengal because they all understand marriage to be a powerful element of state-making and gender-making projects at moments of significant political transformation: civil war and civil rights, revolution, and modern decolonization and independence.]

[Similarly, *States of Marriage* argues that the institution of marriage itself functions as a political force. This book shows how the contours of marriage reform, codification, and debate in the Republic of Mali, known in the colonial period as the French Sudan, can be traced through transformations in the colonial court system, local African engagements with state-making processes, and what rights policy workers call "gender justice." Gender justice refers to gender-based notions and definitions of justice, legal rights and privileges, typically as they are defined by governing and administrative bodies as well as sociopolitical and religious communities.[6] Increasingly, scholars employ the term gender justice critically and analytically to interrogate the social ramifications and historical contexts of gender-based authority and relationships.[7] Justice is a powerful term used to indicate notions of moral or ethical righteousness, upheld by natural or juridical law, or social values and expectations. In this book, I use gender justice to refer to the efforts of social groups, individuals or institutions at defining gendered privilege, rights, and obligations in law and society.[8] However, these efforts were contested and up for debate.

Throughout the book, I ask the following questions: How did state actors marshal marriage as a tool of colonial state making, and what is its role in the definition of gender-based rights and social privileges? In what ways did the actions and decisions of Malian women and men shape the colonial state's understanding of local marriages and gendered forms of familial and marital obligation? Over the course of the twentieth century, colonial administrators in French Sudan increasingly sought to draw African marriages under the purview of the colonial state and render them "legible" and recognizable, in order to create a codified definition of an African marriage.[9] The codification of and concern over African marriages represented a central component of the civilizing mission of French colonial rule. Over the course of the twentieth century, this codification and definition of African marriages, or the "marriage legibility project," as I call it, became entwined with political and social arguments for gender justice, rights, obligations, and privileges. James Scott uses the concept of legibility to describe centrally managed projects of "high modernism" — his examples are the development of *ujamaa* villages in Tanzania under Julius Nyerere, or the Great Leap Forward in Communist China — which sought to render complex and dynamic behaviors visible and comprehensible to bureaucrats, so that they might be managed for the benefit of state development.[10] The marriage legibility project of French colonial administrators is not as easily recognized as an example of violent high-modernism, when compared to ujamaa and the Great Leap Forward. However, as Alice Conklin has noted, the codification of justice in French West Africa — and I include the marriage legibility project in this — succeeded in creating the illusion that human rights were being upheld.[11] It is in part this illusory quality of legibility that conspires to create space for the exercise of violence on the ground in the name of democratic ideals and human rights within colonial contexts. *States of Marriage* illustrates the ways in which such marriage legibility projects formed part of a larger liberal agenda of employing marriage as a means for defining rights-bearing, modern, and gendered subjects both within colonial contexts and an international and global community. In the earlier periods of French colonial rule, efforts to codify African marriages, bridewealth, and divorce were about making marriages legible, and once a certain kind of legibility was achieved, it enabled other, more forceful interventions to shape and reframe these practices.[12] Framing this process as a "project" captures state actors' deliberate efforts to place African marriage at the center of state making as well as the collaborative, contested, and negotiated quality of such an expansive process.

Gender justice, as it was manifested through African marriage reform and customary law, rewarded different genders and certain aspects of gendered obligation at different times. African men's roles as patriarchal heads, family providers, and payers of bridewealth were at times defended by the colonial legal system, whereas at other times African women's abilities to leave unsatisfactory marriages, choose their own marriage partners, or determine the conditions of marriage were upheld. As French colonial state-sponsored definitions of African marriage became more and more fixed through legal decree and code, the less these definitions of marriage reflected the contours of marriages that were actually forged by African women and men. However, some African women and men continued to engage in state-sanctioned legibility projects in forging marriages — but not necessarily for the reasons that the architects of these projects intended.

States of Marriage operates on three interactive levels. The first level is local, in the town of Sikassoville and the outlying region of Sikasso. Sikassoville has grown consistently over the course of the twentieth century and is presently the second-largest urban center in Mali, after the capital city of Bamako. Sikasso is many things: it was the last bastion of African resistance to French military conquest in the region that is now known as Mali; it is a border region that serves as a trade, travel, and knowledge production center; and it is the heart of Mali's agricultural production, critical to the country's internal vitality and place in the global market. Within this multilayered population center, the provincial-level courts of Sikasso provide a glimpse into disputes and discussions between women and men regarding how they defined mutual gendered obligations to one another in marriage, through their roles as fathers, mothers, husband, wives, sons, and daughters. The local site of inquiry allows us to see how individuals engaged — or did not — with the colonial courts in order to negotiate their marriages, bridewealth transactions, divorces, and disputes surrounding conjugal relationships. Here we also see the power of local and regional chiefs as they acted at times as state interlocutors and at times as strategists driven by their own interests. This local context also allows us to trace the relationship between larger sociopolitical changes and the shape of local marriage practices and disputes.

The second level is the colony of the French Sudan. Colony-level decisions and discussions about marriage policy reveal the vision that colonial administrators had of African marriages within the French Sudan, and the places where this vision did or did not line up with local practice. Figures such as governors and regional commandants operating in the service of the governor operated and made decisions based on concerns for a cohesive colony within French West Africa and the French colonial world more broadly. We see at this level the ways in which state actors often had an eye on local variation and innovation while always considering the larger colony-wide legibility project. The goal of the legibility project was to make governance easier and more streamlined, but it was also an effort to delineate, in a paternalistic sense, practices of African marriage that retained what was deemed "good" about African custom while fostering practices that were perceived to be in line with French civilization.

The third level is transnational, and includes flows between Europe and Africa and a wider Atlantic world and twentieth-century French imperial world. The policies implemented on the ground in places like Sikasso were, in many instances, part of a larger vision of a French Republican civilizing mission. The French civilizing mission as it was exercised throughout French West and Equatorial Africa reflected broader late nineteenth- and early twentieth-century concerns, which at times were connected to expressions of paternalistic humanitarianism and antislavery activism. French colonialism unfolded in a context of Western liberalism and the development of universal notions of freedom and human rights, paradoxically enough.[13] This is not to suggest that colonialism was benign, but quite the opposite. In the years following World War II, the global context of universal rights discourse informed human rights activism and colonial governance in ways that affected marriage and family code formation: such codes increasingly emphasized the rights of the individual over the rights of the family, but in ways that did often did not reflect the values of the women and men whose marriages were ostensibly being defined through such codes.

The topic of marriage opens doors onto historical arenas of complex power struggles and social predicaments. It is the site of the "taken for granted" aspects of the so-called private or domestic sphere, which is often the most conservative and retentive site of culture.[14] As such, marriage appears as an important practice of exchange and as a sociocultural institution in number of African historical and anthropological studies. In all of these contexts, it is clear that marriage was central to understanding the operation of power, value-based exchange, and familial expectations within society and as forms of historical transformation.

Marriage, in many locales, is also about garnering wealth—wealth in people and wealth in material goods. When women and men approached the courts in Sikasso to dispute specific marriage-related practices, they were disputing each other's respective rights to such wealth. Wealth in people is a concept that has gained currency in African studies since the late 1970s.[15] In African studies scholarship, wealth in people was an expression first used to describe the accumulation of slaves as dependents.[16] Scholars found that many powerful men were more interested in garnering wealth in people through slaves than wealth in goods. This was because amassing wealth in people was a long-term investment in labor and the accumulation of clients. A useful term stemming from anthropological studies, it was often used to express Marxist and economic practices of acquiring and maintaining dependents for labor resources, often at high material expense and investment.[17] Wealth in people signifies the conjoined relationship between material accumulation and social value.[18] However, the term is also useful as an expression of social and kin accumulation in the form of political followers, religious disciples, and above all, through marriage.[19] Here I renew the assertion of other Africanist scholars that wealth in people is a useful term for describing the nexus of social, relational accumulation and material, and labor practices, but I emphasize that this type of wealth is gendered at its core. Wealth in people is a particularly useful expression that deserves more attention and analysis with regard to marriage.[20] In Sikasso, wealth in people appeared as a generational and gendered concern manifested in marriage transactions arranged by male elders. Older men attempted to garner wealth in young men and wealth in young women at different historical moments. This was due in part to shifting demands on the labor of young men in the 1920s and 1930s. Young women bore the brunt of the absence of young men and slaves in rural regions of Sikasso as they were called upon to replace male laborers. Their value as laborers increased, and their value as a social commodity also increased as it became more difficult for older men to amass material wealth during the Global Depression and throughout the colonial period. By contrast, certain young men gained new access to material wealth through migrant labor and the new cash economy. Young women, for their part, were aware of the attempts of older men to control their movement between households as young wives, and over time worked to devise strategies to loosen the grip of male elders. In Sikasso, women did this simply by abandoning their conjugal homes, or by forging intimate relationships with men that were not based on formal marriages brokered by older generations.

Jane Guyer, and later, Guyer and Samuel Belinga, have argued that "wealth in people" is an expression grounded in Equatorial Africa and should be exported cautiously; nonetheless, "wealth in people" is a power-ful term that effectively conveys relationships of obligation, vulnerability, and authority in colonial Sikasso.[21] Its original application as a concept related to precolonial systems of exchange and value in persons contin-ues to be relevant in colonial contexts, particularly in modern contexts of acute economic stress. I argue here that wealth in people is a highly gendered and generational kind of accumulation, something that cannot go unnoted. The importance of this wealth endured, and in fact seems to have become increasingly vital and contested. This was because over the course of the colonial period, marriage became one of the only sites through which elder men could amass wealth in people and wealth in goods. Marriage and conjugal relationships were relationships bound by mutual obligations and generational and gendered authority. When women and men approached the courts, they worked to contest or uphold these mutual obligations and forms of authority.

Over the course of the colonial period, elder men worked to consoli-date their control over the flows of wealth through marriage, in terms of the exchange of bridewealth as well as the exchange of women between families. Cases that appeared to be about the abandonment of the con-jugal home, bridewealth disputes, or marriage promises were quite often about younger men attempting to claim wealth in people from elder men in the form of wives. Older men of influence worked to wrest control over marriages by requiring higher, more extensive bridewealth payments and labor. They opted in and out of state-sanctioned avenues when it suited their interests. Male elders increasingly demanded more material wealth or wealth in labor in exchange for younger women.

Bridewealth became a more coveted and contested transaction over the course of the colonial period. This was due to changes in the demands on and distribution of labor, which was often an important part of the marriage contract in Senufo society in the Sikasso region.[22] The changing value in bridewealth was also due to the shifts in the economy, household access to material wealth, and conversion to Islam throughout southern French Sudan.[23] By the late 1930s, the interfamilial exchange in women as brides within Senufo communities began to shift toward bridewealth exchange based on money or cattle. This transformation in exchange prac-tice surrounding marriage affected wealth distribution, the capacities of young men to marry, and young women's strategies surrounding marriage.

State actors, such as colonial administrators, elected officials, magistrates, and lawyers in the colonial period, debated the terms of African marriages and marriage law reform while always invoking the potential impact that these legal categories of practice had on women in the family and society. African women resided at the center of contestations between colonial administrators, judges, African chiefs, and male heads of household over issues pertaining to society and Muslim traditions, as well as definitions of modernity and state-formation. African women and their sociopolitical status, especially after 1930, served as a litmus test for French social reformers and colonial administrators who sought to gauge the success or failure of the civilizing mission of the French Third Republic in West Africa. Marriage and gendered contractual bonds served as the lens through which the status of African women as colonial subjects and potential citizens was measured. At the same time, court testimony and records from 1905 through the 1950s, newspaper reports, and oral testimonies by women themselves provide us with a sense of what African women were fighting for and articulating in their own right by bringing marriage-related cases before the courts. Quite often, these two strands of conversation and debate express different concepts of women's experiences and social status, often in relation to religious identity, women's strategies and capacities for self-sufficiency and community reliance, and women's use of the colonial and postcolonial family court system as a vehicle for change.

GENDER, LAW, AND POWER IN MODERN AFRICAN HISTORY

The study of law and society and legal regimes is a main current within African studies, particularly in the fields of anthropology and history. Historians, taking earlier cues from anthropologists, engaged in concerted ways with the question of law, society, and colonial history in the early 1980s, but it would be at least another decade before the field picked up momentum.[24] The 1991 publication of *Law in Colonial Africa* laid the initial groundwork for the development of a methodology for using court cases and testimony in social history.[25] Since then, historians have turned to the themes of divorce and marriage as windows to social history in colonial Africa, and women and gender categories in particular.[26] Much of this work stems from former British colonial Africa, a context where native courts were considered to be a cornerstone of indirect rule.[27] Increasingly, however, scholars of former French colonial Africa engage with this genre of primary sources, in part because so many French colonial administrators trained as lawyers under the Third Republic, when French colonial rule in Africa was at its height.[28]

This turn to colonial courts as primary historical sources is also driven by historians' desire to show that court cases are rich source materials for the reconstruction of the actions of otherwise voiceless and invisible actors—namely, women, slaves, and former slaves—as far as colonial documents are concerned. This scholarship is largely based in the use of court cases to reveal agency and make sense of a larger social milieu, rather than an effort to engage in a structural analysis of legal regimes.[29] If historians of African women have struggled with sources in our efforts to reconstruct perspectives on the past of African women, court records have become a lens onto this past.[30] Women were litigants in African courts: they went to court to dispute their marriages, to fight for inheritance rights, and to defend their property and rights towards entrepreneurship.[31] Consistently, court cases from the early colonial period show that marriage, divorce, and rights over property were the main concerns of Africans, and often times, marriage and property disputes went hand in hand. Regardless of the reasons why women approached the courts or how many other venues for dispute resolution were available, these court cases are significant because they represented a new alternative to individuals seeking formal, even official, resolutions to the conflicts in their lives. Such scholarship on law and history reveals, in a variety of locales throughout Africa, that gendered power and authority were often at stake in legal battles.

However, some read this work, and its adherent focus on the possibility of legal avenues within colonial contexts, as an argument for the power of rule of law and civil legal order for everyday women and men living under colonial rule.[32] The potentially dangerous underbelly of convincing arguments for the recovery of agency as it was expressed in colonial courts is the erasure of violence meted out by the colonial state or on its behalf in the name of law and order.[33] As well, a focus on dispute potentially leads to knowledge of practice surrounding social rupture or exception, rather than successful extralegal strategies of reconciliation;[34] sources that privilege the world of the court may not shed light on the world outside the court, where most of a life is lived.[35]

States of Marriage takes all of these intellectual arguments seriously. As Gary Wilder writes, "Violence, because [it is] pervasive in colonial societies, poses a challenge to scholars who want not simply to describe it or denounce it."[36] Structural violence can be hard to see, and it is frequently masked by uneven benevolence in the form of paternalism and maternalism.[37] The marriage legibility project contributed to structural violence, and it existed alongside the exercise of physical violence, especially the *code de l'indigénat*, a set of laws establishing Africans as legally inferior to Europeans and subject to physical punishment without trial.[38] The marriage legibility project also shaped and organized testimony regarding gender-based violence within African marriages and determined which types of punishment of wives were acceptable and which were "contrary to French civilization."[39] And yet within structures that do violence we may find mechanisms for generative growth and possibility. Feminist scholars have long understood this as an element of patriarchy, and this is in some ways what Deniz Kandiyoti is arguing in her conceptualization of the "patriarchal bargain," a theoretical framework that I rely on in chapter 4.[40]

As a book centered on actions and arguments, *States of Marriage* posits that colonial courts presented both a paradox and possibility for African litigants. Rather than present an analysis of aggregate data and large-scale social process evidenced through court testimony and legal outcomes,[41] *States of Marriage* outlines a history of marriage—a legal contract, as well as a social practice tied to rights, privileges, and obligations—as an element of modern colonial state making and discussions of gendered rights and obligations in the French empire.[42] The chapters in this book deal with the issue of justice, and discussions on the possibility of delivering justice through courts of law and in spite of courts of law. *States of Marriage* is not a legal history per se, but rather a political and social history that engages with questions about the court, law, and justice as part of a larger history of an institution (marriage) and the ways that it is used by state governments and communities on the ground to manage people and order authority based on gender and generation. Along this vein, *States of Marriage* is not an ethnohistory of practice apart from the state; while I am not attempting to further an argument that the colonial state was all powerful and totally hegemonic, I am mainly interested in marriage as an instrument of colonial state making. I believe that it is in looking at marriage in this way that we can see both the overwhelming strength and violence of the colonial state, as well as its weak spots and limitations.

Although it may be ambitious to say that *States of Marriage* connects the rich historiography on African colonial law to the developing fields of human rights history and histories of humanitarianism, this book does make some suggestive nods in the direction of human rights and humanitarian histories.[43] Throughout the twentieth century, international women's rights reformers and colonial administrators viewed the status of Malian women as colonial subjects through the lens of marriage and gendered contractual bonds. This is evident as early as 1905, with the abolition of slavery and the introduction of colonial courts in French West Africa. The language of the regional colonial administrators and the architects of the colonial legal system in these early years described their understanding of "the failure" of African marriages as tied to the fact that "African marriages were akin to slavery." At this same time, the civilizing mission, or la mission civilisatrice, was taking shape as the French ideology of colonial development and uplift.[44] Although some (most notably Alice Conklin) have written about this civilizing mission and the ways in which it was about expressing French republicanism, there have been few discussions about the connections between the civilizing mission and the formation of women's rights as human rights in the colonies within a culture of developing humanitarianism in the early twentieth century. And although historians of human rights and humanitarianism make the connection between antislavery activism and humanitarianism in the early to mid-nineteenth centuries, Africanist scholars are pressed to remind our colleagues that the slave trade within Africa surged over the long nineteenth century and into the twentieth.[45] Thus humanitarianism and discussions of human rights and natural rights—particularly as they occurred before World War II—on the African continent urge us to take notice of alternative trajectories of rights-talk and action. Marriage and the family, as Pamela Scully reminds us, were often at the center of such discussions.[46]

During the period between 1914 and the late 1920s, the colonial state expressed interest in supporting local patriarchal authority and men's claims against women in marriage-related court cases. However, linkages between African women's status in marriage and slave status were made again in the 1930s during the Great Depression, with the resurgence in human pawning of children and women throughout West Africa. At this time, colonial administrators turned their attention once again to the status of African women, but this time, the role of the print media and the intervention of Christian missionaries, notably Catholic sisters, contributed significantly to the conversation.

Later, with the formation of the Mandel Decree in 1939 and the Jacquinot Decree in 1951, we see African marriages taking center stage in gender justice strategies employed by lawmakers in French West Africa. In 1939 the emphasis was on consent and efforts to "rescue" African women from the allegedly slave-like conditions of marriage. In 1951, the emphasis was on bridewealth standardization and minimization—again, an effort to curb what the French perceived to be practices that promoted "slave-like" conditions in marriage, but something else as well: in 1951 the gender justice of marriage reform was as much about men as it was about women. After World War II, in the wake of returned soldiers who had fought for France and the growing sentiments of nationalism, colonial administrators were under pressure to ameliorate some of the generational constraints on young men who sought to marry. These constraints often manifested as exorbitant bridewealth set by elders. In addition, the international context of 1951 significantly reframed the discussion of rights and African marriages: the 1948 Universal Declaration of Human Rights and its article 16, declaring that "men and women of full age, without any limitation due to race, nationality or religion, have the right to marry and to found a family . . . the family is the natural and fundamental group unit of society and is entitled to protection by society and the State."[47] Thus from 1905 through the 1950s to independence, there were different moments of transformation and waves of movement around African marriages.

LOCATING *STATES OF MARRIAGE* IN SPACE AND TIME: SIKASSO IN THE FRENCH SUDAN AND THE WORLD

Ascending Kuluba, the "big hill" or the "hill of power" on the way to various state ministries, the colonial archives, and the presidential palace in the Malian capital city of Bamako, one cannot help but study the murals covering the walls that line the paved road. The murals depict the conquest of the French Sudan and the rise of nationalism and the independent state of Mali. Among paintings of precolonial West Africa leaders, presidents, and freedom fighters, there is a large painting of Babemba and Tiéba Traoré. Kenedugu, the empire of Tiéba and Babemba Traoré, was centered in Sikasso and was the last bastion of precolonial power in the vast West African interior that became the French Sudan. Many Malians, particularly if they are from Sikasso, tell the tragic yet somehow triumphant story of the conquest of Sikasso and the Traoré dynasty. As the story goes, when it became apparent that the French military had penetrated the great walls surrounding Sikasso and protecting the Kenedugu Empire from invasion, Babemba Traoré, who had become the king of Kenedugu after his older brother's untimely death, shot himself to death. Babemba's refusal to accept French occupation and the fact that Kenedugu was the last African empire to fall to colonial domination in the French Sudan is a central component to the narrative of modern Mali. Sikasso also claims some ownership over the nationalist leader and first president of Mali, Modibo Keita, who worked for years as a schoolteacher in Sikasso and who was initially jailed by the French colonial government over his anticolonial publications in a journal he founded in Sikasso, *L'Oeil de Kénédougou*. Thus Sikasso has a claim on the bookends of colonial rule over the French Sudan and the creation of Mali. And yet there is very little written on the history of Sikasso, in French or English, when compared with other towns and cities in modern Mali.

Indeed, the region that became the colony of French Sudan and later the independent Republic of Mali has long captured the interests of travelers, ethnographers, and historians. In particular, amateurs and experts alike have documented and studied the Niger River and its inland delta more than perhaps any other part of the West African interior. This is for many good reasons. The Niger River is one of the major lifelines of West Africa, with its crescent-shaped path beginning in the Guinea highlands, extending north into the West African interior almost to the Saharan desert frontier, and curving dramatically back south toward the Gulf of Guinea. Archaeological sites, namely those located at Jenne-Jeno, indicate that humans have long settled along the river and its fertile inland delta. The precolonial kingdoms of Ghana, Mali, and Songhay were centered along this river zone, and the major towns and cities along the river and the delta—Segu, Mopti, Jenne, Timbuktu—comprised population centers of intellectual, cultural, religious and economic innovation. Research in the French Sudan and Mali throughout the colonial era and the postcolonial era tends to reflect the centrality of the Niger River and its delta region both to the geography and precolonial history of human development and society in West Africa.[48] These works on the precolonial history of the region significantly shaped the historical lens of scholars who studied the transformations of the colonial era in the French Sudan. Modern historical studies of the French Sudan and independent Mali primarily focus on locations along this vital vein.[49]

However, the towns and population settlements off the banks of the river and away from the fertile delta are also an integral part of the history of the region, the colony, and the country.[50] Market towns and villages along the ecological zone fringes of the forest and the desert edge are integral parts of the regional economy and cultural and intellectual vitality of the area, and are epicenters of innovation. Anthropologists have argued that such "out of the way places" are, in fact, quite modern in their own ways and closely connected to larger regional and global forces.[51]

The Sikasso region is the southernmost region in the country of Mali, as it was in the colony of French Sudan, and thus two of its regional borders are also national borders. Sikassoville is far closer to Bobo Dioulasso in Burkina Faso (formerly Upper Volta) than it is to the capital of Mali, and it "faces" northern Côte d'Ivoire, to paraphrase many colonial administrators and politicians. Every day, villagers from Sikasso region cross the border between Mali and Côte d'Ivoire for day labor, to sell and buy in regional markets that straddle international boundaries, or to visit family members. Over the course of the postcolonial period, Sikasso has served as a temporary home to untold numbers of refugees from northern Côte d'Ivoire and Burkina Faso. Many on both sides of the Malian-Ivorian and Malian-Burkina borders do in fact claim common lineage ties, despite modern articulations of the primacy of national citizenship in regional identity politics.[52] Sikasso has historically been and continues to be an integral part of a regional identity at the nexus of three colonies and three countries. A diverse, busy hub with a rich local market, Sikasso was—and is—clearly an important center for many people. Sikasso is not at the heart of the "Mande world," but it is an integral market town and transit point between the forest zone to the south in Côte d'Ivoire and the desert frontier to the north.[53]

French conquest of Sikasso in 1898, the center of the Kenedugu Empire, was the final act of military defeat and "pacification" in the part of the West African interior known as Western Sudan, and signaled the completion of the French military consolidation of the colony of the French Sudan. By the late nineteenth century, the French project of military conquest had shifted—albeit contentiously—away from military rule toward civilian rule. Colonial administrators in West Africa and the minister of colonies in Paris were mainly concerned with the effective formation of administrative units and a system of law through which to govern the vast African population under French rule. The French Sudan and other colonies within the French West African Federation were broken up into subdivisions and districts, which the central administration believed would lead to more effective colonial rule. At the head of the federation was the governor-general, who resided in Dakar, Senegal. The governor-general maintained a direct line of communication with the minister of colonies in France. Under the governor-general presided the governors of each colony within French West Africa, which in 1895 was composed of Senegal, French Guinea, Ivory Coast, Dahomey, and French Sudan. By 1922 French West Africa also included the colonies of Upper Volta and Mauritania.

The governors of each colony administered a region divided into districts, or *cercles*, which were in turn governed by a commandant or regional officer of the colonial government. The commandant was assisted by a *commandant-adjoint*, or deputy commandant, who governed in the commandant's absence and assisted with tax payments and periodic census taking throughout the region. Cercles often corresponded roughly to precolonial regions and polities; for example, Sikasso cercle included Sikasso and the surrounding villages that had been absorbed into the political and military sphere of Kenedugu. Each cercle included many subdivisions, or cantons. Like cercles, cantons also corresponded to precolonial political organization; in the French Sudan, a canton was also known as a *jamana* or a *kafo* in Bamanankan. A canton included many villages, sometimes hundreds. Canton chiefs governed each canton and were the primary administrative intermediaries between the French colonial cercle administration and the local village chiefs and African communities. The smallest administrative units were villages, which ranged in size from a few hundred inhabitants to thousands. Villages were governed by village chiefs, who typically came from local genealogies of authority. When the French military conquered the Kenedugu Empire, they assumed control over an area ravaged by slavery and regional war. However, they also assumed control over an authoritative center—Sikasso—with an organized military and a bureaucratic system based on the political authority of men from specific lineages. As the French presence in Sikasso shifted from military to civilian rule in the early years of the twentieth century, local administrators were eager to understand the political allegiances of these men of authority. These men were integral to the development of a colonial administrative system that hinged on the taxation and pacification of villages that had suffered under the tyranny of the Kenedugu Empire. However, these men were also essential to the formation of a new corpus of expert knowledge on which the colonial administration would come to rely—customary law.

SOURCES AND METHODS

States of Marriage builds on a growing body of literature in African history that examines the practice and meaning of marriage within histories of law. It also benefits from a large corpus of historical work that relies on legal cases and civil disputes to understand social change during the colonial period throughout Africa.[54] I rely heavily on testimony from previously unexamined civil-level and criminal-level court cases as a means for understanding the power dynamics of the legal process, and as evidence of litigants' articulations of gendered marriage obligations. However, while I rely significantly on legal sources, I assert that dynamics outside the court and colonial political offices determined the local meanings of marriage in the lives of men and women, some of whom became plaintiffs and defendants in the colonial courts.

This book draws significantly from civil court records from Sikasso. Although some of these records are classified in the National Archives of Mali (hereinafter ANM), many of the cases examined here were unclassified and located in the archival holdings of the Sikasso Prefecture. The unclassified court records of Sikasso are composed mainly of civil and commercial cases, though there are also select criminal cases located in a separate registry. Three separate registries containing court records were located in arbitrary locations, and some pages of the registries were destroyed by the elements and insects. Therefore, the cases examined here are not a source of comprehensive data on the Sikasso court, but rather a sample of court cases that are available. However, while these cases were unclassified and inconsistent in terms of years of coverage, they were much richer than the classified court cases in the National Archives of Mali. This is because the unclassified court cases contained detailed court testimony, which is absent from the court records that were sent to the lieutenant-governor's office. Although translators and a court stenographer mediated court testimony, such sources provide insight into how men and women articulated their grievances with one another, a process that I outline in greater depth in chapter 5. I choose to emphasize the quality of the court records rather than the information they might provide as an aggregate data set. *States of Marriage* is the first study to use the unclassified court records from Sikasso and is therefore is a significant contribution to the study of Sikasso and the study of customary law and marriage in Africa. In citing court cases from the National Archives of Mali, I adhered to the protocol established by the director, Mr. Ali Ongoïba, and I protected the privacy of all litigants, regardless of the year in which their cases appeared before the court. In the case of Sikasso district tribunal records, I adhered to the United States Freedom of Information Act and the protocol of the National Archives of Senegal and French West Africa in citing the names of litigants, which apply a standard thirty-year access rule to judicial archives. The court cases that I cite in this book are from fifty years ago or more, and therefore the chance that they involve living persons who could be identified is minimal.

In addition to the classified civil and commercial court records from Sikasso in the National Archives of Mali, this study is based on political, economic, judicial, agricultural, and ethnographic reports on Sikasso that were sent to the governor-general in Bamako over the course of the colonial period. These files are rich sources on everyday life in Sikasso through the eyes of the administration. These records are supplemented by files on marriage and African family life contained at the Centre des Archives d'Outre Mer (CAOM). In addition, select records from the White Fathers Archive in Rome provided information on White Fathers priests' perceptions of the status of women and what they perceived to be the corruption of local chiefs in Sikasso. Finally, written travelogues and ethnographies provide narrative, descriptive information on European travelers' perceptions of the region of Sikasso and the people who inhabited the region at different times in the late nineteenth and early twentieth centuries.

Oral interviews conducted in the Sikasso region provide a rich depth to written sources on colonial perspectives of life in Sikasso. Interviews were conducted in a variety of ways. First, some interviews were conducted in a conventional, one-on-one, question-and-answer format. However, some oral data were collected from group settings, which I have identified as "discussion groups." This second format was useful because it provided an informal, social context within which my research assistant and I would discuss, with a number of people, a sociohistorical topic of interest. Participants in these collective interviews seemed to be more candid, and they questioned one another and interjected in illuminating ways. Discussion groups yielded rich data not only on events from the past, but on the ways in which community members worked together to forge or contest a commonly accepted history. Participants in discussion groups provided different cues for one another, laughed together as they recalled certain histories, disagreed with one another, and learned from one another. Although the conventional one-on-one format was useful for gathering information from elders with detailed and formalized oral narratives of the past (for examples, see interviews with Yaya Dow, Cékoura Berté, Bakary Koné, and Aminata Kouyaté), discussion groups were often more candid and yielded surprising insights into the past. I found that younger people and women of common social status were more comfortable with the collective interview format (with the exception of Aminata Kouyaté, who, as a *griotte* and performer, was very self-assured in interview settings and was comfortable with a narrative form). Collective settings are more natural formats for conversation and discussion, and people tended to be less self-conscious in these types of settings. However, both interview formats were useful in different ways, complemented each other, and provided me with rich information that enhanced the written, historical information from the colonial period in Sikasso.

I found that many women were reticent about speaking of "trouble" in marriage, and as a result, the women we interviewed answered most questions about marital rupture and hardship in short and simplistic ways. I also believe that, generally speaking, younger generations and many women believed that they did not have the authority to talk about history or "the way things really happened." It is possible that such hesitation was a response to my status, as well as my research assistant's status, as relative outsiders—for although my research assistant was a Malian woman, she was not from the Sikasso region. Yet our standing as community outsiders could have also freed women up to say things they would not have normally revealed to individuals connected to them through social and kin bonds.

Some women were taken aback by the topic of my research and the fact that I wanted to talk to them in the first place. Here I believe that there were at least two things at play: a common notion that marriage was not a practice with a history, and the idea that women were not the proper transmitters of *History* (unless they were griottes). In Sikasso, a region with a very well defined historical narrative of political and military ebbs and flows, questions about the transformation over time of an often taken-for-granted cultural practice may have been puzzling. Moreover, in a postcolonial (neocolonial?) context wherein foreign (white and female) development workers often interview villagers in search of data with which to construct quality of life metrics, I was perhaps out of context because of the questions I asked. When I consider the responses that we did receive to questions about marital trouble as well as about happiness, I see that they often revealed prescriptive and proscriptive visions. This is instructive because such information reflects ideal norms, which, as the chapters that follow will show, is illuminating.

CHAPTER OUTLINE

States of Marriage is organized into six chapters, an introduction, and a conclusion. Chapter 1 illustrates how myths and ideal stories of marriage practice in Sikasso region—as well as the breakdown of marriages—help us understand the role that marriage practice plays in maintaining political community stability and ideas of just behavior, which rest on gendered roles. At the same time, we see how the history of settlement and conquest of the Sikasso region contributed to different notions of belonging and identity. Through these histories of settlement we see how notions of difference emerged within and among Sikasso communities.

Chapter 2 begins in 1905, a few brief but tumultuous years after colonial conquest. In this year the French abolished slave status and introduced a new colonial court system for African subjects throughout French West Africa. In these first years of the twentieth century in the southern districts of the French Sudan, colonial administrators often confused marriage and divorce disputes with claims of enslavement because of the transactional practice of bridewealth exchange that underpinned local marriages. Chapter 2 shows that from 1905 to 1912, African women in Sikasso district successfully divorced husbands, broke the bonds of slavery, and made claims against figures of patriarchal authority in the native courts. This period marks what I call an emancipatory period in the colonial court system, a time when gender justice manifested as successful divorce cases brought by African women to the provincial-level colonial courts, in a context where marriage and slavery were at times conflated. The emancipatory period of the court reflects early Third Republic and early civilian rule interests in antislavery rhetoric.

Chapter 3 explores the 1914–29 period, a time during which the marriage legibility project rested on the identification and reification of the African family unit. This coincided with a period of restructuring the colonial court system, which introduced more specific language about ethnic differentiation and called for more evidence to support women's claims for divorce. The African family, as it was framed by colonial officials and legal interlocutors, was patriarchal and rested on the ultimate authority of the father. Paradoxically, this entrenchment of patriarchal authority and administrative emphasis on the stability of African families occurred at a time of increased labor and military conscription, taxation, and other state-building practices that tested family cohesion. During this period, it was young men who turned to the courts seeking gender-based and generational justice. Young men found their interests in marriage were not supported by elder men, the latter of whom sought to extract bridewealth and failed to maintain marriage promises. They also attempted to force their wives to return to the conjugal home, relying on the colonial state's desire to uphold patriarchal authority over the family and marriages.

Chapter 4 continues to explore themes of generational tension around the consolidation of patriarchal authority, but addresses transformations in these local dynamics during the 1930s and 1940s. In the 1930s, West

African societies experienced a resurgence in human pawning (putting up a person as a security against a loan), a historical dynamic that has been examined by a number of Africanist historians. It was in this context that the French colonial administration passed the Mandel Decree, which established consent as a cornerstone of African marriages, as well as different minimum ages of consent for women and men. The Mandel Decree signaled a major shift in the French colonial marriage legibility project: a move from efforts to establish marriage legibility to the enforcement of restrictions and definitions of acceptable practice in African marriage. Chapter 4 also reveals that the 1930s was a period in which we see efforts by patriarchal household heads and chiefs to garner wealth in women and wealth in men—a gendered type of accumulation that brought with it different types of obligations, exchange practices, expectations, and outcomes. Colonial administrators failed to understand the impact of the Global Depression on local interpretations of wealth in women and wealth in men, and the resurgence in human pawning sparked a renewed interest among Catholic missionaries and local administrators to eradicate slave-like practices. At the same time, specific Catholic missionaries sought their own form of gender justice: justice for young African women, whom missionaries perceived to be caught in the trap of forced marriage.

Chapter 5 continues to examine the 1930s, the height of the marriage legibility project, but through the lens of domestic violence. Marital murder and domestic violence cases in Sikasso from the 1930s reveal the efforts of colonial state actors to establish what was "contrary to French civilization" in marriage practices and outlaw such practices. The cases in this chapter tell us something about how Sikasso women and men appeared as court actors to make claims about what was acceptable in marriage and what was unacceptable. These cases help us understand more about how patriarchal authority was upheld within marriages and families, and how it was upheld in the courts. Justice for dead women—and for the colonial state—was perceived as prison time for guilty husbands, but we also see different articulations of what it meant to act "justly"—for husbands, who were called upon to correct and punish their wives, and for wives, who argued that their abusive husbands behaved in unjust ways, breaking the moral economy of the family.

Last, chapter 6 discusses the limits and possibilities of the marriage legibility project as a component of state making in the 1950s to independence. Cases from the *tribunal de premier degré* in Sikasso reveal that men in Sikasso sought to validate their marriages through the colonial tribunals in the 1940s and 1950s, partially as a precautionary act against wives who might leave the conjugal home. In 1951 the French colonial government passed the second major marriage-related decree, the Jacquinot Decree. Whereas the Mandel Decree centered on establishing consent as a cornerstone of marriage, the Jacquinot Decree sought to limit the price of bridewealth payments by future husbands and require the signing of a marriage certificate. If a marriage certificate existed, a husband had a better chance of proving that his wife had abandoned the home without reason, thereby securing his entitlement to bridewealth reimbursement or custody of children. At the same time, the definition of marriage was increasingly limited by state regulations. For their part, elder men worked to limit young women's abilities to leave their conjugal households and forge multiple relationships. Men and women who appeared before the civil tribunal in Sikasso articulated marriage-related grievances against one another that showed their dissatisfaction with increasing intergenerational pressures upon them in marriage. In some cases, women responded by refusing to abide by expectations of conjugal life articulated by male lineage heads, fathers, and husbands. Young men decried the bridewealth payment and labor expectations that were placed on them by male elders. By the 1940s and the 1950s, the state had become increasingly interventionist in the arena of African marriage throughout the French Sudan. Some of the claims that young men and women made in court reflected their desire to break with the older generation in the management of their marriages. It is here where we see the innovations of bricoleurs in their engagement with the marriage legibility project: women and men used the certification process and claims-making language supported by the Mandel and Jacquinot Decrees to mitigate vulnerabilities and ensure material and social support. Although the Mandel Decrees and Jacquinot Decrees increasingly emphasized the power of the individual in a liberalizing colonial state project at the dawn of decolonization, African women and men used the processes put in place by the marriage legibility project to reinforce the importance of social relationships and generational hierarchies that defined marital obligation and practice on the ground.

A NOTE ON ORTHOGRAPHY

It is often a challenge to settle on a consistent spelling of names and places when working with multiple languages. For place-names, I use the English translation for the sake of simplicity (hence, "French Sudan" instead of "French Soudan," and "Kenedugu" instead of "Kenedougou" or "Kénédougou"). In the case of people's names, I have maintained the French spelling as it appears in the record (hence, "Fatoumata" instead of "Fatumata"). Sikasso refers to the region, including villages and the regional center, which I call "Sikassoville" for the sake of clarity. Foreign words are italicized only in their first citation and translated within the text. All translations from French are mine unless otherwise noted in the text or notes. All of the translations of oral interviews in Bamanankan cited in this book are the work of Oumou Sidibé.

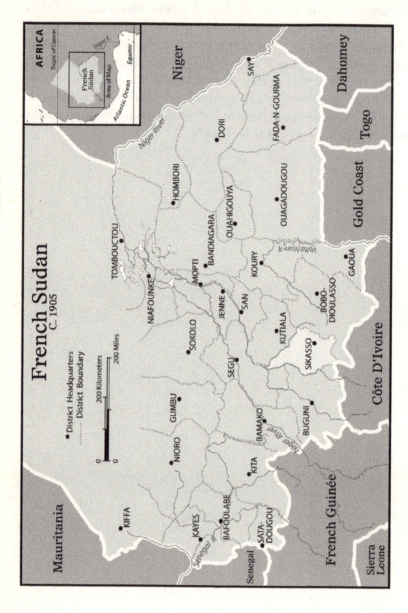

Map 1.1 French Sudan with districts, ca. 1905. Map by Don Pirius

1 ∽ Locating Gendered Knowledge and Authority in Sikasso at the Turn of the Century

THERE IS A TOMB IN THE VILLAGE of Bugula that is said to belong to Momo Traoré, the older sister of Tiéba and Babemba Traoré, warrior kings of Kenedugu. In 1852, Momo, her younger brother, Tiéba, and their mother were sold into slavery after their father, Daoula, was defeated in battle. After three years in slavery, the three were redeemed by their father in 1855, and returned to live in Bugula, the Traoré home in Kenedugu.[1] The experience of enslaved life was galvanizing for the young Momo; it steeled her against the vulnerabilities and political turmoil of life in a conquering and conquered family in late nineteenth-century West Africa. By all accounts, she learned from her experiences in slavery and turned her hardship into her strength. Momo, as a liberated adult, is said to have been a fierce warrior and horsewoman, fearless in battle and respected by all who knew her. Many versions of her story describe Momo as similar to female soldiers from the West African kingdom of Dahomey, and some even claim that she cut off one of her breasts, like a legendary Amazon, so that she could better shoot arrows or fire a rifle.[2] Some stories describe her as having eschewed common marital and maternal expectations associated with her gender, and she is said to have lived her life in a way that was similar to that of her warrior younger brothers.

Stories of Momo are familiar to women and men all over Sikasso district today, from sitting rooms in urban Sikasso homes to courtyards in verdant villages many kilometers off the paved road heading south to Côte d'Ivoire. Yet her history as a woman of note with military authority and expertise is relegated to myth and legend by most professional historians, hidden offstage to the main performances of her brothers Tiéba and Babemba and their *sofas*, or warriors. With the turn of the twentieth century, military and political authority in West Africa became increasingly coded as a masculine enterprise.[3] When the French military formally conquered Kenedugu in 1898, diplomatic measures rested on the establishment of men of authority from specific families who represented particular ethnicities—in Sikasso region, these were namely Senufo and Jula identities. Early French administrators and military leaders perceived these men of authority as imbued with ethnic expertise, knowledgeable in the social and cultural mores of their respective communities and the differences between them. In turn, many of these local men presented themselves as rightful authorities on important matters ranging from land rights to marriage practices. These early colonial processes of rendering political and social practice legible to the new ruling class—French commandants and administrators and their male African interlocutors—established the groundwork for the marriage legibility project that would unfold in the years to come.

A major component of the establishment of gendered authority in the period of conquest and early colonial rule was the delineation of identities into discreet categories of ethnic difference. Whereas local communities identified difference in sophisticated ways, such ideas of difference did not necessarily adhere to a static notion of ethnic category, race, or tribe in the ways that French ethnographers and military leaders sought to find.[4]

To be sure, difference mattered in local communities. However, in Kenedugu, like many other West African places, these differences existed along a variety of axis lines: common ancestor, caste, trade or craft, language, patronym, belief in a common supernatural or invisible power. Some of these markers might change over time in the life of an individual or from generation to generation. Although difference mattered, there was an element of flexibility, or at least contingency, within certain categories of difference between groups or individuals. Differences determined who could marry whom—particularly in the case of caste status. But marriage was also a way of joining households and kin ties and overcoming certain types of difference.

Alongside colonial texts of conquest and travel, there are histories, stories, and myths about late precolonial marital forms in the Sikasso region, which illustrate the ways in which marriage was linked to community cohesion and social order. Such sources allow us to see the ways in which marriages, or at least, ideal marriages, were expressed by embedding oneself in new relationships of obligation and dependence that relied on complementary forms of gendered obligation and knowledge.

Though colonial administrators and lawmakers would seek to disaggregate marriage practices from other social forms and political practices later in the twentieth century, in the mid to late nineteenth century marriage was commonly understood as an element of social and political cohesion. Emily Osborn writes that household making and state making were closely intertwined projects in certain West African locales of the seventeenth and eighteenth centuries, projects that depended on gender norms rooted in complementarity, albeit a hierarchical complementarity.[5] This was certainly the case in Kenedugu and the Sikasso region through the nineteenth century.

STORIES AND MYTHISTORIES OF MARRIAGE AND RECONCILIATION

May it be a serious marriage.

—*Bamanankan marriage benediction*

Family is a well. Once you are in it, you cannot get out.

—*Senufo adage*

Mythic or legendary stories reveal what ideas about the past can do in the service of the present. Stories of the past, particularly when commonly retold or shared within a community, reveal notions about normative expectations and behavior prescriptions.[6] In her work in Hutu refugee communities and camps in Tanzania, Liisa Malkki describes such histories as "mythico-histories." The mythico-histories that appear in Malkki's work are subversive reinterpretations of the past, but they are also stories that "clarify the world according to certain principles."[7] It is the clarifying element of mythico-history that is so powerful: it is not that such imaginings of the past are falsehoods, but rather that they serve explanatory and ordering purposes. Importantly, the Hutu mythico-histories often relied on proverbs as anchors, "devices for persuasion" in the project of creating a world order.[8] Similarly, anglophone historians of Europe have dubbed such stories of the past as "mythistories," as a way of acknowledging the roles that myth and story play in the forging of identities and historical consciousness, a notion that can be traced to Herodotus.[9] Historians of African societies have long recognized the important role that myth plays in the construction of history and historical narrative—the epic of Sunjata, the origin story of the Mali Empire, being an iconic example of the wedding of history and myth—but it took some time within the academy to come to terms with the larger epistemological issue of who could lay claim to an "authentic" voice of the past.[10] In fact, Sunjata serving as the ultimate emblem of mythistory illustrates the problem: myth and story were for so long seen only as viable for political and event-based history, rather than social and cultural histories of value, meaning, belief, and everyday practice. Although we have moved some distance from these debates about political and social history, professional historians still need to turn in deliberate ways toward the various uses of the past in order to construct cultural histories.

Women, particularly elderly women, are often regarded as integral to the teaching of cultural practices and histories of marriage. In African historiography, one salient example of this transmission of mythistory as cultural history is that of Luo *pims*. In East African Luo society, older women who had married into a kin group, women known as *pims*, are regarded as custodians of local history of social practice.[11] The pim is a repository of knowledge about marriage, death, and birth practice within a community, and children, especially girl children, learned about cultural practice from her as they slept in the same quarters with grandmother-pims.[12] The pim's role is important in a patrilocal, patrilineal society: she married into her husband's lineage and moved to his family compound and in so doing, became an insider-outsider who anchored herself to her marital kin group through her mastery of knowledge about kinship history and social mores.

In contrast to pims, Senufo women of Sikasso region married within matrilineal and patrilocal (or occasionally, duolocal, meaning a husband and wife maintained separate households) society. In a matrilineal community the lineage was determined through the married woman's ancestral line, with her brothers and maternal uncles serving as patriarchs. Senufo women with expert knowledge about social custom, particularly marriage practices, were often members of *sandogo*, the Senufo women's secret society. Sandogo is complemented by *poro*, the Senufo men's secret society. Each matrilineal segment might be represented within a village sandogo by one woman, called a *sando*, and in this way, membership is hereditary. A sando's responsibilities and obligations included protecting the sanctity of marriage agreements, interpreting dreams and manifestations of the supernatural, and working to stay in the good graces of the spirit world.[13] Part of this work included learning *tyele*, a form of divination. Although sando women's expertise lay predominantly in the realm of working between the spirit world and the human world, a significant part of her responsibilities included maintaining marital order as an element of social order within her community and passing on knowledge of past marriage practices. This expert knowledge and authority balanced the political power of male chiefly leaders.[14]

Within Mande society throughout West Africa, *jeli* (*jeliw*, plural) or praise-singers, are reserves of historical practice. The jeliw are the keepers of sweeping epics, such as Sunjata, mentioned above, but they are also responsible for songs that offer commentary and advice on common cultural practice. One of the labors of women jeliw, known as *jelimusow*, is performance at weddings. Jeli songs performed at weddings often include benedictions, like the one included in the epigraph above, and prescriptive and proscriptive information about the obligations and demands of marriage.[15] One such song that captures the hardship of marriage for the newlywed woman is the following:

> Stop crying, bride.
> Stop crying and listen to me.
> If your mother-in-law abuses you,
> Just cry, but don't say anything.
> If your sisters or brothers-in-law abuse you,
> Just cry, but don't say anything,
> But leaving your house is not a crime.[16]

Although knowledge about the past is often the domain of cultural practice experts, like the sando and the jelimuso, the popular and everyday production and circulation of notions of past practice informed my understanding of how marriages were maintained throughout the Sikasso region. Many accounts and renderings of marriage in the past that I heard in both Jula and Senufo communities throughout the Sikasso region contained familiar refrains or reference points. More than a few people said something along the lines of "before, we didn't have divorce . . . now, young people do not respect marriage." Another common element was the important role played by a large tree in the village. If a married man and woman were having problems, they would sit under a great tree with village elders, possibly the village chief, and work out the problem. If the problem could not be resolved, they would leave the shade of the tree headed in different directions, signifying the rupture of the marriage. Any tree that cast shade upon those involved in dissolving a marriage would quickly dry out and die.[17] One version of this story even claimed that mentioning divorce or marital rupture under a tree would make the tree die.[18] The role of the tree in these stories is significant; according to local animist cosmologies as well as Sufi Islamic interpretations, trees are important natural sacred sites.[19] Within villages, trees provide shade for gathering, they yield nourishing fruit, they weather storms, and they endure through human generational spans. At the base of a tree, one might offer sacrifices to the ancestors, as the tree served as a ladder to the spirit world. Sacred groves of trees, different from singular trees within the village, are important sites of initiation and sacred society ritual, and are both feared and revered as necessary boundary sites that demarcate inside and outside, the natural and the supernatural.[20] A community benefits from trees and what they offer, in the same way that a community benefits from successful marriages. Likewise, the message is proscriptive in a symbolic way: [if you break a marriage bond, you are responsible for bringing suffering to others and for introducing a destructive element to your community, including the ancestors.]

The tree figured significantly in most stories, but political authority figures also featured prominently. Some stories were of village elders meeting in the courtyard of the village chief's hut to work out a reconciliation with the elder family members of the troubled married couple.[21] Others tell stories about the role that force and submission played in maintaining marriages. Chiefs had the power to send a noncompliant woman back to her marital home, or to inflict physical punishment in the face of a woman's resistance to marriage. One interviewee said that "a woman who wanted to leave her marriage would be beaten [by the chief or on his behalf] until she agreed. . . . It didn't matter how long it took."[22]

In all of the stories and mythistories concerning marriage before the colonial period that I heard in Sikasso region, marriage was idealized and imagined as something where divorce was rare and reconciliation encouraged. Force was not taken lightly, but because of the seriousness of the bond of marriage and the promise in marriage, a woman objecting to her marriage would be beaten into submission. Notions of choice and the agency of the individual, particularly the woman, were not primary factors in determining what constituted an ideal marriage; rather, a sense of duty and obligation and a recognition of one's role, deeply tied to age and gender, were important. The marriage was a constitutive element of larger social forms.

Before entering into marriage, Senufo girls and boys were not expected to be sexually inexperienced. In Senufo society, intimate relationships between girls and slightly older boys or young men were considered acceptable, even encouraged by the girl's family. Typically, such premarital ties ensured the protection of a girl's honor and physical safety, as she was permitted to be physically intimate with her boyfriend but not engage in sexual intercourse. Furthermore, these relationships were not expected to turn into marriages themselves; the boyfriend's duty and moral obligation was to defend a girl's virtue until her marriage to another man. If it was discovered that a Senufo girl was a virgin upon her marriage, her boyfriend was rewarded with gifts from the husband and the respect of the community.[23] In fact, it was ideally the task of the girl's mother to select a boy or to approve her daughter's choice of someone who would be given the responsibility and the right to a premarital relationship with her daughter, explicitly telling him that he was being given her daughter as a friend, not a wife.[24] Ideally, these types of relationships bolstered marriage.

Members within a marriage brought different obligations and responsibilities to the marriage. Bridewealth and marriage prestation, or gifting, undergirded marriage in both Senufo and Jula communities. In Senufo farming communities, a man was expected to provide agricultural labor to his new wife's matrilineal household. This labor would take place over several years, beginning with the initial promise of marriage between a girl and a man, and may even begin before the birth of a girl—that is, a marriage agreement between two kin lines might be brokered before it is evident which individuals from the respective matrilineages will be marrying one another.[25] A Senufo wife was expected to go through her premarital genital excision, bring gifted potteries and cookware into her home, and provide domestic and farming labor to support her household. She was also expected to be sexually available to her husband. If the husband was of a Jula trading family or a blacksmithing or griot family, he would provide bridewealth payment in materials such as cloth, cowries, gold jewelry, or occasionally cattle. The bridewealth payments would not be given to a woman herself, but to her father and mother or to her matrilineage. Although bridewealth will be explored in greater depth in chapter 2, we can understand that these expectations were rooted in the idea that marriage was constituted of parts, the different parts were important to the formation of a whole, and marriage constituted one element of a larger social contract between families, which contributed to the bedrock of a stable society.[26]

The notion of complementarity, or "twoness," appears in many African cosmologies and cultural formations.[27] Twoness often appears as complementarity, but it can also indicate divergence or the possibility of incongruity if not properly managed, respected, or attended to. Twoness frequently appears in binary formations—male/female, woman/man, night/day, life/death—and is essential to something conceived of as a whole. The art historian Anita Glaze identifies twoness as an essential quality of Senufo cosmology, and an essential quality of masquerade and art forms, particularly those that represent gender complementarity. Male power and authority cannot exist without female power and authority, and both have control and mastery of different realms. This is not to say that twoness is antipatriarchal, for the different realms of power and authority are still hierarchically ordered. All things and people embody twoness within them, but larger social relationships are also composed of twoness, ideally setting them up for harmony, symbiosis, and complementarity. Twoness emphasizes complementarity and interdependence within the self and within relationships, including marriages. Recognizing twoness as an integral element of cosmological vision, and as it was reflected in social expectation, highlights the importance of dependence rather than individuality, the latter element emerging as an important component of marriage reform in the mid-twentieth century at the height of French colonial rule. A marriage, for example, is a social form that is ideally defined by twoness, as manifested through a gender binary and complementary roles played by husband and wife. The vast majority of marriages in Senufo and Jula society were polygynous in the precolonial era, and continued to be through the colonial period to the present; thus, the idea of twoness in marriage does not represent the total number of individuals within a man's marriage, but rather, the relationship between a husband and each of his wives. As Glaze aptly notes, "Existential processes such as stress and adjustment, conflict and resolution, characterize social tensions of the real world and potentially threaten the ideal unity and wholeness expressed by the perfect pair."[28] Thus the ideal of twoness is maintained through cultural expression of visual and performance art and divine symbolism, whereas the reality of quotidian stress and conflict is recognized as something that must be dealt with.

Cultural mythistories of Senufo marriage before colonialism suggest that marriage was expected to fulfill a person's obligation to their community. Twoness, or the idea that duality was important for the completion of a whole, illustrates the ways in which notions of sovereign individuality or even consent were not ideas that complied with a sense of self embedded in social expectation or obligation. When conflicts or divergences arose, despite efforts to enforce ideals of mutual yet hierarchical obligation, the ideal goal was to mitigate the conflict and find a way to resolve it.

And yet marital rupture was a reality in both Senufo and Jula society. As the jeli's song above reminds the suffering new bride, it is not a crime to return to your natal home. This advice flies in the face of the expectation that women who return to the natal home will beaten, either by their fathers, uncles, or the village chief, until they return to their husbands — at the very least, the jeli's song complicates this prescription. Here, then, we can see a conflict in norm and expectation of women in marriage, and an acknowledgment that rupture and trouble occur within marriage, perhaps even as a matter of course. Furthermore, among Senufo communities, married women might leave the marital home for reasons of discontent, but this did not necessarily mean that she sought divorce. Théodore André, who lived and worked as a colonial administrator in Sikasso in the early twentieth century, offered this observation in a dissertation on the Senufo in 1913:

> Among the Sénéfo [sic], marriage is, in principle, lasting, but there does exist an absolutely extraordinary custom which is poorly reconciled with the observation that the family, in all other regards, is patriarchal: This customary arrangement allows a woman to leave her husband at any moment to go live with another man, without having to justify this abandonment of the home. The husband, in this case, has no customary power to make her reintegrate the conjugal home. These cases of abandonment usually happen after a correction, or when the husband has had a bad harvest.[29]

Such cases of abandonment were not absolute: rather, a woman might leave the marital home to cohabitate with a man whom fortune favored, but when conditions changed she might return to her husband. The former marriage had not necessarily been dissolved by her departure. The husband in question could regain his wife by paying her family a set amount in cowries and imploring her to return.[30] In cases in which a Senufo wife intended to definitively leave her husband and break the conjugal bond, she would place her cooking pots and the rocks on which they rested outside the door of her hut, and clean all of the ash away from her cooking fire, an unmistakable sign of desire to rupture marriage.[31] In such instances, physical correction by the woman's family in the form of a beating, and reconciliation efforts with the matrilineal head and chiefly authorities were in order. Similarly, if a woman committed adultery, the penalties were very harsh. A woman might be beaten severely by the members of her own household, but according to some sources, the Sando would be authorized to kill her or a member of her family. The man in question would be heavily fined in livestock, cowries, or currency.[32] In these ways, stories, mythistories, and proverbs reinforce notions of marital harmony as underscoring community harmony—while conflicts arose, figures of political and cultural authority were responsible for mediating disputes and working to restore order. Marriage was built on principles of balance and complementarity. Further, marriage unified kin groups into larger networks of belonging, along lines of ethnicity or other common bonds. Just how ethnicity and forms of group belonging became recognizable in the Sikasso region—to people living there, to travelers, and to nineteenth- and twentieth-century conquerors and colonizers—is a matter worth examining.

MAKING ETHNICITY LEGIBLE: CREATING A LEXICON AND ESTABLISHING AUTHORITY

French exploration and military campaigns into Kenedugu in the mid to late nineteenth and early twentieth centuries resulted in the production of a form of travel writing, a body of text that set the ethno-linguistic terminology used by colonial administrators to define the communities over which they ruled and which scholars later inherited. These terminologies were grounded in notions of who constituted insiders and outsiders in the region of Sikasso, their beliefs, the languages they spoke, and their vocations. The lexicon of race and ethnicity was an important part of the colonial project, in part because it was central to concepts of customary law. The vocabulary and categories of knowledge stemming from this literature created distinct categories between Senufo people and Jula, or Bambara people, as well as Fulbe, or Gana, people. These categories, while based on some lived realities of the late nineteenth and early twentieth centuries, solidified ethnic differentiation in the minds of colonial administrators who lived and worked in Sikasso, differences that played out in myriad ways over the long twentieth century. This French desire for ethnic legibility in West Africa did not suddenly emerge in the mid to late nineteenth century, but was part of a longer process of mutual recognition and identification that unfolded between Africans and Europeans in contact with one another over the previous century. What made the French effort to establish ethnic legibility in the West African interior in the 1850s–90s notable was its direct tie to conquest and political rule, rather than earlier relationships of trade and negotiation, which, though marked by historical contingencies and asymmetries of power, were not relationships of conquest and rule under empire. The emergence of colonial ethnic legibility in a larger context of scientific racism, knowledge production, and nationalism—that is, the self-consciousness of European national identity and the recognition of nation elsewhere—contributed to desire to identify and codify discrete ethnic categories, complete with language, body typologies, personality characteristics, and sociocultural practices and beliefs that marked them as recognizable and distinct in a colonial framework — but in ways that presented these categories as precolonial in origin.

French explorers, soldiers, and colonial administrators standardized the lexicon now commonly used by scholars to refer to ethnic identities and languages in southern Mali. René Caillié, Gustave Binger, and Maurice Delafosse were the most influential in the region. René Caillié, the first European explorer to reach Timbuktu and live to recount his travels, passed through Sikasso and present-day southern Mali in roughly 1827.[33] Maurice Delafosse, most often referred to as a hybrid "scholar-administrator" in historical and anthropological literature on West Africa, was a prolific and influential figure in West African ethnography at the turn of the twentieth century. Delafosse's work remains the controversial foundation of virtually all research on ethno-linguistics in former French West Africa.[34] Louis Binger, for his part, explored much of West Africa as a military officer under the grand project of French territorial claims, which resulted in the shaping of colonial boundaries. In particular, Binger was active in what is now Guinea, Burkina Faso, southern Mali, and Côte d'Ivoire. Like many other high-ranking French military men on the ground in Southeast Asia and North and West Africa in the late nineteenth century, Binger transitioned from military officer to governor of Côte d'Ivoire in 1893.[35] These three men, different from one another in many ways, were, to use the words of Mary Louise Pratt, the "monarchs-of-all-they-surveyed," laying expert knowledge claim to and mastery of imperial landscapes.[36] This formation of expertise based on exploration and conquest was the basis of the vocabulary and framing devices used to categorize ethnic difference in West Africa.

Although the terms used by Caillié, Binger, and Delafosse were based on interviews with local people and are therefore accurate in some details, they are imperfect. While passing through southern Mali in the late 1820s, René Caillié wrote of a group of people he described as "Bambara," but who today would call themselves "Senufo."[37] However, even the term "Senufo" is not completely accurate, though men and women today in southern Mali self-identify as Senufo, and it is an acceptable term for scholars of the region. "Senufo," in fact, is a term used to describe a group of people who speak one of two languages, Sienare and Supyire, which are in turn composed of some fourteen dialects. "Senufo" is a Manding/Bamanankan term meaning "Siena speaking," but generally applied to all Sienare and Supyire speakers of the Gur language subfamily residing in northern Côte d'Ivoire, southern Mali, and western Burkina Faso.[38] Thus "Senufo" is one of many terms applied to at least fourteen different dialectic groups located throughout the region of modern-day southern Mali, western Burkina Faso, and northern Côte d'Ivoire.

Maurice Delafosse makes a case that the Senufo were "native to the region" where he encountered Supyire-speaking people in the very early years of the twentieth century.[39] These people whom he described as "Sénoufo" claimed in their oral traditions to be the oldest residents of the region. According to Senufo oral traditions that Delafosse recorded, Supyire-speaking people in Sikasso were elephant hunters who had lived to the northwest of Sikasso in what is today Buguni, but were pushed out of the area by "banmana" people and dispersed into three groups, one settling in the Sikasso region, another further south in Korhogo, and a third in Tengrela, present-day northern Côte d'Ivoire. To the northeast of Sikasso, Delafosse explained, the Senufo subgroup Minianka settled, and despite a significant influx of Mande "banmana-speaking" immigrants to the region, the Minianka were able to retain their distinct identity apart from the newcomers.[40] It is in his description of the Minianka subgroup that Delafosse makes a distinction between the terms "banmana," "Bamâna," and "Bambara," a difference that contributed to confused terminologies of identity that carried through the twentieth century. "Minianka" was in fact a term used by "banmana" neighbors. Delafosse observed that the "Muslims" called the Minianka "Bambara" and that Minianka called themselves "Bamâna."[41]

The conflation of ethno-linguistic terms also reveals an insider-outsider dynamic at play among the groups that served as Delafosse's informants. "Bamana" and the derivations of the word (Bambara, Banmana) are commonly understood as meaning "those who refused the master," or Allah, or those who were not Muslim.[42] "Bamanankan," or "Banmanakan," indicated the language of the pagans, and was often applied to Sienare and Supyire people in the area by Mande Muslims who spoke a dialect often called "Jula," to indicate their affiliation with the Mande trading networks of West Africa.[43] Thus, although in twenty-first-century Mali the term "Bambara" or "Banmanankan" indicates a Mande language or ethnicity that is, in essence, synonymous with "Jula" in northern Côte d'Ivoire, the original meaning of the word was often applied to non-Muslim Supyire- and Minianka-speaking people in the Sikasso region as well as the Sienare people of the Korhogo region of Côte d'Ivoire to the south.

Most ethnographers of the Korhogo region tell us that Senufo people identify themselves as part of matriclans, that they are acephalous, and that they view their ancestors as holding the most politicized authority.[44] By the nineteenth century, the Supyire-speaking Senufo of the Sikasso region had begun to develop self-contained village communities governed by male-elder authorities. Many also built walls around their villages, which served to protect communities from outsiders, but they also made for insular village settlements. This protective action was a response to raiding by Mande speakers to the north and from raids stemming from Kong in the eighteenth century, but it also reflects the decentralized quality of sociopolitical life among the Senufo of the Sikasso region. The result was low-level warfare, but this did not result in the actual demise of villages, nor did it seriously impede economic flows or trade. Rather, the use of protective walls accentuated the decentralization of Senufo villages.[45]

It is not only Senufo and Bambara or Jula identities that are complex in the region. The Fulfulde pastoralists who in the mid- to late nineteenth century settled in Kurala and the area known as Ganadugu are often described as the "Gana." Gustave Binger observed in 1889 that the inhabitants of Ganadugu and Kurala

> are Fula people mixed with the Bambara and Senufo with whom they had had contact. . . . Their houses are constructed like the Bambara, they wear their hair like the Senufo, and their tattoos are a mix of Bambara and Senufo. They are very hard-working . . . but the situation between Segu, Samori, and Tiéba will most likely bring about their ruin.[46]

Indeed, the "situation between Segu, Samori, and Tiéba" significantly affected the people of Ganadugu, as they were situated on the western frontier of Kenedugu, which became a contentious borderland between Tiéba Traoré and Samori Touré in the late 1880s and 1890s. But before we arrive at the "situation between Segu, Samori, and Tiéba," we must explore local histories of settlement that preceded the Kenedugu Empire and its conquerors.

THOSE WHO CREATED IT AND THOSE WHO FOUND IT: ORIGIN AND SETTLEMENT HISTORIES OF DIFFERENCE AND BELONGING

Sikasso has long been a place of diverse settlement and the mixing of communities. Some time before the founding of Kenedugu in Sikasso in the 1870s, the town of Sikasso was established in the region as an important Senufo trading town. Trading in the town and region of Sikasso was based on landlord-client relationships, which ensured an enduring system of accountability, trust, and reciprocity between itinerant merchants coming from the south and their farming hosts in Sikasso.[47] Over the course of many centuries, trading between traveling merchants and farmers developed networks between the town and outlying villages of Sikasso.

The historian Yves Person posits that Senufo people were already settled in the region of Sikasso when "merchants and Muslims" began to arrive in the seventeenth century.[48] In fact, merchant routes and trading relationships in the Sikasso region predated the seventeenth century by some time. Sikasso and the decentralized villages of Wasulu to the west relied on small-scale trading networks with traders from the south at different times over the course of the Mali and Songhay Empires, which spanned the thirteenth to the late sixteenth centuries.[49]

The "merchants and Muslims" of the seventeenth century to whom Person referred were Jula, or Bamanankan-speaking merchants who participated in the kola trade northward into the Sahel region and along the desert frontier.[50] The majority of these merchants were Muslim and belonged to associations based on their religious identity that connected them to larger trading networks throughout West and North Africa. However, not all of the trading relationships between centers such as Korhogo, in present-day northern Côte d'Ivoire, and their customers in market towns such as Sikasso were formalized in these ways. The trading routes in this part of West Africa also existed on a small scale, drawing on direct connections with purchasers and landlords in Sikasso.[51] Traders heading north stayed with local autochthonous landlords, who were often farmers tied to local agricultural production. Oral histories from the region cited in colonial exploration and travel literature describe a long history of Senufo settlement in the large town of Sikasso and in decentralized villages surrounding the town of Sikasso.[52] Villages often formed loose federations for protection from outside invasion and redistribution of agricultural goods in times of uneven harvest or drought.[53]

The kola trade for Jula merchants in northern Côte d'Ivoire and the Sikasso region slowed in the early eighteenth century because of restrictions from the Baule people in northern Côte d'Ivoire, who would not allow any Jula traders to enter the forest region through their well-traveled corridor for kola acquisition and trading purposes.[54] However, this does not seem to have hampered trading relationships in Sikasso. Senufo farmers produced cotton, which they would trade in raw form to Jula traders for kola and salt. Jula women and female slaves would spin the cotton and weave it into strips, which would then be traded back to Senufo clients.[55] These commercial networks between merchants originating in northern Côte d'Ivoire and local farmers and landlords in the region of Sikasso were also the basis for social relationships. Although many villages in the surrounding country-side of Sikasso were predominantly settled by Senufo farming and hunting communities, villages along the itinerant trade routes also had long histo-ries of hosting Jula traders and merchants.

These networks and complementary relationships between farming land-lords and itinerant merchants existed before the founding of Kenedugu; in fact, the success of the Traoré clan empire in the nineteenth century was built on the convergence of warrior, merchant, slave, and farming identi-ties. Oral histories from the village of M'Pegnesso in the Sikasso region help construct a case study to illustrate the relationship between Senufo farmers and Jula traders before Kenedugu.

M'Pegnesso is the official state name of the village historically and lo-cally known as M'Pegnegue, its Senufo name. Village elders trace twelve chieftaincies in the village, placing the village origins well before the ar-rival of the French in the late nineteenth century, and before the ascension of Tiéba and Babemba Traoré and the Kenedugu Empire in the 1870s. According to oral traditions of the founding of M'Pegnegue, the man who settled the village went by the name of Kapitié and came from Faama, a larger Senufo village northwest of present-day Sikassoville. These oral accounts allege that Kapitié was kidnapped after settling in M'Pegnegue, likely during one of the regional wars that plagued decentralized Senufo villages through the eighteenth and nineteenth centuries. At some time during his enslavement, Kapitié was brought to a Jula village. After some time in the Jula village he was either liberated or escaped, and he returned to M'Pegnegue and could speak Jula.

The twisted path of the oral histories from M'Pegnegue tells a tale of en-slavement, adaptation, and transformation. Regardless of whether the story of Kapitié is true and verifiable, that slavery and contact with Jula traders factor into the origin story of the village is revealing. The story highlights themes that are important to the regional history: enslavement, travel, return, and contact with Jula-speaking traders and slavers. M'Pegnegue/M'Pegnesso elders recounted histories of enslavement during the expan-sion of the Kenedugu Empire, the sieges of Samori Touré, and the eventual conquest of Sikasso by the French in 1898. As one older man stated, "We learned Bambara from the Sarakole [Mande people] who took our ances-tors."[56] Many villagers in M'Pegnegue were Muslim, and although con-version to Islam in the southern region of Mali occurred on a large scale only after World War II, M'Pegnegue claimed a connection to Islam that villagers said dated from around the time of French military expansion in the late nineteenth century. The return years later of men and women who had been enslaved during the regional wars of the late nineteenth century seems to have marked a process of conversion to Islam.[57]

In fact, Jula traders from Côte d'Ivoire relied on slave labor for their kola trading caravans and for weaving the cotton cloth that was a popular trade item in the region of Sikasso. The very trade items that lay at the basis of the relationship between Jula traders and Senufo farmers were produced by slave labor. In the eighteenth century, many of these slaves were Senufo or came from Wasulu to the west, and were enslaved through raids stemming from the Kong Empire in the seventeenth and eighteenth centuries. Some also came from areas such as Kabadougou in northwestern Côte d'Ivoire.[58] While enslavement and displacement in southern Mali surged in the nineteenth century, enslavement was also a security issue for decentralized societies in southern Mali over the course of the eighteenth century.[59]

However, M'Pegnegue's/M'Pegnesso's relationship with Jula speakers and Islam stemmed from relationships outside of slavery as well. When asked the question, "Is M'Pegnesso a Jula village or a Senufo village?" one response provided insight into the complex past relationships between Senufo and Jula identity in M'Pegnesso:

> M'Pegnesso is a Senufo place . . . but here it's as if we have two fathers, a Senufo father and a Jula father. The Senufo created the village, but the one who came and "found" it was a Jula who spoke Bambara. . . . He installed himself next to the Senufo, and while the Jula conducted commerce, the Senufo farmed. So these two things, the slavery of our ancestor and then the second one—in fact it's the Bambara that was stronger than the Senufo.[60]

As this question was posed in a large discussion group setting, another older man of M'Pegnesso injected his own opinion on the question and the issue of language and ethnicity in Mali, past and present:

> What the others are saying is true. There was intermarriage (between Jula and Senufo). But if you hear people talking about the "Jula" language, they are talking about Bambara today. There are some who are confused. . . . That which we call "Bamanankan" is the Senufo language. But today, everyone thinks that those who speak Jula are all Bambara, and it's become the national language of Mali.[61]

This exchange illustrates the multifaceted history of linguistic and ethnic identity in many of the villages of Sikasso region. Although today M'Pegnesso is considered a "Senufo place," it clearly has a history infused with Jula language and settlement. Most of the inhabitants of M'Pegnesso spoke Senufo at home, but informants indicated that almost all of the men, and many of the women, spoke Jula as well.[62] The practice of intermarriage reinforces the understanding that marriage and cohabitation between Senufo women and Jula traders reinforced small-scale and long-distance trading networks and eased the pathways and connections between landlord and stranger.[63] In nineteenth-century Jula communities located in present-day northern Côte d'Ivoire and southern Mali, intergroup marriage was seen as a safeguard against caravan plundering.[64] In some Jula communities, intermarriage within clan wards (*kabilaw*, *kabila* sing.) who shared the same patronym was promoted. Such marriage practices created multiple strands of relatedness between any two individuals.[65] Robert Launay tells us that in Korhogo, Côte d'Ivoire, marriage negotiations were never directly carried out by a groom's kabila, but rather a negotiator from outside the kabila, known as a *furusirima*. The furusirima came from the same conglomerate of kabilaw, known as a *makafo*, and kabilaw from the same makafo would help each other with the brokering of marriages.[66]

Other regional origin stories of pre-Kenedugu times weave themes of migration, settlement, marriage, and political ascendancy. Bakary Koné, an elder of Sikassoville, recounted the following story of pre-Kenedugu settlement in the Sikasso region, which he had learned from his own father. According to Koné's oral history, the first Traoré *faama* (king) of Sikasso was a man named Tenemakan. When Tenemakan and his two brothers were young men, they left the Kong Empire, in present-day northern Côte d'Ivoire, on the advice of a *marabout* (a Muslim religious leader) who instructed them to leave Kong in order to find political success. This was essential, in part, because the ruling dynasty of Kong was the Wattara family, adversaries of the Traorés. According to the oral histories, the way in which the Traoré brothers expanded their power was by settling in villages and marrying local women. However, one element of the history of pre-Kenedugu settlement is particularly notable. Koné recounted the following:

Tenemakan, who was the youngest, left his brothers in an effort to continue their expansion north. He found himself in a village called Sofarasso, about 45 kilometers from where we are now [Sikassoville].

Figure 1.1 Bakary Koné, Sikassoville. Photograph by author

They told him there that there existed a village called Kofilaben where the village chief was a woman. Tenemakan was very happy to hear this, but would not tell anyone why. He took his leave from Sofarasso in the direction of Kofilaben. He arrived in Kofilaben and found that it was true: the chief of the village was a woman named Naabo Koné. Naabo's father had been the much-loved chief, but his daughter became the chief after he died.

The tradition goes on to recount that all the villagers were working in their fiends when Tenemakan arrived, with only Naabo to be found within the village. As a good host, Naabo fed Tenemakan and offered him drink. Tenemakan asked for the chief, to which Naabo responded, "You are looking at the chief." Tenemakan asked again, and Naabo responded, "You think that a woman cannot be chief. Why else would you continue to ask for the chief when the chief stands before you, healthy and well?" At this point, Tenemakan was certain that Naabo was telling the truth and that she truly was the chief. He explained that he was a hunter and that he wanted to remain in Kofilaben to hunt. However, he felt that he could not be hosted in a village with a woman for a chief. To this, Naabo responded that the village needed hunters, as they were a village of farmers. Naabo offered to step down from the chieftaincy and offer the position to Tenemakan, as she felt that this was a sacrifice that the village needed. However, in order for this political shift to work, Tenemakan had to agree to marry the daughter of Naabo, a girl named Momo, and he had to build Naabo her own residence in the old *fonio*, or grain, field. Tenemakan complied, and became a very powerful and successful hunter. Momo, the daughter of Naabo, was the namesake of Momo Traoré, whom we met at the beginning of the chapter. The location of Naabo's residence in the old fonio field became the center of the present-day village of Finkolo.[67] This oral tradition recounts a trajectory unrecorded in written narratives of Kenedugu's past: a history of migration and political expansion out from Kong, which was entirely contingent on hosting and marriage with local women. But even more than this, Koné's oral tradition tells a story of the possibility of women's political leadership—this leadership, however, was contingent on men of authority and could be relinquished in the service of great men. The marriage between Tenemakan and the first Momo highlights a number of themes: intermarriage between Senufo and Mande communities, the important symbiosis between hunters and farmers, and the centrality of households to political authority.[68]

Other oral traditions recount the departure of the Traorés from Kong in slightly different ways, but do not contradict the tradition told by Bakary Koné. According to these narratives, by the sixteenth century, the Traorés had established themselves throughout what is today southern Mali, northern Côte d'Ivoire, and western Burkina Faso, primarily as traders. The Traorés experienced a significant generational split when Kancina Traoré abandoned trading in order to become a hunter and warrior.[69] This was how the Traorés became known as both traders and warriors, long before the time of Tiéba and Ba Bemba Traoré in Sikasso in the mid-nineteenth century.[70] The Traorés, as trader-warriors, settled among the Senufo state-less societies, and according to oral traditions and French travel accounts, they passed on their patriclan name.[71]

In Sikasso today, the generally accepted narrative of Traoré settlement in Sikasso and the consolidation of Kenedugu recounts that Daoula Traoré (Momo and Tiéba's father) and the Wattara clan of Kong engaged in pro-tracted warfare in the 1840s.[72] As Kong began to disintegrate, the Wattaras and other powerful merchant-warriors left the area and headed north to-ward Sikasso, resulting in regional political friction and reconfiguration. This culminated in a battle between Daoula Traoré and the Wattaras, with Senufo farmers caught in the middle. Farming villages offered allegiances to the party that seemed most likely to protect their village settlements. The majority of Senufo villages sided with the Wattaras, as did Bobo-speaking villages to the immediate north.[73] These militarized struggles decimated any Senufo villages between them that showed shifting allegiances, with the Wattaras eventually being pushed back to the east and toward Bobo Dioulasso in present-day Burkina Faso. Local written and oral sources de-scribe the period of the 1830s through the early 1850s in Kenedugu as a fraught time marked by protracted armed struggle and political upheaval between the Traorés and the Wattaras. In 1852, Daoula Traoré's children, wives, and most of his belongings were captured by the Wattaras and their warriors. A few years later, Daoula recovered some of his wealth and was able to buy back Momo, Tiéba, and their mother.[74]

In approximately 1855, Daoula Traoré established military and politi-cal authority around the settlements of Bugula, Niaradugu, and Fama, and claimed Kenedugu for the Traorés.[75] Under Daoula, Kenedugu grew, with Bugula as its center. When Daoula died in 1860, the Traoré dynasty had built up a solid military and had developed a reliable tribute and agricul-tural system based on the surrounding Senufo villages. Following Daoula's death, the Traoré successors struggled to reestablish authority, until Tiéba Traoré, Daoula's son, ascended to the head of the Kenedugu empire. Tiéba expanded the Kenedugu empire through military conquest of outlying vil-lages and demanded tribute in return for protection. However, tribute pay-ment was not equal among villages. Certain villages were required to pay very high tribute, in the form of agricultural goods and food grains, as well as slaves and women. Other villages that had shown their loyalty to Kenedugu and which had been incorporated over a longer period of time had lighter obligations.[76] Villages absorbed into Kenedugu through military conquest and the exaction of agricultural tribute were transformed into allies, headed by locally appointed chiefs and warriors.[77] Thus, by the apex of Kenedugu

Figure 1.2 The wall, or *tata*, of Sikasso. Photograph by author

in the mid to late nineteenth century, Senufo slave warriors and local male authorities had joined the administrative body of Kenedugu as chiefs and military leaders. These Senufo slaves were absorbed into the warrior class of Kenedugu or traded outward for other regional commodities.[78] Expansion through war and enslavement helped Kenedugu develop and become a formidable political entity in West Africa.[79]

Under Tiéba Traoré, Kenedugu reached its height as a West African empire. Tiéba continued to build a military in Kenedugu, and moved the capital to Sikasso, where he commissioned the construction of a *tata*, or fortress wall, around the city, replicating the walled villages of the countryside surrounding Sikasso. Sikasso was a natural center for Kenedugu because it is located in an area that is naturally protected by different hillocks and rivers and can be attacked only at a diagonal. It was this latter reason that had the greater impact on Kenedugu and its position vis-à-vis other West African leaders such as Samori Touré and its influence in the eyes of the French military, and later the nascent French colonial administration in the Sudan. Tiéba created a commercial empire in Kenedugu, one that was built on a hierarchy that rewarded youth, that depended on the work of Jula trading and regional surveillance networks, and the productivity of

Figure 1.3 The placemarker for Tiéba's grave, Sikassoville. Photograph by author

Senufo agriculturalists. Kenedugu was a fortified, militarized, commercial center that built its success on cultural and religious moderation.[80]

Historians and the people of Sikasso disagree over whether Tiéba and his brother and successor Babemba Traoré were Jula or Senufo.[81] These are not mutually exclusive identities, and the debate reveals more about the formation of binaries in the colonial period and the colonial record than the historical realities of their time. Mamadou Traoré, a descendant of Babemba, explained, "The Traorés of Sikasso are Mande, but we married Senufo, Gana, and other types of women."[82] In this explanation, Traoré explains that his forefathers became locally relevant and entrenched through intermarriage. Such intermarriage practices recognized difference—indeed, intermarriage was built on difference—but difference was malleable and useful in the service of social formation.

ESTABLISHING LOCAL MEN OF AUTHORITY IN SIKASSO AFTER FRENCH CONQUEST

The making of ethnic pathways and categories in the nineteenth century provided the foundation for the marriage legibility project in the twentieth century. Through this process of forging ethnic legibility, four important local leaders emerged from the fall of Kenedugu to become canton chiefs in the colonial administrative district of Sikasso. These men represented local figures of authority that the administration would come to rely on for local governance and in the formation of categories of customary law and knowledge in colonial Sikasso.[83]

While Babemba perished in the fall of Sikasso, many of his closest advisers and lieutenants survived and played important roles in the establishment of French rule in Sikasso. Some oral accounts of Kenedugu's fall attribute the French military's success to treason stemming from those closest to Babemba.[84] Many of these elite soldiers from Tiéba and Babemba's inner circle were rewarded with leadership roles in the new government of Sikasso. The men of authority who rose out of the ranks of Kenedugu represented a precolonial establishment of authentic African leaders, in the eyes of the French military leaders such as Captain Morisson, Commander Quiquandon, and Colonel Audéoud, all of whom left written accounts of their military campaigns to establish French presence in West Africa. Early commanders in Sikasso were hesitant to turn to Babemba's and Tiéba's immediate successors, yet they wanted to rely on men who had some sort of authoritative claim on the precolonial past of Sikasso. French commandants on the ground in Sikasso viewed these men in terms of Senufo and Jula identity categories, which set the tone for local rule.

Oral accounts of the fall of Kenedugu, as well as Kélétigi Berté's biography, recount the divisions that occurred immediately following French conquest. Tiéba's sons, Fo and Amadou, fled and joined Samori's army. Upon French conquest of Samori later in 1898, Fo and Amadou, also known as Madou, were captured and sent into exile in Timbuktu. They were allowed to return to Sikasso in 1906.[85] Samba Tiémoko Traoré, Bembanitieni Traoré, Kélétigi Berté, and Kolondugu Sanogo remained. These four men were important war chiefs under Tiéba and Babemba, and Samba Tiémoko Traoré and Bembanitieni Traoré were the paternal nephews of the Traoré kings. Kélétigi Berté and Kolondugu Sanogo were leaders who rose through the ranks from slave soldier backgrounds to powerful positions of authority in Kenedugu.

Kélétigi Berté was one the most influential of these local men of authority. Berté came of age as a soldier in Tiéba's army, fighting alongside other young men of his age-grade who had been conscripted into Kenedugu's army. According to Berté's biography, written by his son Oumar, Berté's identity was shaped by his relationships with men of his age and elders in Kenedugu. His coming-of-age was shaped not by notions of ethnic distinction or ethnic identity, but by his gendered role as a warrior engaged in local warfare.[86] According to his biography, Berté was a member of a multilingual, multiethnic group of men who perceived insider-outsider identities along lines of gender, generation, and geography.[87] Berté, and warriors like him, were more concerned with solidifying their allegiances to Tiéba and pacifying newly incorporated villages than with distinctions between Jula and Senufo. These notions of insider and outsider shifted with French conquest.

By the time Kenedugu fell in 1898, a precedent for French administration of its West African territories had been established, first in Senegal and later through the conquest of West African centers such as Segu. Colonel Louis Archinard, the supreme military commander of the French military in the region of Western Sudan from 1888 to 1893, established the groundwork for French rule in the colony of French Sudan by establishing regional district officers in the capacity of commandants des cercles. As interim lieutenant governor of the French Sudan colony, Audéoud named Captain Coiffé, one of the primary military leaders in the siege on Kenedugu, the first commandant of the administrative cercle, or district, of Sikasso. Within each district, several cantons were composed of federations of villages, each one headed by a canton chief who reported to the commandant. In this sense, the canton chiefs were powerful intermediaries between local village chiefs and the colonial authorities. Under Coiffé and his successor the following year, Sagols, canton divisions were quickly established.

After military conquest, it was imperative to "pacify" the population and establish French authority. This establishment of French authority was based first on conquest and, second, on the founding of the *mission civilisatrice*, or the civilizing mission. The civilizing mission was an imperial doctrine based on the idea that rule of native populations should be executed based on the principle of French superiority—superiority in culture, thought, and capacity to govern effectively and justly.[88] In this way, French colonial rule was rooted in the idea that certain principles of civilization could be brought to African subjects over time—thus, although the civilizing mission was a coherent concept, the elements of its mandate would change over time in accordance with principles of uplift. From the beginning, native justice was at the center of the civilizing mission.

Part of the civilizing effort included drafting an ethnographic history of the conquered region, establishing important ethnic groups and languages, social mores, and practices.[89] The decision to create an administrative territory out of Kenedugu along the preexisting lines of the four most important *jamanaw*, or cantons of Kenedugu, came to Audéoud on the battlefield after the breach of Sikasso's *tata*.[90] The cantons of Bugula, Kaboïla, Natie, and Fama were the most important cantons of the administrative district of Sikasso, in part because they were literally at the center of Kenedugu. The four cantons met at crossroads of Sikasso town, or Sikassoville, and replicated the village federations with the oldest allegiances to Tiéba and the Traoré dynasty in Kenedugu.

After meeting with Audéoud and Coiffé in the week after Sikasso's fall, Kélétigi Berté was named canton chief of Kaboïla. The naming of a canton chief for Bugula was more complicated. Bugula, long considered the home of the Traorés and the residential seat of Kenedugu, was the domain of the Traorés. Audéoud and Coiffé refused to recognize Tiéba's sons, Fo and Madou, as canton chiefs because of their opposition to the French. Samba Tiémoko Traoré was named canton chief, in recognition of his initial participation in the rebuilding of Sikasso.[91] In the years that followed, succession disputes plagued the canton of Bougoula, as the colonial administration privileged the descendants of Samba Traoré as opposed to Fo and Madou Traoré.[92] Similarly, Bembanitieni Traoré, the cousin of Tiéba and Babemba, became the canton chief of Fama. Finally, Kolondugu Sanogo was named canton chief of Natie.

These four men—Kélétigi Berté, Samba Tiémoko Traoré, Bembanitieni Traoré, and Kolondugu Sanogo—represented the past glory of the warriors of Kenedugu, but they also signified the willingness of certain among them to become power brokers for the colonial state. For the French commandants, they each represented access to local knowledge along ethnic lines. Berté and Sanogo, whose patronyms were of the Senufo language, became informants of Senufo custom and practice. The Traorés, by contrast, were regarded not only as repositories of Kenedugu's oral traditions, but experts on Jula practice. Their *carnets du chef*, or chief's notebooks, which were held by the commandant's office throughout the colonial period, marked the Traorés as "Jula-Musulman" and Berté and Sanogo as "Senoufo-Musulman."[93] Their *carnets* report how important these four men were to establishing customary knowledge in the district of Sikasso. Samba Tiémoko was often cited as "an excellent chief, noble, quite, obedient and obeyed," indicating his willingness to serve as an intermediary in the French colonial enterprise.[94] Bembanitieni Traoré was described as "excellent, methodical, devoted to the cause."[95]

All four canton chiefs were integral in the drafting of the "Monographie du Sikasso," which was recorded for the district's administration and sent to the governor-general's office. The monograph is a detailed, multipart study of the history, organization, ethnic background, and practices of the inhabitants of the colonial administrative unit of Sikasso. There is no date or author noted on the monograph, but according to its file and the information contained within it, it was drafted between 1900 and 1907, likely by the commandant of Sikasso. The monograph represented the early colonial commitment to identifying native custom and tradition, which they believed played a large role in the pacification of rural populations and the establishment of the French administration as the liberators of newly conquered territory.[96] The monographic study is replete with references to the distinctions between Jula and Senufo lifestyles and population settlement. According to the monograph, the Senufo inhabited the "wide band of territory across the southwest and northeast, passing through the center of the circle . . . including the cantons of Natie and Fama . . . they are occasionally found in Bugula and Kaboïla."[97] By contrast, Jula "are numerous in Kaboïla and Bugula. . . . They originate from Kong. They arrived in Sikasso at roughly the same time as the Traorés. Their villages dot the route of conquest."[98] Jula, furthermore, were "at once cultivators and merchants," whereas Senufo were "exclusively cultivators. . . . They also make excellent soldiers."[99] These distinctions in practice and ethnic identity were significantly informed by the earlier work of travelers in the region, such as

Caillié and Binger, but also by the oral histories produced by the members of the Traoré, Berté, and Sanogo families.

The monograph concludes with a note on the political and judicial organization of Sikasso at the turn of the century: "Native justice ignores any mechanisms of instruction, as well as the idea of an audience." So-called native forms of justice were perceived as potentially problematic or inadequate, but the author was also careful to note the need to recognize native forms of authority and justice and bring out their natural strengths. "There are natural arbitrators in Sikasso . . . these are the canton chiefs," the author concluded. The canton chiefs, and particularly the four chiefs of Bugula, Kaboïla, Fama, and Natie, would serve as judges on the local tribunals. Conveniently, these four were equally divided along ethnic lines, in the eyes of the commandant. With two Senufo judges and two Jula judges, the canton chiefs were equipped with the perceived inherent knowledge necessary for the formation of a basis of customary law. As Archinard had established earlier in 1893, native justice was to be left to the "natural judges"—that is, canton chiefs and village chiefs.[100] Together, chiefly men of authority would work with the local commandant to establish local custom that would prevail in the colonial courts and in the administration of each of the cantons of the district of Sikasso.

This chapter sets the historical and regional context of the study by outlining late precolonial patterns of settlement and historical transformations. By the mid-nineteenth century, a localized system of exchange between merchants and farmers in southern Mali contributed to local economies and societal development. French explorers and travelers who passed through the region beginning as early as the 1830s perceived distinct ethnic and linguistic differences between these merchants and farmers, which were partially rooted in localized differentiation, but also in the perspectives of the travelers themselves, who were looking for distinctions and division.

By the 1870s, the villages surrounding Sikasso became the epicenter of the Kenedugu Empire, a nineteenth-century kingdom that stemmed from the Kong Empire to the south. Kenedugu was built on the groundwork of the merchant routes into the Sikasso region, and expansion was made possible through commercial relationships, enslavement, and military conquest—but it was also made possible through marriage alliances. The leaders of Kenedugu, the Traoré patriclan, claimed a Mande heritage rooted in the Kong dynasty, but their history was also marked by integration with Senufo farmers throughout the region, as well as enslavement. Despite previous and future emphasis on ethnic distinction in the administration of the region, Kenedugu was built on a blending of different identities, which, although distinct, were not entirely divisible in clear ways.

When Kenedugu fell, the French military leaders involved in the conquest quickly established relationships with the warrior chiefs and authoritative figures of Kenedugu. These men had ties to the Traoré dynasty and the prestige of Kenedugu, but they were also amenable to new political authorities and were keen on being involved in the new administration as regional canton chiefs. By the turn of the century, the chiefs of the four most important cantons of Sikasso—Bugula, Kaboïla, Fama, and Natie—emerged as integral members of the colonial administration. These men would prove important to the formation of customary categories in the years to come and served important roles in the formation of native justice.

Although the dominant narratives of the settlement and European conquest of the West African interior focus on the rise and fall of political men, this chapter suggests that marriage also served as a stabilizing social and political force in precolonial Sikasso region. Marriage created inter- and intracommunity cohesion, and it was regulated by men and women in figures of authority. The story of Momo, which opens this chapter, reminds us of the importance of marriage as an element of state making: named after a woman who was central to the building of Jula-Senufo alliances underpinning the Kenedugu Empire, Momo Traoré was a symbol of the exceptional women at the root of the Traoré family in Kenedugu. However, with the fall of Kenedugu to the French and the rise of new forms of governance and justice, the people of Sikasso would see women like Momo move into the background of myth and story. This shift would happen as certain ideas about marriage and ethnicity began to congeal in the early years of French colonial rule.

2 ⌇ Contesting Slavery and Marriage in Early Colonial Sikasso

IN JUNE 1908, A WOMAN NAMED MA SIDIBÉ of Ganadugu-Nord canton approached the French colonial commandant's office in the district of Sikasso. She was there to report that a man by the name of Fadogoni Sountara of Banzana village in Ganadugu-Sud canton had enslaved her daughter and sold her to a man named Pé Konaté in the neighboring administrative district of Buguni. The two men involved in the alleged enslavement were held in the local prison as a preventative measure while the colonial administration in Sikasso investigated the charges. Days later, the men were released, and all charges of enslavement and trafficking were dropped, as the colonial administrator concluded that the case "was not a question of trafficking [slave trade], but of marriage according to local custom."[1]

As it turned out, Ma Sidibé herself had been a slave in the village of Banzana. During the local wars that ravaged the Sikasso region in the late nineteenth century, Ma Sidibé was captured and enslaved in Banzana, after which she became a member of the household of Fadogoni Sountara's brother, where she lived as his wife.[2] Upon her husband's death, Ma Sidibé became the wife of Fadogoni Sountara, who had inherited his deceased brother's wives and property according to local custom. However, at the time of the levirate transfer, Ma Sidibé's father intervened and paid Sountara a sum, releasing Ma Sidibé from any contractual bond to

Fadogoni Sountara.[3] This would have settled all matters of Ma Sidibé's relations with Fadogoni Sountara if it were not for the three children she had by his deceased brother. Sidibé left her two oldest children with Fadogoni Sountara, but kept her baby girl, who was still nursing. Sidibé returned to her natal village with her youngest daughter, but as the girl grew older she began to make visits to her paternal uncle's home. When the girl was five years old, Fadogoni Sountara promised her in marriage to Pé Konaté, a cousin of Sountara's living in a nearby village. The girl was brought to her betrothed's village in order to meet his family, who wanted to ensure that she was healthy and worthy of marriage. The Konaté family determined that she would make a good wife, and a bridewealth price was agreed on between Pé Konaté and Fadogoni Sountara. The conditions of the bridewealth transaction called for the girl to remain at her uncle's house until she reached a suitable age, whereupon Konaté would pay a portion of the bridewealth (a cow, a steer, and an acceptable number of kola nuts). On the day of the marriage, Konaté would pay the remainder of the bridewealth (a heifer and three sheep). Ma Sidibé played no role in her daughter's marriage arrangement.

When these matters became clear to the colonial administrators in Sikasso, they asked Ma Sidibé if she understood and recognized the rights of Fadogoni Sountara over her youngest daughter, to which she responded that she did. At this point the colonial administration dropped any investigation into the case, remarking that the bridewealth agreed on for the girl was good, in fact very suitable and appropriate for the cantons of Ganadugu in the district of Sikasso.[4]

Ma Sidibé's complaint against Fadogoni Sountara appears in the colonial Sikasso political reports and trimestral judicial reports for June 1908, but she never went before the provincial tribunal as a litigant in a civil case of child custody, unlike many others in Sikasso and throughout the French Sudan between 1905 and 1912. Why, if she was willing to go before the colonial administrator and claim that her daughter had been enslaved, did Ma Sidibé ultimately acknowledge Fadogoni Sountara's rights over the girl and choose not to bring her case to court? We will never know the inner life of Ma Sidibé or the outward pressures placed on her in this negotiation, but the way in which her actions were framed within the colonial administrative report as an abrupt about-face provides a glimpse of the sort of bet hedging by those, who, on a day-to-day basis, worked to shape the contours of their own lives and the relationships of power and authority that affected their actions.[5]

This chapter examines a relatively short span of years surrounding the French colonial conquest of Sikasso in 1898 to the beginning of World War I in 1914. In 1903, a new unified legal system for the Federation of French West Africa was created, establishing a three-tiered court system for African subjects: the village tribunal, the provincial tribunal, and the district, or cercle, tribunal. It took two years for the courts to be implemented, and by 1905, African litigants were bringing their complaints before the village and provincial tribunals. In the same year, slaves throughout the French Sudan initiated a massive exodus, part of which became known as the great Banamba slave exodus in the colonial historical record, and the French administration issued a decree throughout the colonies outlawing slavery as a legal status. By 1912, the colonial administration revisited the colonial legal system and instituted changes and reforms to its structure and policies. This period between 1905 and 1912 in the French Sudan has been called a period of "linked transformations of French conquest, the end of slavery, and the operation of the new courts."[6] In Sikasso these linked transformations were certainly momentous, but they were also contested. Not only was there localized resistance to French rule, there was also a persistence of slavery and inconsistency in use of the new courts. The end of slavery by French decree had a varied impact on the ground in the French Sudan; for the most part, it succeeded in abolishing legal status within a colonial framework and curtailing slave trafficking, but it did not effectively end slavery.[7]

It is during this period of linked transformations that we begin to see the emergence of a marriage legibility project, as administrators attempted to render certain African practices tied to marriage as legible or understandable within a colonial framework. These early processes of dissecting African marriages were about disentangling marriage from slavery and determining which local African practices were "acceptable" in the eyes of the colonial administration, and which were "contrary to French civilization." These discernment practices drew on the Enlightenment-based concept of natural rights, but they also stemmed from colonial readings of Islamic law, specifically Maliki law as it pertained to marriage and divorce.

Documents from the early establishment of colonial state institutions, such as tribunals and the commandant's administrative posts at the colonial district subdivision, show the ways early colonial administrators attempted to resolve marital conflicts according to their understanding of local custom and their desire to create customary laws in the nascent colonies. Women and men of Sikasso introduced these conflicts as they attempted to gain control over the direction of their lives after the dissolution of Kenedugu and the resultant local transformations of everyday life. Quite often, efforts to achieve stability in familial and social networks resided at the heart of such struggles. Stability, in such contexts, was grounded in authority and protection—authority over junior members of a household, such as wives and slaves, and protection within patriarchal systems of belonging. However, as women and men struggled in their processes toward establishing stable lives, they instigated moments of conflict and rupture that sometimes pushed against gendered structures of authority at both the family and administrative levels.

In examining certain marriage and divorce cases in the provincial tribunal of Sikasso from 1905 to 1912, we see the ways in which women and men expressed ideas about different types of gendered rights and obligations, as well as gender justice. Many women who appealed to the colonial tribunals claimed that it was the obligation of men to pay bridewealth, and in the event that bridewealth was not paid, they claimed that it was their right to leave the marriage. Women who approached the courts also argued that it was the obligation of husbands to provide shelter, nourishment, and care for them and their children. In turn, many husbands who appeared in the courts recognized that it was their obligation to provide for their families in material and emotional ways, but they also argued that it was their right and obligation to find work, which quite often took the form of migrant labor in the early twentieth century. Men who approached the courts in marriage cases argued that it was their right to seek a form of gendered justice by requesting that the courts assist them in requiring their wives to return to the marital home. Child custody cases resided in an arena where women and men challenged one another's claims for gender justice.

When African women in the French Sudan approached the new colonial courts for divorces, very often the courts viewed their demands as a reflection of the failures of husbands to uphold the gendered rights and obligations attached to marriage. At times, the provincial court seemed to view the complaints of women as an extension of slavery-based notions of rights and obligations, thus requiring colonial legal intervention. In these cases, African marriage trouble converged with questions of bondedness. Ma Sidibé's predicament highlights the deeply embedded obligations that defined relationships between a slave and a master, a husband and a wife, an uncle and his brother's children. Whereas legal status shifted, networks of human connections, regardless of how uneven they may have been, persisted beyond colonial bureaucratic transformations.

If we are to consider Ma Sidibé's complaint in context, we need to understand that the region of Ganadugu sustained significant suffering and human loss during the wars of Samori and Tiéba; it witnessed a major population exodus in the late nineteenth century followed by a wave of returnees in 1905–6; and it was administratively divided into different cantons with new figures of authority governing each canton.[8] Sikasso-based colonial administrators remarked on the high agricultural yields coming from the Ganadugu region, the ability of its inhabitants to pay their taxes as a result of the land's abundance—and the fact that the brutality of the indigénat—the punitive system that allowed local-level administrators to punish and "correct" African subjects who committed any of a series of offenses against the colonial state or its subjects, without any recourse or due process allowed the so-called perpetrator—was applied from time to time in order to exact these taxes. The Sikasso commandant also documented the corruption of the canton chief of Ganadugu-Sud, his abuse of power in adjudicating a domestic dispute, and ultimately the fact that the commandant was "required to correct" the canton chief (though the canton chief remained in power).[9] Ma Sidibé approached the office of the commandant of Sikasso in this context of such undulating power plays and shifts of fortune. She called attention to the fact of slavery as it undergirded her daughter's relationship to both Fadogoni Sountara and Pé Konaté, and she acknowledged the practices of kinship and adherent obligations. Slavery and kinship were the bonds that tied, and for women like Ma Sidibé, these ties were not necessarily antithetical to one another. Ma Sidibé, her daughter, and Fadogoni Sountara were connected through interlocking bonds according to their gendered roles of obligation and indebtedness, bonds that were ultimately thrown into relief through a marriage promise. However, Ma Sidibé, and others like her, regarded some of the social bonds that made them vulnerable to others as negotiable in the early colonial period, a time when avenues of power and individual status were undergoing transformation. Their bonds of obligation and hierarchy were not completely eradicated, but the end of the legal status of slavery and the introduction of colonial tribunals provided the opportunity to test social contracts and status. Though Ma Sidibé's situation occupies but a few pages in the colonial records of Sikasso, it illuminates the complexities and contingencies of marriage, divorce, child custody, and the end of legal slave status in the early colonial years of Sikasso and the colony of the French Sudan.

QUESTIONS OF CUSTOM IN THE COURTS: MARRIAGE, DIVORCE, CHILD CUSTODY, AND SLAVERY

Although French West African civil and commercial legal procedure has been described at length elsewhere, it is necessary to provide a brief historical overview of colonial legal categories and the architecture of the court system and judicial process at work at this time in Sikasso and the French Sudan.[10]

The Third Republic of France ushered in many policy-related and practical changes in French West Africa. By the turn of the century, France generally moved away from military expansion and rule in the French Sudan toward civilian rule, a shift that was deeply tied to late-nineteenth-century French metropolitan desires to separate militarism (often associated with extreme power and the monarchy) from a Republican ethos of civilian rule and natural rights.[11] The consolidation of bureaucratic authority in the governance of the colonies under the Ministry of the Colonies in France in 1894, a reform that included the establishment of the governors-general of French West Africa, signaled this shift in the mission of colonial rule from military expansion and consolidation to civilian rule.[12]

It was also during this time that the colonial administration endeavored to create the foundation for the rule of law that would uphold categories of rights and recognize the rights-bearing individual.[13] This was an important cornerstone of the principles of the civilizing mission. However, concepts of rule of law and rights-bearing individuals in colonial contexts were ideologically paradoxical, let alone practically challenged. Some in the colonial government in French West Africa were particularly concerned with the establishment of a judicial system that would counterbalance the indigénat.[14] Although some colonial administrators as early as 1905 were critical of the indigénat, many commandants throughout the French Sudan used it excessively in their exercise of local power. For example, the indigénat allowed for the immediate imprisonment of men like Fadogoni Sountara and Pé Konaté, and it underpinned the Sikasso commandant's "correction" of an allegedly corrupt canton chief in Ganadugu. The punitive and violent indigénat would not be replaced by a civil, commercial, and criminal law system, but would rather exist alongside it. It was the simultaneous existence of the indigénat and the multitiered legal system for African subjects that highlighted the limitations and fictions of the civilizing mission and its application in French West Africa: the rights-bearing colonial subject was an individual with heavily circumscribed access to formal justice, a type of justice defined by the colonial power itself.[15] In such a context, justice would be served if it were in line with specific French notions of civilization, and so long as it did not upset the French citizen-and-subject hierarchy.

As the governor-general of French West Africa, Ernest Roume saw the new judicial system as an imperative component of the new colonial administration in the twentieth century but was concerned with upholding the treaties signed with African leaders that promised the allowance of customary practice and law.[16] In this sense, he was reluctant to enforce many French legal principles and practices, but he wanted to be certain that the colonial judicial system would be able to distinguish between what were considered "acceptable" customary practices, and those practices that were deemed contrary to French civilization.[17] However, he was also careful to note that acceptable customary practices could gradually be brought in line with "natural rights, the foundation of all legislation"—something he distinguished from republican notions of law.[18] Natural rights ultimately informed the basis of the privileges and rights protected by republican law. However, natural rights were regarded as inherent to personhood and as existing before political rights, and were ultimately available through reasoning processes.[19] Thus, if "reason" was encouraged through the civilizing mission, then Africans would come to realize their natural rights and adapt their "acceptable" customary practices accordingly. In the interest of allowing for customary practice—the types of practices that might eventually be "brought up" to natural rights standards—marriage disputes and family-related cases were to remain largely untouched by French legal intervention.[20] Roume made his views on this clear by stating, "We will under no circumstance alter especially those essential rights that result from the husband's authority over his wife, the father's authority over his children or guardianship" (my emphasis).[21] In this sense patriarchal rights appear as natural rights. However, it was not only the perceived rights of husbands over their wives and children—that is, the right to paternalism and to patriarchal authority—that concerned administrators in the early years of the court system. In fact, some disagreed that local marriage practice should remain outside the realm of French legal intervention. In 1905, the commandant of Sikasso lamented:

> Women are inferior in Black Africa. . . . It is for this reason that they are always the ones to introduce the divorce request in the indigenous tribunal, for motives that are generally futile. . . . The [native] judges rarely rule in favor of women. Furthermore, indigenous custom is very imprecise on the matter of a wife's rights in marriage, and the husband's authority is always what matters.[22] (My emphasis)

There is some irony in the commandant's concern over African women's rights, as French women were also regarded as legally and politically "inferior" (particularly in marriage, property, and citizenship rights) in 1905.

But his observation that indigenous custom was "imprecise" or vague—illegible, even—on the question of women's legal rights in marriage underscores the challenge that administrators faced in determining customary law practice, particularly which practices were acceptable and which were contrary to French civilization. The distinction between the individual rights of a woman in marriage, suggested in the quote above, and the patriarchal rights of a man points to the larger concept of gender-based justice at the root of the colonial legal system.

In July of 1905, the commandant of Sikasso expressed frustration over the fact that customs were not written down and were therefore difficult to understand relative to marriage, divorce, and bridewealth practice.[23] This was partially owing to the prescriptions of Colonel Archinard in 1893, which recommended that local justice in the French Sudan be left to native judges, as we saw in chapter 1. Yet Colonel Trentinian, who became governor of the French Sudan in 1895 within the context of the transition from military consolidation to civilian rule, had commissioned a study on "native law" and "Muslim law" in the French Sudan, from which a rudimentary set of written customs did result.[24] Trentinian's study, based on communication with commandants posted throughout the colony, created a stark binary between "native" law and "Islamic" practices of justice. Native customary law practice was seen as governed by magic, sorcery, and the occult, whereas Islamic law was described as "providing some comprehensible structure" to legal practice.[25] "African justice is simple," wrote Lieutenant Sargols, posted in Segu, to Colonel Trentinian. He continued, "They use poison, kola nuts, and cowry shells—a state not far from barbarism." By contrast, Sargols believed that "populations which have submitted to Islam have an organization of justice that is more rational and based in written custom."[26] According to such views of arbitration and justice, there was little legitimation or "legibility" ascribed to the women of sando and their divination, instructive songs of the jelimuso, the furusirima and his processes of bridewealth negotiation, or reconciliation efforts that might take place under a village tree.

Trentinian called for local chiefs, elders, and qadis (Islamic judges)—local men of respect and authority—to assist in the adjudication of civil affairs before 1900, so as to lighten the load of colonial administrators.[27] In Sikasso, the men of authority whom we met in chapter 1—canton chiefs Kélétigi Berté, Kolondougou Sanogo, Samba Traoré, and Bembanitieni Traoré—all contributed to the shaping of customary law according to Senufo and Bambara/Jula custom.[28] Berté and Sanogo claimed Senufo identity and Samba Traoré and Bembanitieni Traoré claimed Bambara/Jula identity; nonetheless, all four men were Muslim and were recognized as Muslims in the colonial record. Although the colonial administration sought to distinguish between "indigenous" and "Islamic" practices in the late nineteenth century and then apply them in the early twentieth-century court system, certain elements of local practice were often read through an Islamic lens. That is, practices that were associated with "indigenous" or "fetishist" customs were more likely to be regarded as contrary to French civilization, and practices that resembled Islamic legal thinking were the most legible and informed the standard to which native customary practice was held. The Maliki *madhab,* or school, which constitutes the dominant Islamic legal tradition in West and North Africa, was translated into French and codified in 1854 in French colonial Algeria. The translated code became standard reading for French colonial administrators in Senegal and the French Sudan; so it is no surprise that by 1905, when administrators went looking for legal practice and custom, they kept coming back to Maliki law as a precedent or a guide.[29] According to Maliki principles, particularly as they were understood according to the French translation, when a woman initiated a divorce—called *khul'* in Arabic—she was expected to reimburse her husband at least a portion of his bridewealth payment. Likewise, a wife could ask a qadi for divorce if her husband failed to provide, if he abandoned her and was absent for an extended period of time, or if she could prove that he was excessively abusive.[30] These standards of ruling appear throughout the provincial court records of Sikasso from 1905 to 1912.

In Sikasso, colonial administrators understood marriage as an arrangement between families that rested on a bridewealth transaction, much like the one outlined in Ma Sidibé's case. Bridewealth was the exchange of goods or currency between families for the transfer of a young woman in marriage to a man of the opposite family, something often labeled as "*dot*" in the colonial archive.[31] Bridewealth is exchanged in both Muslim and non-Muslim communities in West Africa. Among Muslim Bambara or Muslim Senufo communities, distinguishing which parts of the exchange were "Muslim" and which parts were "Senufo or Bambara" would have been challenging. Any descriptive accounts of bridewealth exchange from the early colonial period come from colonial ethnographies or oral traditions, both of which tend to represent normative and prescriptive notions of practice. However, they are useful for establishing standards of cultural practice around marriage, practices that reinforced certain ideals of social harmony and behavior expectations.

Bambara or Jula bridewealth payments could take place over a long period of time and take a variety of forms, depending on the castes of the two households involved and the region in which they lived. In the Sikasso region, bridewealth payments among Jula households typically began with an initial gift of kola nuts and cloth given to the father or guardian of the intended bride. A second installment of payment occurred at the moment of the *woro siri*, a stage in the marriage known as "tying of the kola."[32] The gift or payment given at the woro siri would have typically been a specified amount of cowries, which later in the colonial period would become coin. This moment of tying the kola signified the solidifying of the compact between two families. The marrying man's family also paid for the cost of the bride's genital excision, which included a goat or animal to slaughter for the celebration, woven mats, special homespun cloth for the newly excised woman, and the cost of the excision implements and medicinal remedies.[33] Excision was to take place before the *furu siri*, the second stage of marriage, translating as "tying the marriage." The furu siri may have taken place at the same time as the woro siri, a month after, a year after, or even longer. In some ways, the ritual itself is similar to the woro siri, but the furu siri was seen as completing the religious aspect of the marriage. The gifts given at the furu siri ceremony were considered to be the actual price of the marriage, and these gifts were typically not to be returned in the case of divorce or death.[34] Furu siri gifts also depended on caste, status, and region. However, such gifts might include cloth for *pagnes* (wrap skirts) for the bride's mother, grain or agricultural products, as well as chickens or livestock for the father, and a variety of different gifts for the bride herself (cloth, shea butter and beauty products, and cooking implements). Fulbe marriage payments in the Gana region, like the one described in Ma Sidibé's case, were very similar to Bambara bridewealth payments, and ideally a significant portion of the payment would consist of cattle and livestock.[35]

The complexity and intricacies of bridewealth payment, as illustrated above, call into question what exactly was to be paid as indemnity or reimbursed upon divorce in the colonial tribunal. Because colonial administrators would have looked for something resembling a contract—something they would have found in Islamic law, but something that would have been more elusive according to non-Islamic practices—it would make sense that the woro siri would be the payment signifying the formal marriage to the colonial tribunal, and therefore the amount to be reimbursed on divorce. The woro siri gifts closely resembled *sadaq*, the marriage payment given to the bride on the signing of the marriage contract, according to most interpretations of Islamic law. According to Maliki law, and specifically the translated and codified standard used by French administration, a wife was required to reimburse *sadaq* upon initiating a *khul'* divorce.[36] Here, then, we see another example of French interpretations of Islamic law informing the application and codification of customary law in instances of divorce.

Senufo marriages, in contrast, had a very different process of payment and exchange that accompanied them. Ideally, the marrying man and his brothers would perform specified agricultural labor for the household of the bride-to-be from the moment of the marriage arrangement until shortly after the birth of the couple's first child. Typically, the only thing resembling a prestation would be the gift of a large pottery water jug to the bride, which would sit in a prominent position within the marital home.[37] However, French administrators also found that a common practice among the Senufo community at the time of conquest in Sikasso was exchange marriage, or sister exchange. This involved two families exchanging girls or young women from their families to men in the opposing families, which tied the families together in social and familial bonds and eliminated the exchange of labor or material bridewealth. In late 1905, the commandant in Sikasso recommended that this practice be eradicated, and instead, Senufo families should "pay a bridewealth in currency, and renounce this practice." He went on to note "such practice is sensitive, and in fact touches upon political issues as well."[38] Exchange marriage was sensitive because it was exactly the kind of practice that seemed "contrary to French civilization," but it was also political because the administrator likely realized that nonrecognition of such types of Senufo marriages would significantly affect the administration's relationship with many Senufo villages. Efforts to monetize Senufo bridewealth would prove challenging, but such goals point to the larger project of legibility: a concerted effort to create a practice that resembled a contractual obligation, and which would not resemble an exchange in persons or slavery.

Beginning in 1905 with the implementation of the new legal system, the Sikasso provincial tribunals focused on eradicating wife-exchange practices. When cases involving Senufo exchange marriages did appear at the tribunal, they were either not recognized or the court attempted to monetize a bridewealth exchange to render them acceptable in the eyes of the court. For example, on 6 September 1905, Kananbé took Norobé to the provincial tribunal in Sikasso. Norobé had married the sister of Kananbé, and following Senufo exchange practice, promised their firstborn daughter to Kananbé as a wife. Kananbé argued that Norobé had not fulfilled his side of the contract. The tribunal ruled that Norobé must pay bridewealth in currency to Kananbé.[39] Similarly, on 5 January 1912, Fansé brought a man named Mori to the provincial tribunal. Fansé requested that the sister of

Mori be given to Fansé in marriage, in exchange for one of Fansé's sisters who had been given to Mori's father some twenty years ago. The court dismissed the case.[40]

Throughout the French Sudan, when African litigants did approach the colonial courts in 1905, most opted out of the village-level tribunal, where village chiefs presided, and brought their cases before the provincial tribunal. The colonial commandant appointed a chief to preside over the provincial tribunal, who was assisted by two court assessors, also appointed by the colonial commandant.[41] Customary law, as opposed to French civil code, ruled cases at these civil and commercial levels of the new colonial court system. Customary laws were subjective interpretations of culture and society, which is to say that they represented normative and often privileged perspectives at a particular moment, and were formed as a result of the expert knowledge of chiefs and interpreters and their exchanges with colonial administrators. The customary laws pertaining to marriage and divorce most often concerned rights to bridewealth and proper bridewealth payment, marital consent, as well as rights over children. Customary marriage law also established behavior expectations for men and women in marriage, and claimants and defendants used behavior expectations and articulations of marital obligation to justify their allegations in the provincial tribunal. Given the main sources of information on local custom in Sikasso at the time—Muslim men in positions of authority—in addition to the biases which emerged from the Trentinian inquiry at the end of the nineteenth century, it is not surprising to see that local "custom" was framed through the lens of Maliki law as well as the binary relationship between what was "acceptable" and what was "contrary to French civilization."

As in many other places throughout French West Africa, the early courts in Sikasso received an abundance of divorce requests in the early years of the native courts, which started hearing cases in 1905. In April of 1905, the commandant of Sikasso observed that the most common cases seen at the tribunal were accusations of theft, while the second most common was divorce.[42] Some women who initiated these divorce cases before the provincial tribunal contested their status in relation to the men whom they opposed in court. These questions over slave status and marital status rested on testimony and proof, the later of which was grounded in the exchange of bridewealth.

The marriage, divorce, and child custody cases heard before the provincial tribunal during its first few years of operation highlight the tensions between the definition and application of customary law, particularly around bridewealth exchanges and practices. It became quite clear in the early years of native court operation in Sikasso that bridewealth resided at the core of most divorce and child custody cases. What remained a challenge was the navigation of individual interpretations of bridewealth payments, whether or not they had been completed, and how bridewealth applied to the demands that men and women made in the civil courts.

African litigants were just beginning to bring their disputes before the native tribunals in 1905, but 25 of 31 cases brought before the Sikasso tribunal that year were marriage, divorce, or cases related to child custody. Court cases from 1905 to 1912 in Sikasso reveal that women introduced approximately 80 percent of the total divorce cases (42 of 52 cases). However, only 24 percent of these cases (10 cases of 42 cases) were dismissed or ruled against women. The administrator who commented that women almost always introduced divorce cases was correct, but he was incorrect when he noted that judges did not rule in their favor—village-level tribunals may have been inclined to rule against women, but this was not the case with the provincial tribunal. Women won divorce cases at the provincial tribunal under the following conditions: if bridewealth payment had not been fulfilled, if their husbands were gone for an extended period (one to five years qualified as abandonment in the courts), or if women sustained unusual physical abuse or were mistreated through unreasonable labor demands. Again, these standards applied to customary law courts stem from French understandings of Maliki law as it was codified in the mid-nineteenth century.

Failure to pay bridewealth and reimbursement of bridewealth were the most common elements of divorce cases at the provincial tribunal. Most divorce cases on the basis of nonpayment of bridewealth were quite straightforward, in terms of their representation in the tribunal record. For example, on 14 November 1905, Bélé asked for divorce from her husband. Her case stated that he failed to pay any bridewealth to her family. As a result, divorce was pronounced, and there was no appeal.[43] Many of the divorce cases recorded in the tribunal records between 1905 and 1912 reflect such characteristics, and in any case where a woman could prove that her husband had not paid bridewealth, her claims were successful. However, some divorce cases revealed other elements at work, such as abuse or failure to provide. On 14 February 1908, Batouli went to the tribunal to ask for a divorce because her husband had only paid 5 francs of his bridewealth payment to her family. She also argued that he did not feed her or their child properly. As a result of her claims and the husband's failure to pay bridewealth, divorce was pronounced.[44]

In cases where women sought to initiate divorce and promised to repay bridewealth, the court often ruled in their favor, so long as there was an acceptable reason for divorce—that is, if they could prove abandonment, mistreatment, or failure to provide. On 15 February 1907, Diaara approached the tribunal to demand divorce because of physical mistreatment. Her husband, Mamadou, stated that he would be willing to accept the divorce if his wife reimbursed bridewealth. Diaara agreed to reimburse him 200 francs, and divorce was pronounced.[45] Although failure to pay bridewealth was a common complaint of women seeking divorce, failure to provide due to abandonment or lack of resources and physical mistreatment were also regular complaints. In March 1907, a woman approached the provincial tribunal to request divorce from her husband, claiming that her husband did not provide for her. Divorce was granted.[46] Divorce claims on the grounds of abuse and mistreatment were very difficult to prove, and women did not always win their cases. On 3 May 1907, Dio requested that the court grant her a divorce from her husband, Traoré, because he had been physically abusing her for fifteen years. The tribunal refused her request.[47] However, on 18 October of the same year, Natogoma requested a divorce on the basis of mistreatment and was granted a divorce, on the condition that she relinquish custody of their older child to the husband, and that she promise to hand over their younger second child in six years.[48] Women had a difficult time claiming mistreatment because a certain amount of physical punishment was seen as acceptable in marriage, in the eyes of both colonial administrators and local African leaders and patriarchs. In order to claim mistreatment, women would often have to be willing and able to prove it through evidence on their bodies or through witness testimony, the latter of which was often difficult to obtain. However, this sampling of different types of divorce cases, alongside the percentages reflecting outcomes, shows us that most women who approached the court seeking a type of gender justice—divorce in instances where men were not upholding their obligations in marriage—were successful.

In Sikasso, over the course of the years 1905–12, marriage cases—that is, cases brought by husbands against their wives after their wives had abandoned the conjugal home—decreased in frequency at the provincial tribunal. Although there are multiple variables that contribute to the reasons for this shift, it at least indicates that men stopped approaching the colonial tribunal for assistance in requiring their wives to return home. One reason may have been that occasionally men approached the courts seeking support from the court in the return of their wives only to find that the court ruled in favor of their wives and granted divorce. Cases such as these were almost always situations where the husband was found to have failed in his fulfillment of bridewealth payment. For example, on 6 October 1905—shortly after the tribunals began to function in Sikasso—Soriba approached the provincial tribunal to request the return of his wife, Fatimata, who had left the conjugal home. Fatimata claimed that Soriba never paid bridewealth, which was found to be correct. Divorce was pronounced.[49] Likewise, on 13 September 1907, Mama took his wife, Aoua, to court demanding that she reintegrate the marital home. Aoua claimed that Mama had never fulfilled his bridewealth payment, and as a result, the court pronounced divorce.[50]

However, the tribunal did successfully help some men in seeking the return of their wives. Moussa appealed to the provincial tribunal on 19 September 1905, for assistance in the return of one of his three wives. Moussa was absent for three years because of his work in commerce. During this time, one of his wives, Nialle, left the marital home and moved in with her lover. The court ruled in Moussa's favor and commanded that Nialle reintegrate the marital home.[51] This case is somewhat curious because it goes against the tribunal's rulings of divorce in cases where women argued that they had been abandoned by their husbands for extended periods of time. However, it might point to the court's early working out of particular categories of "customary" behavior. Cases such as this also suggest that there were tensions in the courts between upholding a system in which men were obliged to participate in labor that took them away from the marital home, and punishing men for abandonment of the home—something that was seen to be in accordance with reified notions of customary law.

The gradual decline in marriage cases corresponds with a similar, gradual decrease or leveling off of divorce cases over the same time. Although this is a very small window of time, it seems to show that the first few years after the creation of the courts and the abolition of slavery were particularly contentious in the courts. While the courts attempted to establish customary practice and indigenous law, women in unbearable conjugal relationships attempted to break away or challenge those bonds, even if they knew that bridewealth payments or manumission payments effectively tied them to men.

The first case of child custody in Sikasso appeared on 18 September 1905. Disputes over rights to children were sporadic in the first few years of the tribunal in Sikasso, but steadily picked up in 1909 and 1910. Disputes over child custody generally took three forms: fathers bringing mothers to court for custody over children when the mother had abandoned the home; paternal uncles or other male relations on the father's side, seeking custody over children from their mothers after the father has died; or mothers seeking custody from the father or father's family. At times, a woman appeared before the provincial tribunal to ask for divorce and in doing so would also request custody of her children, making child custody a secondary claim.[52] In cases of divorce or death of a husband, women infrequently requested custody of their children from the provincial tribunal. If bridewealth was given to a woman's family as part of a Bambara or Jula marriage agreement, the expectation was that the children of that union ultimately belonged to the father and his lineage.[53] However, instances of women asking for custody of children, when "customarily" they would not have access to them, are suggestive of alternative practices at work in daily life. The frequency with which fathers and paternal uncles petitioned the courts for custody of children indicates that there was individual struggle or contestation over this "customary" claim to children on the part of mothers. As Martin Chanock has observed, "custom" was a weapon in the battle against the economic independence of dependents.[54]

The persistence of child custody cases does show that although women increasingly lost custody, some women may have perceived the provincial tribunal as a mechanism for change and challenge to authority over the domestic sphere. If it is true that authority over children lay in the hands of fathers and uncles, then the courts presented a potential alternative venue through which women might gain authority over their children. In the early years of the provincial tribunal, women were typically more successful in their claims for children in the courts. More frequent, too, were cases where ex-slaves sought custody of their children from former masters. For instance, on 1 March 1907, a former slave woman brought her former master to court in order to regain custody of her children, and the tribunal ruled in her favor.[55] On that same day, a former slave owner brought the widow of his slave to court over custody rights to their child. The mother was awarded custody.[56] In these cases, women prevailed over men of some power, and they may have encouraged other women to seek custody of their children in the hopes that the court would challenge their husbands' rights to them. Throughout French West Africa, the decline of slavery initiated disputes regarding parental authority over children, and questions over the status of children from slave-master relationships were central to these disputes. These instances of official articulation of the distinctions between slavery and patriarchal authority rights are evidence of confusion on the part of local administrators regarding the status of women and the possible rights of women and men over their children, as slavery was abolished as a legal status.[57]

Indeed, in the first years of the tribunal, slavery-related claims appear throughout the run of marriage, divorce, and custody cases. For example, on 19 May 19,1905, Soungourou approached the tribunal with a male relative, Birama.[58] Soungourou had been a slave, and was married to Dielimory, an African soldier for the French, or tirailleur, at the fall of Kenedugu in 1898. When Soungourou followed her husband to his natal village, she found that life with him was very difficult and she was beaten regularly. Birama offered to pay Dielimory 150 francs, an amount determined to be the reimbursement of bridewealth. Dielimory accepted the payment, and divorce was pronounced. Here, the case reads as a reimbursement of bridewealth upon a woman's initiation of divorce, but there is clearly much more going on under the surface. There is no indication that any bridewealth was paid for the initial marriage between Soungourou and Dielimory. Indeed, what we know of them is that Soungourou was a slave and was likely taken as a spoil of war by Dielimory. Although the payment of 150 francs might be interpreted by the court as reimbursement of bridewealth, it could also be read as a slave redemption transaction.

Similarly, on 30 June 30 1905, the Sikasso provincial tribunal heard the following case. Mory married the daughter of an older woman. As bridewealth, he offered the old woman the domestic services of a young girl, whom he claimed was a relative of his. The wife left Mory, and Mory approached the tribunal requesting that either his wife or the young servant return to his home. The tribunal declared the marriage to be annulled, and that the young servant girl, who was determined not in fact to be a relative of Mory but in fact a slave, was to be brought to a slave liberty village. The tribunal declared that Mory had no right to claim damages from this annulment.[59]

In another case later that same year, Ténékoro appeared before the tribunal to claim the return of Karidia to his home. On interrogation, it became clear that Karidia was a former slave who had been redeemed by Ténékoro at the price of 200 francs. After redemption, the two were to be married. However, she later reneged on this agreement and decided that she wanted to leave Ténékoro, who wanted the price of her slave redemption returned to him. The tribunal ruled that Karidia could leave if she reimbursed the price of her redemption.[60] Although it is unclear if Karidia, for example, was able to pay back her redemption price and leave—or if she tried alternative venues for leaving or breaking her bond to Ténékoro— this case does point toward the ambiguities of men's and women's relationships where enslavement and emancipation are involved. For the French colonial officials overseeing the local magistrates' rulings in the tribunal, it was especially difficult to determine customary practice regarding marriage in this period of slave emancipation. Karidia could have potentially benefited from this murkiness, but a former slave redeemed by another was frequently in a position of indebtedness to her liberator, as her status often remained subservient.[61]

SLAVES AND WIVES: INTERPRETING SOCIAL AND LEGAL CATEGORIES IN THE HISTORICAL RECORD

How do we begin to understand where slaves and wives intersect in the historical record and why? Slaves and wives were distinct categories of status and identity, but at times the boundaries between them became blurred.[62] In early colonial Sikasso, and elsewhere in the French Sudan, a man might have asserted to a tribunal that a woman was his wife while she argued that she was his slave. It was not uncommon for a colonial administrator to write in his monthly political report that local marriage practices and bridewealth exchanges were similar to slave trafficking, contributing to the construction of narratives such as Ma Sidibé's story. In fact, observations that African marriage was "slave-like" became integral to political debates over marriage decrees and laws later in the twentieth century.

One fundamental reason that slaves and wives intersect is the fact that the majority of slaves in the Western Sudan throughout the nineteenth century and during French conquest were women.[63] Slave women were valued for their productive and reproductive labor; they performed tasks such as cooking, gathering firewood, working in agricultural fields, and other domestic chores associated with nonslave women's work. Many slave women also became concubines and sexual laborers. Some have argued that slave women were not only valued for the basic qualities of their labor, but because they could be easily captured and absorbed into their adoptive societies.[64] Enslaved men often worked as porters and field hands, but recovered slaves were also conscripted into the French armies as tirailleurs for conquest of African states and empires. Coerced laborers constructed the new railroad system that the French built in the West African interior.[65] Enslaved women, often included in the spoils of war, served the tirailleurs as cooks, porters, wives, or concubines, and were integral to the maintenance of the military camp.[66] Female slaves outnumbered male slaves throughout Africa, and studies of slave markets indicate that female slaves consistently brought higher prices throughout the Western Sudan.[67]

The convergence of gender and slave roles contributed to the concealment of slavery in the presence of a colonial administration, and slave-master relationships persisted well into the colonial period. Moreover, the perpetuation of slavery through venues sanctioned by the colonizing mission made it increasingly difficult to deal with abolition, particularly with regard to women in slavery. The early colonial administration in Senegal allowed slavery to persist, setting a precedent throughout French West Africa. Slaves were permitted to enter French protectorate territory as members of trading caravans, in an effort to protect colonial interests in trade, social welfare, and overall efforts toward empire building. Administrators turned a blind eye to coerced domestic labor in St. Louis, the French capital of Senegal. When colonial initiatives were directed eastward, the carving out of the interior of Senegal and the Western Sudan stimulated the production of slaves. The economy of expansion in the Western Sudan relied on slave labor and exchange of slaves by the colonial military, as they could not rely on significant state support from France to carry out their colonial agenda.[68] In this way, slaves were produced through wars of expansion and conquest of local populations.[69] The essential reliance on slavery for colonial expansion, coupled with the militaristic quality of the development of the colonial state until the 1890s, challenged moves toward abolition.[70]

The continuation of slavery in the early years of colonial rule throughout French West Africa was due in part to the fact that in practice and policy, France vacillated between complicity with slavery and the eradication of the practice.[71] Mid-nineteenth-century reliance on slave women by the French military in state-building projects and colonial military expansion extended into the twentieth century. After military conquest, as French colonial administrators laid the groundwork for civilian rule, they struggled against the legacy of the nineteenth-century military expansion that resulted in the conquest of Kenedugu and Samori.[72] At the center of this struggle was continued reliance on slavery and the colonial government's ambiguous relationship with enslaved women and women seeking to sever their ties with male husbands or masters.[73]

By 1905 one of the realms of local practice seen as requiring French legal and moral intervention was the slave trade and the eradication of slave status. On this point, Roume declared, "Every day the abuses [of slavery] become more rare and will become even more so when the administration becomes better armed, legally."[74] Regional slave exoduses and the abolition of slavery in 1905 resulted in large numbers of people returning to Sikasso, Buguni, and neighboring Wasulu in order to reintegrate into their households and communities.[75] This shift came in waves; people returned one by one, in families, over the course of a few years. Colonial administrators and locals in Sikasso noted the return of people who had been enslaved and brought to the Banamba slave market. In the May 1906 political report for Sikasso, the colonial administrator noted that between 11 May and 1 June, 197 people passed through Sikasso, on their way home from Banamba. The majority of them went on toward present-day Côte d'Ivoire, to Folona and Nanergue. Another group of approximately 100 slaves entered Sikasso during these weeks of May, but these people settled in the various villages or cantons of Sikasso. Samori had enslaved many of them and sold them to the Banamba market, and others had been purchased for salt or cloth on one of the Maraka slaving trips down to Sikasso in the late nineteenth century.[76] The pattern of freed slaves settling in Sikasso or passing through the colonial district went on for years after 1905. Their return home corresponds with the establishment of a colonial court system for African subjects in the French Sudan. Thus at the same time that administrators and local African magistrates struggled to define customary practice in the realm of marriage, they also faced a growing population of people with shifting slave and free status.

From the viewpoint of many state actors, slave emancipation was ideally to be followed by the socially reconstitutive powers of family formation and marriage.[77] In twentieth-century French imperial and postslavery contexts, some colonial administrators had such visions of a postemancipation world, but they were also more focused on and concerned with how emancipation would affect labor projects such as the construction of the railroad and the cultivation of essential cash crops. In this way, the goal was to create free workers who were also subjects of the colonial state. However, the view of development in the pre–World War I period, something the overseas France administration called *mise en valeur*, centered—at least rhetorically—on engaging in infrastructural development programs such as road and rail construction while promoting a moral agenda.[78] In the pre–World War I period, slavery and abolition framed the French colonial moral agenda, particularly the message that French colonial rule would bring emancipation from African forms of slavery to the people, notably in the hinterland. One initial concern was for the potential emancipatory power of the courts, in the case of women who sought to leave marriages that seemed akin to slavery. Thus we see two interests at odds with each other in the early years of the practice of French colonial family law: a colonial moral agenda based, paradoxically, on liberal notions of individual rights, and therefore invested in eradicating slavery and bondedness; and a practical and political interest written into colonial policy that called for African family disputes to be "left to custom" in an effort to protect the patriarchal authority of husbands and fathers. In both cases, the interests were rooted in a French colonial paternalism. African women were perceived as being in need of uplift and rescue (though we might understand African women as exercising some form of circumscribed agency by going to the courts), and African men were in need of reinforcement by the French colonial state—so long as the interests of African men did not fly in the face of "French civilization" or challenge the limits of their colonial subjecthood.

Despite the legal abolition of slavery in the early years of colonial rule, the practice of enslavement and slaveholding persisted largely because those in the position to buy slaves continued to procure them. In the same political report that outlined the story of Ma Sidibé the administrator from Sikasso wrote:

> There are more serious charges weighing against N. Taraoré, chief of the village of Kaboïla, and his accomplice, Nampé Diamatane. It seems as if Diamatane, under orders from Taraoré, took two daughters from one of Taraoré's servants and sold them for 200 francs and 175 francs. One of them has been recovered and reunited with her mother, but we are still looking for the other child.[79]

That the slave seller in question was a chief is no coincidence, but rather explains the enduring hierarchies of power and the implication of village and canton chiefs in the persistence of slavery and the maintenance of many precolonial systems of power and control over subservient women and men. This anecdote embedded in a political report from 1908 is emblematic of many other similar situations where men in authority, particularly chiefs, continued to exercise their power and influence over slaves and junior members of society, despite shifts in legal status and procedures made available to men and women living under French colonial rule.[80]

Given these historical variables of social transformation, the productive question to ask is not simply why slaves and women intersect in the historical record, but rather, *which* women and slaves intersect in the historical record.[81] This is an important distinction if one is concerned with the localized intimacies of everyday life that occurred with the end of the legal status of slavery and the introduction of colonial courts and the colonial task of codifying customary practice and ethnic ways. Asking "which women?" in the study of women and slavery in African historical contexts reveals the ways in which broadly applicable terms such as "slave," "woman," or "wife" have locally derived contingencies and definitions. Women who had been slaves, women with questionable bridewealth agreements, junior wives—that is, any wife who was not the first wife in a polygynous household—and wives of men whose slaves departed during the great slave exoduses of the early twentieth century intersected often with slaves in the historical record.

If we return to the story of Ma Sidibé, we see that her own relationship with slavery reveals the continued bonds of slavery after its abolition and the resonance of slave-master relationships. A woman such as Ma Sidibé found herself in a peculiar predicament; she joined the conjugal home of a man as his wife during a period of enslavement and warfare. It seems that no bridewealth was given to her father, or at least there was no adequate "proof" given to the colonial administrator handling the affair to indicate otherwise. As either his slave or wife, Ma Sidibé was subject to the custom of levirate transfer to the deceased man's brother. However, her father effectively freed her of individual obligation to the brother by paying an acceptable sum, a practice that would be followed to either manumit a slave or reimburse bridewealth. The place where Ma Sidibé's situation most closely corresponds with the intersection of slavery and marriage is in her claims over her child. In either a case of slavery or divorce, a woman would not typically have rights over her child which would supersede the rights of the father of that child. Ma Sidibé, in her assertion of rights over her child as a socially "absorbed" slave mother, was acting the same way so many wives and recently divorced women behaved before the colonial tribunal in Sikasso in the early years of colonial rule. Ma Sidibé continued to experience the bonds and relationships of dependence, as well as the obligations of slavery, even after the legality of slave status was nullified. Such bonds would continue well into the twentieth century for some women, while other women would sever their ties with men who increased their burdens at the end of slavery's legal status.

By 1911, many administrators on the ground understood the importance of bridewealth in the contractual nature of a marriage, but at the same time they were confounded by the fact that there was only proof of marriage through testimony of bridewealth payment—that is, there was no record to indicate that bridewealth had been paid. Furthermore, some families spent their woro siri bridewealth as soon as they received it, at a time when local markets were just beginning to stabilize, and when the colonial administration through their intermediary canton chiefs were exacting tax payments. Though French administrators understood the existence of practices such as bridewealth exchange, they did not seem to understand the nature of local marriages and the role that they played in maintaining social harmony—unions over which their colonial courts presided in divorce, marriage, and child custody cases through the local provincial tribunals.

MARRIAGE AND CHAOS: CONSOLIDATING AND CONTESTING GENDERED AUTHORITY IN EARLY COLONIAL SIKASSO

In March 2005, Yaya Dow of Kaboïla village in the Sikasso region told the following story of the first years of French colonial rule of Sikasso, based on his own memories and the stories recounted to him by his father and the elders of his community:

> There were seven women from Niabory's household who left because they were not married to him. My mother left with them, and said that she would not go anymore with my father . . . and my father was no little marabout![82] At the [tribunal] judgment, my father said that she would never leave with his son. I was there, as well as my father, Niabory, Kourouma, Kélétigi, Saaba Tiémoko, Kolondjougou, Zemanjini, all the canton chiefs. The commandant asked Niabory, "So, what are we going to do with your wives?" Niabory told him, "Leave them, as they were not my wives but my slaves. I took them when they were very young as wives. If they do not want to stay with me, if they say that they are not married, fine, let them leave. I can always get more." But my father said no, that he for his part wanted his child. The commandant asked my mother, "And you, will you go with your husband?" She said, "No, I'm not going with him because I am not married to him, and my child is not going with him either." The commandant said to my mother, "For you, it is not a problem." But the whites are craftier than we are, for afterwards, the commandant asked Fassala Kanté, the interpreter, to ask me if I wanted to go with my mother or my father. I said, "Huh?? Follow a mother! I'm going with my father!" My mother threw herself on the ground, crying, and put me down in front of the [commandant's] desk. It was actually another woman who brought me here [to the village of Kaboïla].[83]

This recollection was in response to a very basic question posed in order to get to know Dow better and gain a sense of the themes that he believed were important to the history of Sikasso. He started with the generally accepted narrative of the betrayal of Tiéba and Babemba, the simultaneous cruelty and appeal of Samori, and how many warriors who managed to escape the French attack on Sikasso fled to join forces with Samori, including Tiéba's sons. He then told us that many men who fought for Tiéba and Babemba were captured by the French, and subsequently imprisoned. According to Dow, his father and his father's patron, Niabory, were held in prison under the indigénat for a prolonged period. The imprisonment of the surviving men of Sikasso and aligned villages such as Kaboïla, Bugula, and Natie significantly upset the balance of power and divided households throughout the region. As a result of the imprisonment of warriors and other powerful men, many women slaves and junior wives may have chosen to leave their masters and husbands.

It is powerful that this was the curve of Dow's narrative on the early years of colonial rule in Sikasso. Some may question Dow's use of dialogue to recount events that took place when he was a small child, and consequently, the veracity of the oral history itself. However, we can interpret his use of dialogue and first person as an effort to emphasize historical dynamics, which he asserts, shaped the course of his life.[84] Dow related an exchange between the imprisoned men, the commandant, and the women that revealed common assumptions about accepted gender roles, authority, historical processes, and their outcomes. The more powerful of the two men, Niabory, was defiant in the face of the French colonial authority that had imprisoned him and effectively driven away the women of his household. He emphasized his friction with the colonial regime by saying that he could always get more women through similar means. Dow's father's concerns reflected the notion that children belonged to their father, regardless of the status of the mother. The colonial commandant in Dow's story was both underhanded and effective in his arbitration of the situation. Dow was illustrating, through a personalized story, something that historians understand from reading secondary material and colonial reports of the time period: challenges to the authority of certain men in power created an opportunity for those people under their power—such as wives and slaves—to leave unsatisfactory situations, or to seek out other patrons. It does not really matter whether or not Dow truly recollected the details of conversations that occurred surrounding the separation of his parents so many years earlier. What is noteworthy is that this is the memory and the association that he and others constructed around the early years of French colonial rule in the Sikasso region. And in fact, the written record throughout West Africa is littered with anecdotal evidence of women doing just what Dow describes in his story about his mother and father at the time of Sikasso's occupation and early French colonization.

The years from 1905 to 1912 were a time of tremendous transition and change due to the legal end of slavery, the establishment of a colonial court system, and the resettlement of freed persons throughout the communities of Sikasso and neighboring regions in the French Sudan. Oral history, court cases, and other written sources reveal the ways in which everyday social transformations that accompanied these transitions had a significant impact on gendered forms of authority in marriage and the family. Many women and former slaves were in a position to test the reconfiguration of labor and bondedness in the new provincial tribunals. At the same time, the stories of Ma Sidibé and Yaya Dow tell us that not all women who tested their relationships to former masters used the new courts to do so.

Likewise, the stories of Ma Sidibé and Yaya Dow's mother reveal the interconnectedness of marriage and slavery for many women in the early twentieth century, a phenomenon that is reinforced by testimony and records from the provincial tribunals of Sikasso. Slave women who had children by their masters or junior wives (second, third, fourth, or greater) often occupied a space where enslavement and wifely status and expectation were blurred categories of belonging. This was because of the blurred categories of gendered and bonded labor demands, including sexual labor and availability, but this was also because of the perception that French colonial administrators had of both African wives and African slaves. Concisely stated, many in the colonial administration regarded African wives *as* slaves—marriage was perceived as slave-like for African women. Thus liberal initiatives such as the civilizing mission created a native tribunal system within the French colonial legal system that was potentially *emancipatory*—former slaves could seek justice, particularly in cases of property claims and disputes over contracts, and women could seek divorce from husbands who did not pay their bridewealth, abandoned their families, or placed unreasonable labor demands on their dependents.

But the courts did not neatly occupy an emancipatory space, nor was the colonial administrative position, in practice, so liberal. Many local colonial administrators, such as the commandant of Sikasso, were concerned about the social upheaval created by massive slave exoduses, and they were especially concerned with the impact on labor stability and access to cheap, free, or compliant workers. They were also concerned with disturbing any goodwill or diplomatic relations with local men of authority (village chiefs, canton chiefs, powerful household heads), goodwill that may have eroded with the departure of too many former slaves or unhappy wives. Furthermore, the colonial mission itself had been built on slave labor and relied on the support system created by slave women. Thus the colonial administration was in a tenuous place with regard to the role that the provincial tribunals played in the early colonial state. This uneasy balance would persist throughout the twentieth century in different ways.

Bridewealth resided at the center of most marriage and divorce cases in the Sikasso tribunal in the early twentieth century. The cases from the Sikasso provincial tribunals from 1905 to 1912 indicate that women had certain advantages in some circumstances, such as divorce requests, but very often they were not seen as having legitimate claims over their children in the eyes of the colonial state or local men of authority who wielded power and were seen by the colonial administration as local experts on customary practices. Likewise, the provincial tribunal provided a new avenue for men to request the return of departed wives in marriage cases. However, in order for this strategy to work to their advantage, bridewealth payment must have been completed, in accordance with colonial interpretations of customary practice. If we are to take customary practice at face value—or rather, if we are to assume that colonial interpretations of customary practice were heeded, then women were circumscribed in many ways by the provincial tribunal, but at the same time, men were also bound by certain formalized practices, such as bridewealth exchange—and many women held them to this practice. Ma Sidibé, and many women who brought their claims over children as cases to the provincial tribunal, found that they were perceived as not having rights over their children. This is not surprising; according to French divorce and family law, as well as Maliki law, women were not seen as having rights over their children. Yet many persisted in their efforts to keep their children, retain custody, and obtain rights over their children.

The early stage of the provincial tribunal at work, before World War I, was a time when customary categories were tried out by court assessors and colonial administrators—customary categories based on ethnicity and religious faith. As we will see, these categories became more galvanized in the courts after World War I. Regardless of the numerous customary practices that were reified and created, however, one customary practice seemed to transcend rigid ethnic categorization in the eyes of the colonial administration: bridewealth exchange. The centrality of bridewealth, the changing value and practices of bridewealth in local communities, and efforts to identify it as a practice would become increasingly important over the course of the twentieth century.

3 ⤚ Returned Soldiers and Runaway Wives

*Defining the African Family in the
French Sudan, 1912–30*

Each family constitutes a state, which is universal
in West Africa.

—*Maurice Delafosse, Haut-Sénégal-Niger*

ON 10 APRIL 1919, BINTOU TRAORÉ, residing in Bugula and of
Muslim status, addressed the subdivisional court in Sikasso on the matter
of the divorce case that she brought against her husband, Daouda Traoré,
also residing in Bugula and of Muslim status. Days before, Bintou made a
verbal request for a hearing by approaching the commandant of Sikasso.
"I do not want to stay with my husband," she stated. "He does not provide
for me. When he left prison, he punished me severely for being poorly behaved while he was away." Bintou Traoré requested divorce and custody of
her child with Daouda, a girl named Diara. When Daouda took the stand,
he responded that he did not accept the divorce request, and argued that
he did, in fact, provide for his wife. He further claimed, "My wife lied to
me. She has a lover, whom she took while I was in prison." Bintou Traoré
refuted the claim that she had a lover. Neither party brought witnesses with
them to the court. The court ruled in Daouda Traoré's favor, and Bintou
Traoré was ordered to return home, or, in the language of the court, "reintegrate the conjugal domicile." The court's reasoning was "based on general native Muslim custom of the region." Daouda Traoré accepted the
ruling; Bintou Traoré stated that she would appeal the ruling.[1]

After 1912, we begin to see in the colonial courts an effort to codify practice according to religion and ethnicity, but often in ways that were ambiguous and ill-defined in the court archive. These codification practices

often focused on identifying litigants according to Muslim and non-Muslim status. However, as we learned in chapter 2, Sikasso court assessors and colonial administrators often read African customary practices through the lens of codified Maliki law and Muslim practices, particularly bridewealth and divorce. Thus the court's disaggregation of Muslim and non-Muslim categories of practice was, at its foundation, based on European formations of customary and Muslim practice. These changes began to unfold in the years following the first implementation of a legal system in French West Africa in 1905, as we saw in chapter 2, and they accelerated after 1912. The 1919 case of *Bintou Traoré v. Daouda Traoré* is an example of this shift, but this case also reveals much more.

If the earliest colonial courts in the French Sudan privileged a type of gender justice that benefited women's desires to leave marriages and which rested on a concern for the similarities between African marriage and slavery, the second phase of the courts signaled a conservative turn away from such interpretations. After 1912, colonial court assessors in Sikasso handed down rulings that tended to strengthen the position of the patriarch in question, whether he be the father of the married woman or the husband who had paid bridewealth in good faith. This approach to marriage and divorce emphasized the importance of the notion of the African family to the greater project of the stable African colony. Such ideas of the stable and recognizable family were important in a context of increased labor migration, as well as military and labor conscription. If we return to the idea first suggested in the introduction of this book that the illusory quality of the legibility project masks the violence that underpins colonial state projects, the period of World War I and the 1920s is quite instructive. The African family was reified, quantified, and discussed in colonial ethnographies and administrative memoranda, but the harsh realities of life under colonialism challenged household stability throughout the Sikasso region.

This chapter addresses the ways in which the ideologies of scholars and administrators such as Maurice Delafosse and Governor William Ponty shaped administrative understandings of African ethnicity, gender, family, and marriage. For them, the legibility of African marriages rested on identifying patriarchal uniformity within families and across African households. According to such views, the stability of a household and a family rested on a single patriarch's capacity to maintain and control his family, by mitigating circumstances in which married women might become "runaway wives," ensuring that bridewealth agreements were properly honored, and by providing in material ways for his dependents. However, these understandings of patriarchy and family cohesion did not account for certain matrilineal practices of patriarchal authority, wherein male power was diffuse, and they did not account for some Senufo women's marriage negotiation strategies that tested the authority of husbands.

Beginning in approximately 1912 the colonial court began to turn away from women's interests in divorce and marriage cases, a trend that would continue through the 1920s. A few years later, the global event of World War I deeply affected local households and gendered authority throughout the French Sudan. Obligatory military conscription, new forced labor projects, and aggressive taxation during the war effort underscored the violence that defined the realities of life under the "civilizing mission."

Debates between colonial administrators such as Ponty and Delafosse over African ethnicity and political authority significantly contributed to the colonial state's framing of the African family, as well as African marriages and their place in society. Men of authority such as Ponty and Delafosse sought to make ordered sense of the world around them, and in so doing fashioned a model for defining the African family in society and the African family as a microcosm of the state. Both Ponty and Delafosse's notions of the African family in French West Africa, and in the French Sudan in particular, framed the normative family as a measurable patriarchal entity headed by a male elder, typically within a larger patrilineal kin group. When Delafosse wrote that "each family constitutes a state, which is universal in West Africa," he invented a truism that would gain currency among the colonial administrators whom he educated at the French École Coloniale: African families were uniformly coherent and naturally predisposed for governance by a modern state. According to such logic, this organic, family-based patriarchy—bound together through marriage—is what would prepare African women and men to evolve as modern colonial subjects of the civilizing mission.

Such understandings of "the African family" as uniform and organically—as well as recognizably—patriarchal contributed to administrative understandings of familial and marital order, and therefore had an impact on legal reform. Although the early years of the native civil and commercial courts in Sikasso allowed for junior members of households, such as young wives and former slaves, to test some of their bonds, this changed after 1912. In Sikasso after 1912 until the late 1920s, two shifts occurred in the subdivision tribunal (which replaced the provincial tribunal in 1912): the number of civil and commercial cases brought to the colonial tribunal appears to have declined, and marriage-related cases brought before the court often resulted in rulings that reinforced elder male authority over marriages.[2]

This entrenchment of elder male authority in the realm of marriage was tied, in part, to the reinforcement of patriarchal authority under the Ponty administration and according to the formation of colonial expert knowledge by men like Delafosse, but it was also the result of conflicting elements in the formation of native civil law and custom. Colonial administrators continued to be torn between supporting "customary practice" and eradicating practices that were "contrary to French civilization," that dichotomous construction that would persist in administrative dialogue pertaining to native legal courts throughout the colonial period. Administrators on the ground, such as district commandants and their deputies, realized that social order rested on working relationships with local leaders and male elders. Increasingly, this was the case with the advent of World War I.

Young women, for their part, often found themselves at the center of intergenerational conflict between young men and elder men. Marital conflicts, stemming from the departure of a married woman from her household, which was labeled "abandonment of the conjugal home" in the colonial legal context, were often much more than this. Such cases mark tensions between young men and older men, as fathers of brides attempted to exact bridewealth from young men under tremendous labor pressures. These cases also gives us a sense of how the colonial state legal apparatus—as constructed by men such as Delafosse, Ponty, district-level colonial administrators, canton chiefs, and litigants—reinforced a particular idea of marital best practices, based on an idea of patriarchal yet companionate marriage. At times "abandonment of the conjugal home" cases did center on women who wanted to end their marriages. However, not all women brought to court for abandonment of the conjugal home intended to divorce, and were instead engaging in other types of conjugal and extramarital strategies.

Colonial projections of what constituted the African family were cruelly ironic in the context of the years surrounding World War I in Sikasso and the rest of the French Sudan. While ethnographers such as Maurice Delafosse wrote of the "little states" dotting the West African countryside, and Governor William Ponty railed against the corruption of Muslim canton chiefs and the need to liberate Africans from oppressive regimes, women and men throughout the colony found their families upended by forces around them. The forced conscription of soldiers for the war effort, coupled with the coerced recruitment of workers for colonial projects, pulled young men, often thrust forward by elders in the community in the first place, into the French quagmire of colonial state building. Such historical transformations had a deep impact on marriage and family formation in Sikasso and elsewhere in the French Sudan.

IDEOLOGIES OF PATRIARCHY: *POLITIQUE DES RACES* AND THE 1912 LEGAL REFORMS

As early as 1908, French colonial policy shifted toward a focus on local practice and customary law. In this year, William Ponty took on the role of governor-general of French West Africa, replacing Ernest Roume, who had been governor-general since 1902. During his tenure Roume was primarily concerned with uniformity in the legal system itself. Though he did encourage colonial administrators and African court assessors to identify prevailing customs on the ground, this was to be done in an informal manner.[3] In 1912, Ponty decreed a restructuring and reformation of the native courts. In doing so, he called for a renewed emphasis in policy on local knowledge and practice, and attempted to enforce a standardized, colony-wide process of litigation. These transformations of the colonial legal system were the first to take place since its 1903 inception, and were based largely on Ponty's policies concerning African religions, ethnicity, and politics in French West Africa, known as his *politique des races*. Politique des races was both controversial and innovative, calling for the eradication of some forms of African political authority and questioning Islam as a locally relevant faith in sub-Saharan Africa.[4] Some administrators and administrators seriously critiqued his reforms, Maurice Delafosse most notable among Ponty's critics.[5] Like Ponty, Delafosse worked in the colonial administration as a young man, but the two men's different experiences and perspectives on the local populations that they encountered significantly affected their ideologies and opinions regarding African forms of ethnic identity and authority.

For Ponty, such an initiative was centered on at least two factors. First, he believed that if authentic African practices were codified and supported by the colonial administrative apparatus, then the external effects of Islam, in particular Islamic practices that he saw as "imported" from north of the Sahara Desert, would be minimized. Second, Ponty desired a more transparent and efficient adjudication process, namely one that did not rely on canton chiefs. This adjudication process was to be expeditious as well as financially affordable. Above all, Ponty believed that this reformed native court system would provide African litigants, as colonial subjects, with the tools necessary to fully engage with the civilizing mission.[6] Ponty's interpretation of the civilizing mission at this time rested on a belief that the democratizing efforts of the French Republic would lift African subjects out of feudal political systems, which Ponty equated to a pre–Revolutionary France.[7]

Politique des races was a philosophy of ethnic particularism based on the idea that Islam, particularly the Islam of the military and political leaders of nineteenth-century West African revolutions that had swept across the region, was an invasive force in rural West Africa. Ponty believed that Islam shrouded otherwise authentic West African cultures and customs, preventing Africans from evolving according to enlightened, liberal, and ultimately republican notions of civilizing progress.[8] Ponty was unhappy with the trend established in the earlier years of the court that relied on Muslim practice as a framework for considering custom. As he wrote to the lieutenant-governor of the French Sudan in 1910 leading up to the 1912 reforms, "It was never the intention of our native policy to favor Muslim influence."[9] The way toward this African ethnic renaissance, according to Ponty, was to eliminate the canton chiefs, many of whom—particularly in the French Sudan, and certainly in Sikasso—were aligned with the precolonial leadership and were therefore corrupt in Ponty's eyes. Rather than work through canton chiefs, Ponty desired an administrative style of direct engagement with village chiefs and heads of households. His desire was to streamline communication and the paths of uplift that would be so central to the success of the civilizing mission. This uplift was to be guided in an instructional sense, much like the way in which a mentor relates to his tutor, or a father to his child.[10] But rather than turning "Africans into Frenchmen," a notion popular along the coast of Senegal in an earlier French colonial period, West Africans would still retain their authentic Africanness—they would gradually be guided away from repugnant social practices and cultural values.[11] In a sense, politique des races was a project of making the noble savage more noble.[12]

Ponty was certainly paternalistic in his view of the relationship between the French colonial administration and African customs, but he was also committed to a notion of freedom and liberation rooted squarely in patriarchy—that is, the freedom of men to head their own households and derive wealth and labor from their dependents. Like Roume before him, Ponty was concerned about patriarchal rights. However, whereas Roume emphasized a foundation of natural rights and stressed the fact that these preceded French republican values, Ponty made a direct link between the support of patriarchal rights and the maintenance of French republicanism and the rights of man.[13] Such simplified visions of the locus of household and family power did not account for other sites of African authority or expertise, and they do not capture the ways in which junior members of households—including wives and younger brothers—might have contested power and authority. Court cases from the subdivision level in Sikasso reveal such contestations.

Ponty had some powerful allies, such as Paul Marty, the head of the Bureau of Muslim Affairs in French West Africa, but he also had influential critics. Maurice Delafosse's views on Islam were almost diametrically opposed to those of Ponty and Marty. Both Marty and Delafosse conceptualized an "Islam Noir" based on the blending of pre-Islamic African belief and Islamic practice, a type of Islam that was seen as specific to sub-Saharan Africa. However, whereas Marty regarded Islam in sub-Saharan locales such as the French Sudan as a lesser form of the faith, almost inauthentic, Delafosse believed that Islam in West Africa was an organizing force within African communities, one that did not threaten colonial order and thus one that should be respected.[14] William Ponty and Maurice Delafosse departed from each other in significant ways when it came to the empire, particularly on views regarding Islam, canton chiefs, and local authority in West Africa. The two men were often at odds on many issues. However, a point of tacit agreement existed between the two men: they shared a common understanding of the definition of patriarchal power in African societies, most notably, the idea that patriarchal power was an organic force with universally recognizable characteristics.

Both Ponty and Delafosse generated ideologies of patriarchy that had an effect on administrative notions of local household authority and community leadership throughout French West Africa. Administrative notions of African cohesiveness and the possibility for social and political order rested on the conviction that men naturally presented themselves as the protectors and leaders of their families and households. Colonial administrators believed that patriarchy, or respect for the authority of the father in what they recognized to be a household, extended directly to the village chief and to the canton chief. The father in many French Sudanese societies was viewed as a "little chief," in administrative writings. Such ideas were tied to Maurice Delafosse's assertions that the "patriarchal form of the family was the basis of native West African social and political institutions."[15] Although Delafosse surely understood the complexity of social forms and historical variations throughout West Africa, he made sweeping and reductive observations of the African family, drawing comparisons to French family structures of authority: "Each family has a chief, a patriarch, who is . . . the oldest of his generation. . . . He exercises over all members of the family the same authority that the father in our own society exercises over his children."[16] Delafosse based his assertions on ethnographic observation, and used such statements to support his position that the authority of chiefs was familiar to African subjects and not resented or seen as disruptive of local order—that chiefly patriarchal authority stemmed from a familiar form of familial authority rooted in the father and patriarch.[17]

In preparation of the 1912 legal reforms, the French Sudanese governor's office circulated a questionnaire asking district level administrators to define the organization of the "African family" in their regions. The commandant of Sikasso provided particularly clear and precise responses, reflecting the ways in which he perceived the patriarchal and patrilineal unit around him:

Q. How, in general, is the family organized? Is there a "*chef*," a head, and who is it?

A. All members of the same family are grouped under the authority of a head of household [*chef de famille*]. In the beginning, at the death of the founding father, the title would be passed to his oldest. In the case where the head of household has no brother, the title would go to his eldest son.

Q. Does this head or chief depend on another "tribal chief" [*chef de tribu*] or village chief?

A. The head of the household is himself dependent on the village head or chief, who in turn is dependent on the provincial chief or the canton chief.

Q. Does the organization of the family rest on the patriarch [giving authority to the father] or the matriarch [passing authority to the mother's side, as well as the order of succession]?

A. The organization of the family rests on the patriarch.

Q. What does "family" mean in the indigenous sense: Is there a father, a mother, and children, or do we mean all the descendants of one common ancestor, united under the same authority?

A. The "family," in the indigenous sense, includes all the descendants of one common ancestor, united under the authority of one "*chef de famille*."[18]

The questionnaire, although issued in order to collect information on the family and the household in the Sikasso region, was mainly concerned with identifying different figures of authority. The linkage between the head of household to the village chief indicates how important it was for the colonial administration to identify direct connections between the governance of the state and local society. The conclusions drawn from this questionnaire and other types of inquiries like it were that the male head of household, in the form of the eldest male, who was the father to children and the husband to wives, was the political representative of the household, and the only one, at that. The invention of tradition in colonial Africa often took the form of invented monarchy, but this invention goes even deeper to an invention of patriarchy as a family form recognizable to European observers.[19]

These observations regarding family organization, patriarchal heads, and the relationship between households and local government are particularly confused for the Sikasso region. Although patrilineal kinship structure—which the commandant invokes in his responses regarding matriarchy, patriarchy, and descendant patterns—would have made some sense for some Jula or Bambara households, it would not have applied to all of the Senufo inhabitants of Sikasso region, some of whom recognized matrilineal kinship. This is not to say that matrilineages were not patriarchal, but rather, the patriarchal authority in a matrilineage was more diffuse, distributed between maternal uncles and fathers. Accordingly, it was a woman's brother who had authority over her children in terms of the labor provided by the sons and the marriage arrangements for her daughters. Although a matrilineal Senufo husband was not powerless, he was not at the top of a hierarchy made up of his own descendants and wives.[20] With the conquest of Kenedugu and the consolidation of precolonial imperial authority through canton chiefs such as the Traorés, the Bertés, and the Sanogos, the form of patriarchal authority that the state recognized as legitimate adhered to patrilineal form. The Bertés and Sanogos were Senufo—but "Senoufo-Musulman"—which meant that their interpretation of patriarchy and male authority in the family recognized patriarchal structure through Islam as well as Senufo matrilineal descent.[21] Because the local men of authority who informed the colonial administration in Sikasso came from these chiefly families, the expert knowledge constructed around family and household order reflected this reification of patriarchy based on a patrilineal model.

Such imaginings of patriarchal order not only discounted matrilineal forms of patriarchal authority, but they also failed to consider the power that some women might hold within patriarchal family structures. In poly-gynous communities in particular, first wives, or *muso folo* in Bamanankan, held tremendous power. As discussed earlier in chapter 1, the majority of households in Sikasso and the French Sudan generally throughout the twentieth century were polygynous. In such scenarios, the first wife was a powerful figure. Although the first wife was not always the oldest wife, she could often wield power over any wives who came after her, and it was she who was responsible for setting the terms of the labor distribution among the wives within a marriage.[22] The normative notion of the first wife was that she was better treated than her junior wives and that she could compel her husband to "correct" disobedient wives. The hierarchy of wives in such a patriarchal frame suggests that it would be worthwhile to know whether women who introduced divorce cases, or women who left their marital homes under different circumstances, were first wives or junior wives. The historical record of the Sikasso subdivision court does not include this in-formation, which reveals that the court assessors and the tribunal president did not regard it as significant. This erasure of the nuances in power among wives is noteworthy and further suggests the oversimplification in the con-struction of legible patriarchy in African families at work in the colonial tribunal.

Although the dynamics of polygyny and the power that wives held do not frequently appear in the court record, there are glimpses of polygyny at work. On 18 May 1922, Coumba Sall and Ma Diarra, of Muslim status and residing in Sikasso, brought suit together against Sidi Mohammed, also of Muslim status and residing in Bamako. The two women sought divorces from their husband because they claimed that he had not paid bridewealth, and that despite his desire for them to join him in Bamako, he had not sent them any support or funds to pay for their travel. The tribunal granted divorce to the two women.[23]

In a different case, Daouda Traoré, of Muslim status, brought suit on 13 March 1919, against his three wives, Aissata Traoré, Samoradi Berté, and Nalohouna Traoré, all of Muslim status, in the Sikasso subdivisional tri-bunal. Daouda requested that the court compel his wives to return to the marital home. Daouda had been imprisoned in Sikasso from 1917 to 1918, and during that time his wives left him. Aissata claimed that she wanted a divorce because Daouda never paid bridewealth, while Samoradi stated that she never got along with Daouda, even before he was sent to prison. For her part, Nalohouna stated that she did not get along with Daouda and he had never paid bridewealth. Nalohouna, who appeared in court with a baby on her back, refused to reveal the identity of the father of her child, but maintained that it was not Daouda. Aissata's father appeared as a witness to the case and confirmed that he had never received a bridewealth payment, which Daouda himself confirmed. However, the father of Samoradi also appeared in court and stated that Daouda had paid bridewealth and that "he could not understand why his daughter would leave the marriage." The court declared a divorce between Aissata and Daouda, but the fates of Nalohouna and Samoradi were more complicated. Although the court recognized that both women had established new domestic relationships in their husband's absence, it ordered that both women return to the marital home of Daouda Traoré.[24]

These two cases are interesting because the court regarded the women's complaints as the same, rather than giving each wife her separate case against the husband in question. In the case against Sidi Mohammed, his wives appear to be acting together as a unified front by bringing suit against him. Although Daouda Traoré brought one suit against all three of his wives, the conditions of each woman's relationship to Traoré were different. These cases reveal the expectations of model patriarchal behavior—payment of bridewealth, capacity to provide for all wives—and the challenges to these expectations of patriarchy—imprisonment by the colonial state and labor migration.

Theodore André made the following observations of Senufo patriarchy in his 1913 law dissertation. He wrote:

> Thus we find in the organization of the Sénéfo [sic] family the essential characteristics of the patriarchal family: the allotment of inheritance to the oldest son from the head of the family; extensive authority over the younger brothers under the direction of the eldest brother. The government of the village chief is equally patriarchal and is exercised, above all, through persuasion. This is found not only among the Senefo; each race in Haut-Sénégal-Niger seems to be organized according to this patriarchal authority.[25]

André was able to identify patriarchal forms within Senufo matriliny: for him, the recognizable patriarch was not the father, but the eldest brother. The village chief's authority over household heads, in this sense, replicated the eldest brother's authority over younger brothers who lived within the same enclosure or compound. As for the role of marriage, André asserted that although "marriage was the base of all family organization," in places such as Sikasso, "the patriarchal regime, in maintaining the individual in a tight dependence vis-à-vis the community of which he or she is a part, takes away the freedom to unite with a person of his or her own choosing."[26] In this sense, the patriarch is organic, recognizable, and legitimate, but at the same time seen as curtailing an important freedom: to choose whom one marries. The latter issue would pose challenges to colonial notions of evolved marriage, but it would take some time for this to develop as a strategy of reform.

For Ponty, the African patriarch was someone who could combat the effects of Islam on local society and authority. In Sikasso the approach to Ponty's initiatives on this front were conflicted; Sikasso administrators recognized the effectiveness of Muslim canton leaders, particularly men such as Bembanitieni Traoré and Kélétigi Berté. Furthermore, they understood the importance of Jula economic networks, which had long defined the success of the Sikasso market and which were often based in religious affiliations. Still, it seems that there was a concern about the influence of so-called "bad" Muslims on the local population, and the administration hoped it might enlist in the authority and assistance of "acceptable" Muslims (specific canton chiefs and others who worked for the colonial project and could be monitored through surveillance) to weed out the negative influences of Islam. The commandant of Sikasso issued a directive to his council of notables to keep tabs on itinerant Muslims passing through Sikasso, particularly those who might be interested in "bringing about dissension" among animist families, thereby upsetting a "natural patriarchal order of the family, in which the authority of the chief is all-powerful."[27] Thus from the perspective of many in the local colonial administration, the struggle was to maintain rightful patriarchal authority in the family throughout Sikasso.

There were limits to Ponty's politique des races and its application on the ground in Sikasso. Although the colonial administration developed a principle of direct engagement with colonial subjects, this was logistically impossible and undesirable to many commandants at the district level throughout the French Sudan. Canton chiefs allowed for streamlined governance, particularly in the French Sudan, which was vast and contained many thousands of villages of various sizes. In regions such as Sikasso, Ponty underestimated the importance of the former sofas, or warriors, of Tiéba and the descendants of the Traoré family. For some cantons in Sikasso, the men of the precolonial regime were the only effective chiefs and interlocutors of French colonial rule. For example, the chief of Folona canton from 1908 to 1921, Daba Bamba, was noted as one of the most effective chiefs in the region, deriving his influence from his family's longtime authority in the region, predating the rise of Tiéba. When Bamba died in 1921, he was replaced by his younger brother, whom the colonial administration regarded as being of the same disposition.[28] For the local colonial administration, the precolonial authority of some of the canton chiefs proved useful for taxation as well as the formation of customary categories of civil and legal status. This was because many canton chiefs claimed to have extensive knowledge of the populations over whom they presided. These men came from particular lineages whom local administrators in Sikasso regarded as representing specific, ethnoreligious identities central to colonial conceptions of the southern Sudanese landscape. Among other things, they were instrumental in the functioning of the subdivisional court.

According to records from the Malian National Archives and the unclassified Sikasso district archives, the court functioned from 1918 to 1930, but sporadically. Some years are better represented than others in the subdivisional court records, and certain categories of disputes stand out. For example, 1913 to September 1918 were unavailable in both the Sikasso archives and the National Archives of Mali in Bamako. This lack of records might be understood as a reflection of the demands of war. The monthly political reports for Sikasso during this time simply indicate that native justice was "functioning normally" and that interested parties should consult the quarterly and monthly judicial reports. It appears, however, that the governor of the French Sudan's office received from Sikasso only one trimestral report from 1913 and another in 1920, and no reports from the war years.[29] Furthermore, in October 1914, the commandant of Sikasso crossed out the section heading of "justice indigène" of his monthly report, writing in an official request for increased staffing in Sikasso instead, stating that "the European personnel in Sikasso is greatly reduced."[30] The subdivisional court did not hear as many cases during the war years because these courts did not function regularly during that time. Despite the archival silences, the 1918–27 cases provide a glimpse into legal disputes over marriage in Sikasso during the interwar years, even if they are incomplete. They also offer a perspective on how the colonial administration in Sikasso regarded native marriage during this period, and how Sikasso women and men engaged with the apparatus of the court.

Like the divorce cases between the years 1905 and 1912, described in chapter 2, women were often the initiators, citing failure of husbands to pay bridewealth, abandonment, and mistreatment as their reasons for seeking divorce. Yet as we see from the case of *Daouda Traoré v. Aissata Traoré, Samoradi Berté, and Nalohouna Traoré,* the court was hesitant to grant divorce if bridewealth had been paid, even though the husband had served time in prison and could not therefore provide.

We also see the significant appearance of "return of wife/reintegration of conjugal domicile" cases, which were often cases between men, centered on the extramarital relationships between wives and their lovers. "Reintegration of the conjugal home" cases reflect a concern for controlling, and punishing, the so-called runaway wife. A third category of case which appears for the first time during this period is "validation of marriage." Husbands brought validation of marriage cases against their wives when wives left their husband's homes on the grounds that bridewealth payments had never been completed. Men claimed, in validation of marriage cases, that the marriages were in fact legitimate according to local practice, and the fact of the outstanding bridewealth payments was part of a normal but incomplete process. In such cases, men sought the return of their wives, which places such cases in a category similar to that of "reintegration of conjugal home." However, in validation cases, men maintained that the premise of their marriages was valid and often took their wives to court to work out the terms of the bridewealth completion. If we know, from chapter 2, that the most common complaint in successful divorce cases initiated by women in the early years of the court was nonpayment of bridewealth, this new category of case may point to the court's interest in maintaining men's marital interests. It may also point to the fact that by 1912 the court realized that bridewealth was a long-term investment and payment strategy.

Many of the subdivisional cases in Sikasso reveal the marriage-related tensions presented by returned World War I soldiers. Some of the cases indicate that fathers hedged their bets regarding soldiers; while men were away at war, fathers and their daughters sought out alternate marriage options in the event that these men did not return. Such option-building was important for families during a war when so many did not return, and when households relied on the financial and labor support of men who were present. Although elder men might have been otherwise entrusted in helping absent men with their marriage contracts, the World War I period introduced a number of challenging variables.

Testimony from the subdivisional cases shows the shortcomings of the politique des races in practical terms. Although Ponty's reforms created categories for "Muslim" and "non-Muslim" status, there is little indication in the historical record what these labels meant in terms of notions of customs. Rather, it seems that the judicial reforms that came out of the politique des races created a language for justifying certain rulings. Expressions such as "according to Muslim custom of the land" and "according to local custom" were commonly invoked in rulings, as we see in Bintou Traoré's case at the beginning of this chapter. However, there is little to no indication of what this notion of customs was based on, other than the discretion of the court assessors.

TABLE 3.1 CIVIL CASES OF THE SIKASSO SUBDIVISION COURT, 1918–27

Cases organized according to year and type of civil claim

Type of case	1918	1919	1920	1921	1922	1923	1924	1925	1926	1927	Total
Divorce	–	5	–	3	8	–	3	2	5	3	29
Return of wife/reintegration	–	8	1	–	–	–	–	–	–	3	12
Validation of marriage	2	–	3	6	–	–	1	–	–	–	12
Child custody	–	3	1	–	1	–	2	–	–	1	8
Inheritance dispute	–	1	–	3	2	–	1	–	–	1	8
Marriage contestation	–	1	1	–	–	–	–	–	–	–	2
Bridewealth dispute	–	1	–	–	1	–	–	–	–	–	2
Levirate	–	–	–	–	1	–	–	–	–	–	1
Marriage custom	–	–	–	1	–	–	–	–	–	–	1
Marriage annulment	–	–	–	–	–	1	1	–	–	–	2
Debt	–	–	–	–	1	–	–	–	–	–	1
Engagement rupture	–	–	–	–	–	–	–	–	–	1	1
Fishing rights	–	–	–	1	–	–	–	–	–	–	1
Total	2	19	6	14	14	1	8	2	5	9	80

Source: Tribunal de Subdivision de Sikasso, 1918–27, Sikasso *cercle archives*, unclassified. A digital archive of these unclassified records has been made for the Office of the Prefecture, Sikasso, Mali.

As the table shows, there were eighty cases uncovered from the Sikasso subdivisional court over the course of 1918–27; however, it is unlikely that this was the total number of cases heard at the Sikasso subdivision during this time. The archival holdings at the Sikasso prefecture were not classified at the time that research on this project was conducted. Thus the subdivisional cases used in this chapter are the only cases that have been uncovered for the period. However, they serve as a useful sample, and testimony is rich in detail that allows for useful historical analysis.

RETURNED SOLDIERS AND THE REINFORCEMENT OF PATRIARCHAL AUTHORITY IN SIKASSO

The years between 1912 and 1930 in Sikasso were a time of increased colonial development and programming. At the level of the colonial commandant's office, this often manifested as persistent requests to the governor-general's office for increased staffing to carry out more tours and censuses of the district, recruitment of soldiers and laborers for public works programs, and the surveillance of "foreign Muslims" and itinerant teachers. The close-to-the-ground labor for these projects was largely carried out by canton chiefs and *gardes de cercle*, local men hired to be the enforcing and punitive arm of the colonial state. This period signals the transition from assimilation policy—a policy that existed largely as myth for the vast majority of people of the West African interior in the late nineteenth and twentieth centuries, and which had greater meaning for small cadres of elites in the Four Communes of Senegal than anything else—to association policy.[31] Association policy from 1912 through the 1930s exemplified what Sara Berry has called "hegemony on a shoestring"—the exercise of infrastructural and sociopolitical authority on a restricted financial budget.[32] Association required the labor, will, and force of men-on-the-ground, a type of colonial service rooted in violent extraction of various kinds and predicated on competing models of legitimate masculine authority. Association emphasized the need for variation in colonial practice and the retention of native institutions.[33] In this sense, Ponty's politique des races contributed to an overall association policy. But association was more than collaboration with chiefs and a concept of local variation of custom, and in many ways it contributed to the exploitation of power.

Recruitment for World War I deeply affected life throughout French West Africa. In August 1915, the commandant of Sikasso noted that 34 soldiers "had volunteered themselves" as part of recruitment campaigns under way throughout the colony.[34] To be sure, such volunteering occurred within contexts of tremendous pressure and coercion. In February of the following year the commandant was disappointed to report that only 130 soldiers had been conscripted since December in Sikasso. He recommended that recruitment operations recommence in Sikasso as soon as the commission for recruitment completed their work in the neighboring district of Buguni, a district from which many recruits originated.[35] Near the end of the war the commandant's reports to the governor-general had become more impatient: "I can assure the superior authorities that I can manage neither the time nor the trouble to recruit the estimated goal of 800 soldiers." The commandant complained of the extreme shortage of European personnel at the administrative district office, arguing that it was difficult enough to make sure that taxes were collected properly and in due course.[36] Progressively over the course of World War I, the colonial administration found itself spread thin with shortages in funding; it was understaffed and burdened with tasks such as labor and military recruitment. African men and women bore the greatest burden of the colonial project and the war during these times.

Although the tirailleurs Sénégalais existed as early as 1857, there was a dramatic shift in recruitment and objectives for the tirailleurs beginning in 1912. Owing to difficulties in voluntary recruitment in the early years of the colonial period, Ponty decreed that conscription, or drafting, would make up a percentage of the recruitment efforts throughout French West Africa.[37] The reasons for conscription in 1912 were to assist with continued "pacification" efforts in Côte d'Ivoire and other areas considered to be rebellious throughout French West Africa, and to fight resistance to French colonial rule in Morocco. The majority of recruits and coerced volunteers for the tirailleurs in the early years of colonization originated from districts with high slave populations, including Sikasso.[38] The sheer numbers reflected in the political reports from Sikasso do not reflect recruitment totals; it is estimated that between 1910 and 1919, enlistment in the tirailleurs rose from 13,000 to 180,000. While these enlistment numbers include soldiers from throughout French West Africa, recruits from the French Sudan made up the majority of the total number. Data from the interwar period indicate that the southeastern French Sudan produced the greatest number of young men for the draft in all of French West Africa.[39] Conscription for military service and forced labor under the auspices of the mobile draft boards throughout French West Africa removed young able-bodied men from their communities. The crucial decisions of which men were fit for conscription were made not only by the draft boards but also by canton chiefs.

As a result of understaffing, commandants and their deputies turned toward canton chiefs to assist with tax extraction and local administration. William Ponty expected commandants and their assistants to conduct frequent surveillance trips throughout their regions in order to gain local knowledge and enforce colonial rule; during wartime, such trips were virtually eradicated because of personnel shortages. However, the intense recruitment process that came out of the 1912 shift toward conscription required commandants to keep detailed censuses of the young men who would become eligible for recruitment and conscription. Commandants relied on the canton chiefs to identify the young men who would be sent to the draft board at the district headquarters. In certain Sikasso cantons, such as the four cantons of Bugula, Natie, Kaboïla, and Fama, canton chiefs could rely on their political authority to determine who was "eligible" for conscription and who was not. Most of the men conscripted into the army were of ex-slave status or from underprivileged families.[40]

The departure of these young men for the war removed them from the process of marriage preparation, or in cases where they were already married, from maintaining their marriages. Conscripted men were also removed from labor obligations at home and relationships of work that contributed to establishing an interdependent relationship with elder men, particularly in agricultural areas such as the Sikasso region. Ideally, a young man's elders and younger brothers might assist him in the preservation of marriage ties, either by completing bridewealth payments and labor on his behalf, or by providing for his wife in his absence. But in the context of rising taxation and increased labor extraction, providing this support labor and payment was difficult. Fathers who had arranged the marriages of their daughters to men who went off to war found themselves in the hard position of honoring the agreement, particularly if bridewealth payment had commenced. But things did not always work out in ideal ways.

Court records reveal the intricacies of intergenerational tension and marital pressures on young women and men during the period of the post-1912 reforms and World War I. Coercive military conscription was not the only form of aggressive extraction associated with colonial projects during this time in French West Africa. Raw material extraction increased significantly during the Great War. After the war in 1918, the implementation of public works projects such as irrigation systems, road works and railroad development, and farming of export cotton, shea, and caoutchouc (natural rubber) grew exponentially.[41] Many of these extractive initiatives were tied to Ponty's plans for colonial development and the implementation of mise en valeur, or development programs.[42] From the southern Sudanese regions of Sikasso, Buguni, and Koutiala in particular, increasing numbers of young men migrated to northern Côte d'Ivoire to seek labor on plantations in order to enter the cash economy in more formal and lucrative ways.

Soldiers returned from the war often found themselves faced with broken marriage agreements. Traoré Bengali, of non-Muslim status, living in the village of Klela, brought Pere Diarasiambo to court on 18 December 1919. Bengali claimed that before he left with the military regiment, it was arranged that he would be engaged to the daughter of Pere Diarasiambo. Bengali argued that he worked in the fields of Diarasiambo for four years toward the marriage agreement. On returning from the war, he discovered that his fiancée was married to another man, and thus Bengali wanted to claim her as his wife. But the father, Diarasiambo, made the following statement, "When I promised my daughter in marriage to Bengali, she was just a little girl. Bengali worked in my field for one year before he was recruited into the military. However, the father of Bengali did not approve the marriage arrangement after Bengali left for the military. So when my daughter grew up, I appealed to the father of Bengali once more. He did not respond, so I married her to someone else." A witness to the case corroborated Diarasiambo's version of the broken arrangement, and testified, "Twice Bengali's father refused the agreement on behalf of his son. As a result, Diarasiambo married his daughter to someone else." The court ruled in favor of the defendant, Diarasiambo, citing that although non-Muslim custom requires that the groom pay the father of the bride in installments through goods or through field cultivation, the fact that the parents of Bengali refused the marriage agreement rendered it void.[43]

Similarly, on 12 June 1919, Sékou Traoré, a retired soldier, appeared before the subdivision in Sikasso with a claim against Diakité Konaté, in a case labeled by the courts as a "dispute over engagement." Traoré explained, "Before my departure for the war, I was to marry Dourouba Dembélé. My father was supposed to give 100 francs in bridewealth payment on my behalf. On my return from the war, I found her married to Diakité Konaté. I claim the woman who was to be my wife." The defendant in the case, who was the man who allegedly "took" Traoré's wife, explained to the court, "I never heard that my wife, Dourouba Dembélé, was promised to a soldier. She has been with me for a long time. I have yet to pay my bridewealth, but I have 30 francs with me now [to put toward bridewealth]."[44]

The first witness called in the case was the woman at the center of the dispute, Dourouba Dembélé. A woman of twenty years, listed in the record as being of non-Muslim status, Dembélé stated, "I do not want to follow this soldier. He never gave me anything. On the other hand, my husband has yet to pay any bridewealth, and he hits me. Recently, he slapped me because I did not want to rest with him in the afternoon." The second witness called in the case was Dourouba Dembélé's brother, Kélétigi Dembélé, a thirty-five-year-old farmer, listed as being of Muslim status. Kélétigi Dembélé affirmed that his sister was married to Konaté. The court concluded that since Traoré could not prove that Dourouba Dembélé was promised to him in marriage and considering that no bridewealth had ever been paid on his behalf for a marriage to her, his claim was void. The court stated that this was "in accordance with Muslim custom in the country." Dembélé's statement that she was unhappy with her current husband and that he had never paid bridewealth was of no consequence in this hearing.

World War I undermined young men's autonomy and their choices in marriage, as it bolstered the authority of elder men, fathers, and chiefs. Bonds of obligation between young and older men were thus tested as the young men who went to war left behind home-based labor obligations that were supposed to contribute to both maintenance of the household and the creation of material gains that would be drawn on to pay taxes. Such dynamics were a contributing factor to intergenerational tensions that arose in the subdivisional cases from Sikasso following World War I.

In 1922, Alima Touré approached the subdivisional court demanding divorce from her husband, a former soldier whom she had married when he was stationed in Chad. The thrust of her argument rested on her claims that he beat her and that she believed him to be insane. Further, she noted, they were "of different races and religions." In this case, Touré was a Muslim woman of Bambara or Jula ethnicity, while her husband was of non-Muslim status and of Fula ethnicity. The court pronounced a divorce, and the bulk of the ruling rested on the fact that the two were of "different races," rather than the claims of abuse and insanity, but with little to no discussion of what these differences meant to the court.[45]

On 20 April 1922, Zanga Berté, of non-Muslim status and a former soldier, in temporary residence at the military base of Kati, filed a request for a divorce hearing at the subdivision court of Sikasso. Although Zanga Berté made the request while on leave, the court was not prepared to hear his complaint until after the expiration of his leave from the military base at Kati, near Bamako. Because of the demands of his service, he was represented at the subdivision court by his brother, Oumar Berté. The case was brought against Niri Kondé, also of non-Muslim status, who appeared at the court in person. Zanga Berté was absent over the course of ten years due to military service. Returning to Sikasso on leave, he found that his wife had formed a conjugal relationship with Yayou Diabaté in the village of Dieou. He immediately came to the commandant's office and declared that he had been with his wife for twelve years and that they had a son together, and that he had heard that she still considered herself his wife during his absence. But at the hearing it became clear that he had never sent news from the front, nor sent money for her—furthermore, his wife and her family assumed that he had died. As a result, divorce was pronounced. No appeals were issued.[46]

Administrators became increasingly concerned with the rights and privileges of returned soldiers in marriage-related affairs. In many ways, these concerns contradicted the renewed emphasis on elder male authority. One administrator from Sikasso wrote that the absence of their husbands during the war allowed brides to take on lovers, at times multiple lovers, in an attempt to maximize their options. "It is, nevertheless, not rare to find in these cases clever women who take advantage of both sides. If they live with the family of their spouse they benefit from the stipend given to the family through the Colonial Budget; on the other side, they receive gifts and allowances from their lovers."[47] Such strategies were perceived as abuses against the soldiers. The administrator's perspective on this dynamic is quite clear; he placed the blame squarely on the young women, as opposed to the men who brokered their marriages. By the 1930s, colonial administrators would encourage soldiers to solicit a marriage declaration from the civil state. But in the years immediately following World War I, there were no mechanisms in place to support returned soldiers in their claims against elder men responsible for brokering the marriages of their daughters and the young women under their authority.

THE TROPE OF THE RUNAWAY WIFE

Throughout many parts of colonial Africa, a familiar figure features in the historical record: the runaway wife. She turns up in the Tanganyikan native courts beginning in the 1920s, simultaneously a passive victim of seduction and a disobedient daughter who complicated the bridewealth arrangements between her husband and her father.[48] The runaway wife appears in the Gold Coast in the 1920s and '30s as an adulterer.[49] She shows up yet again in the Zambian Copperbelt in the 1930s, forsaking life and marriage in the countryside for labor and lifestyle opportunities in the growing towns.[50] In the 1940s she appears in the British colonial records of Gusiiland, Kenya, as a woman fleeing forced marriage with an older and wealthy man, whose only redeeming quality is that he can afford soaring bridewealth prices.[51] The runaway wife in the French colonial courts in

Kayes, the French Sudan, was a law-breaking woman escaping domestic violence.[52] Pervasive and unruly, the runaway wife appears as a transgressive figure that upset the moral economy of patriarchal forms and whose actions reveal the breakdown of the African family writ large.[53] Her enduring presence in the historical record points to common dynamics and transformations in colonial African societies, especially from the 1920s through the 1940s. These transformations include dramatic changes in labor, the growth of urban centers, and shifting bridewealth requirements to meet the demands of a monetized economy. However, the runaway wife is an archetype standing in for so many individual women who both respond to complex hierarchies and initiate actions to serve their own interests.

Some women who became runaway wives in the colonial record were in fact trying to negotiate their own interpretations of marriage and conjugality in a context of increasingly closed definitions of marriage and family.[54] This is not to say that they were forsaking marriage, but rather that they sought to shape their marriages in ways that met both their own interests and those of the larger community. In critically examining the local Sikasso archives, commandant's administrative reports, and the published documentation of administrator-ethnographers, we see that women deemed runaway wives in Sikasso from the 1920s through the 1930s were doing at least two things: they were seeking to break unsatisfactory marital bonds or they were using culturally appropriate leverage to negotiate the terms of their marriage.

On 27 March 1927, Loungara Courobary, a resident of Ferkessedugu, Côte d'Ivoire, sued his wife, Ma Diarra, in the tribunal subdivision court of Sikasso, for abandonment of the conjugal home.[55] Courobary, of non-Muslim status, explained to the court that and his wife had been married for a number of years. However, he acknowledged that he had not completed bridewealth payments. After they had been married for a few years, his wife's sister died. Courobary gave his wife permission to return home to Sikasso for a condolence visit. She remained for some time, finally writing to him and declaring that she would not return and that they were no longer married. In response, Courobary sent Ma Diarra 300 francs. She refused to accept it. As a result of these actions, Courobary explained, he sought the tribunal's assistance in forcing her to return to him.

In return, Ma Diarra explained that Courobary treated her very poorly, insulted her, and drank *dolo*, or beer, all the time. She declared that she did not love him and that he had not paid the bridewealth for their marriage. The tribunal then posed the following questions:

Q. Before you married him, did you know that Loungara Courobary drank *dolo*?

A. Yes.

Q. You have no other motive for divorcing him other than his bad character?

A. No, but he really does make me suffer. He beat me.

Q. Did he wound you?

A. No.

Q. Who arranged your marriage?

A. Mamadou So.

Q. Does he have rights over you?

A. No.

At this point, the tribunal questioned the wife of Mamadou So, Mama Kouyaté, as she was residing in Sikasso at the time. Kouyaté explained that she and her husband knew Courobary, as they had been traveling in Côte d'Ivoire. She also explained that she was neither a relative nor a close ally to either party involved in the case. When Kouyaté and So were in Côte d'Ivoire, they were approached by Courobary, who asked if Kouyaté could assist him in obtaining a wife. On her return to Sikasso, Kouyaté asked Diarra if she would consent to marrying Courobary. She agreed, and went with Kouyaté to Ferkessedugu, Côte d'Ivoire. Kouyaté testified that she received a total of 75 francs from Courobary, and that the two of them had agreed on a bridewealth of 300 francs for the marriage. Taking all things into consideration, the tribunal ruled that the marriage was null and void because neither Kouyaté nor So had any familial authority over Ma Diarra. The nonpayment of bridewealth made the decision easier to maintain. Nowhere in the verdict was mention of Diarra's claims of abuse or dissatisfaction with the marriage.[56]

On 16 June 1921, Abdoulaye Traoré approached the court and declared that his wife, Sita Traoré, was constantly leaving their home, and at the moment that he brought their case to the court she was no longer living with him. The canton chief, who was also the head of the family, Tiémoko Traoré, attempted to reconcile the two, to no avail. Their marriage, the court assessor noted, was arranged according to Jula custom. Sita explained to the court that she was the daughter of Tiéba Traoré, and that her husband was the son of Babemba—hence, the two were cousins. She argued that the marriage was arranged for political reasons, that the two had been promised to one another since childhood, but she could not remain within the marriage because of her husband's violent character. Neither litigant brought a witness forth in the case. The president of the tribunal, who on that day was Kolondougou Sanogo, assisted by two notables of Muslim status and the secretary of the court, M. Perron, the deputy commandant of Sikasso, ruled thusly: given that the two were legitimately married according to Jula custom and that they come from the dynastic Traoré family, and that Sita cannot provide any proof of her mistreatment, Abdoulaye's claims were deemed legitimate and he is "authorized to compel his wife to return to their home." No appeals were issued.[57]

However, some women who fit into the category of the runaway wife were not seeking to leave their marriages. As shown in chapter 1, on occasion, it was culturally appropriate for Senufo women to leave their conjugal homes to go live with another man, without justifying the departure and without signaling the act as a move toward permanent divorce. She might do this after being physically punished, or in the event that the husband had a bad harvest and times were difficult for the household. If she took such action, the husband was not seen as having corrective power over here; rather, it was his task to win her back, often with the payment of cowry shells or other material offerings.[58] Bohumil Holas, an ethnographer who conducted fieldwork in Senufo communities based in Côte d'Ivoire and the French Sudan between 1946 and 1955, did not find evidence of this practice.[59] However, Holas conducted his research some thirty to forty years after André, and Holas conducted all of his ethnographic interviews with men of influence: village and canton chiefs and poro society members, in addition to male intermediaries or "middle figures"—colonial interpreters, teachers, and doctors. Even if such practices were still in existence in the post–World War II period in Senufo communities, these men may not have characterized women's departures from the marital home as part of a normal course of action.

These cases reveal concerns that overshadowed other issues that emerged from the subdivisional cases in Sikasso immediately following World War I: numerous parties were invested in marriage and therefore attempted to interfere in marriage negotiations or broker marriage arrangements; and returned soldiers struggled to uphold their marriage contracts and the marriage agreements that they had procured before leaving for the war.

The authority of fathers and questions over who had rights to broker and benefit from a marriage were issues that concerned colonial administrators. On 5 October 1920, the office of the French West African governor-general issued a memo to the lieutenant governors of the colonies addressing a survey on the "legality and morality of native marriage" that was conducted by local district administrators. "Fathers possess the ability to contract the marriages of their daughters, from the time of their infancy. . . . [This is] a custom that is incompatible with the principles of our civilization, constituting a form of slavery."[60] As a result, the memo suggested, judges of native tribunals and commandants should be careful to limit the influence of family members and other people on the constitution of a marriage arrangement—the only person who should be allowed to interfere with a marriage arrangement in the legal sense should be the father of the bride. According to the memo, "The problem posed herein touches upon one of the most delicate points of native, individual rights: the constitution of the family and the rights coming from paternal authority, a guardian's authority, or marital authority. . . . This is not only a philosophical point of view, but a political and judicial point of view."[61]

This 1920 memo highlights the challenges of early policy on marriage: the balance between individual rights and patriarchal authority, particularly as they pertained to women. After some fifteen years of civil cases in the native courts, colonial administrators struggled to draw the line between unlawful coercion and customary practice—that is, acceptable multiparty involvement in the marriage of young women. *Courobary v. Diarra* exemplifies this problem. Although the defendant in the case cited at least two reasons why she wanted to dissolve the marriage, the one reason that swayed the court assessors to rule in her favor was the question of who had arranged her marriage. The person who benefited from her marriage was not a male family member, and therefore the marriage was rendered invalid.

Many cases labeled as abandonment, issues of "runaway wives," or disputes over marriage engagements were situations determined not by the woman in question, but by her father or the man responsible for arranging her marriage. Male elders who were responsible for arranging young women's marriages became increasingly relevant to the ruling marriage-related cases. Testimony from all of the cases examined here reveals that young women's concerns in marriage were not at the center of the rulings. Rather, the question rested on the agreements between the male elder responsible for brokering her marriage and the man to whom she would be married. This was a departure from the focus of the tribunal de province cases before 1912. This shift was supported by the renewed interest and reliance on patriarchs and male authorities.

The colonial administration in the French Sudan, particularly under the direction of Governor-General William Ponty, had a vested interest in supporting, defining, and reifying patriarchy in African families. This was an extension of a liberal political investment in notions of freedom and liberty, but it was also a reflection of Ponty's desire to circumscribe the influence of Islam on local communities. Ponty, and many other like-minded political actors, interpreted liberty as the rights of the father or the man to be the head of his own family and household, unencumbered by a monarch or government interference. This notion significantly affected colonial interpretations of family order and kinship on the ground throughout West Africa, and it reinforced the notion that the legibility of African marriages rested on the identification of a patriarchal figure.

Although Ponty desired a reform of the canton chief system, a system of authority that he believed to be a corrupt throwback to precolonial Islamic revolutions in West Africa, the colonial administration relied deeply on canton chief authority. This was due to the onset of World War I, and the fact that commandants on the ground believed it unrealistic to eliminate the canton chief system. Thus canton chiefs continued to exercise tremendous authority throughout the countryside, benefiting from an administrative ideology that privileged patriarchy as an organic and familiar foundation of society. This emphasis on patriarchy reinforced administrative designs on modern colonial state building.

Although the early years of the native civil and commercial courts in Sikasso allowed for junior members of households, such as young wives and former slaves, to test some of their bonds and use the courts as a venue for determining which relationships were worth renegotiating, cases from the Sikasso subdivisional courts after 1912 reflect a reinforcement of elder male authority in the marriage-related cases of younger men and women. Here we see a shift in the type of gender-based justice that the subdivisional court reinforced. The historical record from the subdivisional court in Sikasso reveals intergenerational tension and marital pressures on young women and men during the period of the post-1912 reforms and World War I. These pressures stemmed from the consolidation of male elder authority in civil court rulings. To a degree these rulings were rooted in Governor-General William Ponty's politique des races, a political philosophy that privileged local varieties of custom in the execution of French colonial rule. However, the silences in the court record are deeply revealing: women brought their divorce and marriage-related troubles with much less frequency to the colonial courts as litigants, and increasingly appeared in court as defendants in marriage-related cases.

The demands and concerns of returned soldiers in turn raised concerns for administrators. By the mid-1920s, it became increasingly clear that it would be challenging for the courts to both uphold elder male authority and support the demands of young men in the civil courts. These intergenerational crises of masculinity would continue to challenge state making in the French Sudan and the shape that marriage reform would take throughout the twentieth century.

Map 4.1 Sikasso region with specific cantons, ca. 1930. Map by Don Pirius

4 ⮑ Wealth in Women, Wealth in Men

The Global Depression of the 1930s,
Competing Labor Obligations, and the
Mandel Decree

THE MANDEL DECREE OF 1939 WAS THE first state-mandated marriage reform in French West Africa and French Equatorial Africa. The decree, named after France's Minister of Colonies from 1938 to 1940, Georges Mandel, was a formative step in the development of a vocabulary and a policy on marriage and women's rights in West African politics. Reformers who actively pushed for the Mandel Decree devised a template of concerns based on their own notions of women's rights and their own interpretations of the restrictions of those rights in Africa. Such concepts of rights and the ways in which they were restricted were not rooted in nuanced understandings of the historical, locally grounded variables of marriage and the intimate links between marriage, economics, power, and work. Marriage practices and the status of women were often examined apart from other practices. They were often regarded as static ethnographic curiosities. Marriage and religion were understood as linked only insofar that Muslim men could have many wives. "Fetishists" were perceived as treating their wives like livestock to be traded. Those who argued for marriage reform and the rights of African women posited that so-called primordial African practices were not in line with French civilization. According to this position, the unchanging mores were to blame for the low status of the African woman and her position in marriage. After World War I, marriage practices in Sikasso changed in part because of colonial dynamics such as military conscription, migrant labor, the *mise en valeur* agenda, the consolidated power of the canton chief, who served as an intermediary to the local colonial administration, and the effects of the Global Depression.

From the late nineteenth century through the 1920s, French colonial administrators attempted to render certain marital practices legible according to customary law; however, the 1930s heralded a period in which the state attempted more forceful interventions in African marriages through top-down decree issued by the Minister of Colonies. Within this context, ideas about gender justice were based on a major shift in the marriage legibility project: a move from efforts to establish marriage legibility to the enforcement of restrictions and definitions of acceptable practice in African marriage. The Mandel Decree of 1939 is illustrative of this shift. However, reformers failed to understand the impact of the Global Depression on local interpretations of wealth in women and wealth in men. Resurgence in human pawning and the monetization of marriage arrangements sparked an interest among Catholic missionaries and local administrators to eradicate such practices, which they regarded as "slavelike." At the same time, specific Catholic missionaries sought their own form of gender justice: justice for young African women, whom missionaries perceived to be caught in the trap of forced marriage and commoditized marriage.

This chapter links the changing economic and agricultural practices among Senufo communities in Sikasso to changes in local marriage practices in the 1930s. Among these changes was an increased monetization of marriage transaction, often in the absence of ritualized prestation that underpinned the forms of bridewealth discussed earlier in the book. Such marriage arrangements resembled human pawning to local administrators and Catholic reformers. Pawning was the act of giving a dependent, often a woman or a child, in exchange for a loan in currency or other necessary resources. A human pawn could be redeemed, but oftentimes, particularly in cases in which the pawn was a woman, she would be incorporated into her new household upon the failure to redeem. Pawning and the monetization of marriage transactions increased during the Global Depression of the 1930s. Some Catholic reformers and colonial administrators used these practices to call for a more interventionist marriage reform strategy on the part of the colonial state. It was in this context that the Mandel Decree of 1939 emerged, a decree that established consent as the basis of legal and legitimate African marriage.

Normative accounts of Sikasso's past, in the form of ethnographies and oral accounts, depict turn-of-the-century marriage in Sikasso as a regulating force in Senufo society. Although such accounts most likely do not capture the real, lived experience of marriage during the period, they do represent ideal expectations, particularly those of elder men in positions of authority. Such men, particularly heads of household or fathers or uncles of girls, strove to maintain certain marriage patterns reflected in these accounts. Accordingly, Senufo men could gain wives in a number of ways that reinforced various units of membership—the virilocal household, the matrilineal descent group, age-grades and secret societies, and the village. The myriad paths toward marriage complemented and contributed to these units of belonging, and maintained a political balance that privileged the authority of the matrilineal patriarchs of a community as well as the chief. In practice, however, increased pressure on men's labor pulled young men away from their farming obligations, thereby upsetting the balance of power and mutual obligations that contributed to community cohesiveness. Matrilineal elders in Sikasso began to lose authority over young men and their labor, while village and canton chiefs consolidated their power as intermediaries under the colonial state. However, matrilineal patriarchs could combat this loss of power and imbalance by enforcing avenues to marriage that required prolonged labor obligations on the part of young men and by restricting access to daughters.

Against this backdrop of pronounced change in regions such as Sikasso, colonial administrators and Catholic missionaries identified what they saw as a crisis in African marriage and the plight of African women. Pawning, which increased in the 1930s throughout West Africa, was both the result of the pressures of the cash economy and efforts to redistribute wealth in people and social obligations in a time of crisis. Missionaries and administrators who worked in West African villages and towns identified the resurgence in pawning, which more often than not targeted young women of low social standing. Colonial administrators such as Jules Brévié concerned themselves with identifying rights, which they believed to be universal and inalienable. Once such rights were clearly identified, colonial officials could go to work ensuring that these rights were protected by the colonial state itself. Driving these reforms was the concern that local African patriarchs—and the sociocultural practices that undergirded their authority—threatened African women's human rights, namely through forced marriage and the act of marrying off girls to older men.

The concern that African women were forced into marriage and exchanged as brides often stemmed from ideas that African marriage and the position of African women were timeless and unchanging and that they could only advance with the uplifting assistance of missionaries and the colonial state. Most colonial officials, missionaries, and activists failed to realize that there were local processes of negotiation and contestation of marriage practices taking place concurrently with their bureaucratic efforts to reform marriage in French Sudan. Furthermore, they failed to see the historical and social changes taking place in regions such as Sikasso, changes that affected marriage practices and access to economic and social resources. It was within this context that the colonial state devised its first marriage reform decree.

COMPETING LABOR DEMANDS OF THE 1930S: WORKING FOR THE STATE AND WORKING FOR MARRIAGE

In the early 1930s, Sikasso served as a crossroads for the interregional markets of West Africa. This was something about which administrators could do very little, despite their wishes to direct market energies toward France rather than within the West African regional economy. The commandant of Sikasso noted in 1933: "As usual at this time of the year, there are a number of caravans passing through Sikasso—they go to the south with dried fish, or come north from Côte d'Ivoire with kolas."[1] The regional food market in Sikasso did quite well in the first half of the 1930s according to colonial reports. Unlike most other areas of the colony, the men and women of Sikasso were not only feeding themselves throughout the 1930s, but they were also feeding communities located in other districts. Colonial administrators remarked that the Sikasso-based cultivation of millet was bountiful enough not only to draw clients from surrounding villages and cantons but also from Buguni, Koutiala, and Bobo Dioulasso.[2] Sikasso growers produced fonio, yams, potatoes, peanuts, and manioc, and sold them in the regional market. Shea nut collection and shea butter production were successful over the same period, with vendors coming up from Côte d'Ivoire to purchase the product for resale in the south.[3] Abderahamane Berté, the influential canton chief of Kaboïla who replaced his deceased father, Kélétigi, petitioned for a sheet-metal roof for the Sikasso market, arguing that the thatched roof was not ample for the vendors and that its dampness encouraged mosquitoes.[4] The local market was not only sustaining Sikasso; it was sustaining the broader region.

However, men and women throughout the Sikasso region did feel the effects of the Global Depression. The Global Depression of the 1930s hit France in 1931, and the effects were soon felt throughout French West Africa. The Depression hit the French Sudan hard, as France's response was to increase taxation in the colonies. Under such conditions, African farmers were responsible for increased cash-crop production, but this would be contentious, as colonial efforts would compete with preexisting regional trade networks and markets. As a major agricultural, cash-crop producing area of the French Sudan, Sikasso farmers experienced tremendous pressure during the Global Depression. Colonial administrators struggled to harness what they believed to be the full potential of Sikasso's growing capacity. They quickly realized, however, that it was difficult to control the directional flow of crops out of Sikasso, the quantity of cash-crop production, and the types of crops that Sikasso peasants would cultivate. In 1933, the colonial administrator from Sikasso complained that it was extremely difficult to convince cotton producers in Sikasso to sell their cotton on the European markets. He noted that producers were taking at least half of their cotton and trading or selling it on the local transregional markets with Côte d'Ivoire.[5] Colonial administrators also encouraged peasant women to devote their energies to the cultivation of groundnuts instead of the collection of shea nuts, as groundnuts provided a more regular harvest and had a wider appeal on the international market at the time. Colonial administrators considered developing rice paddy production in the Sikasso region as well. As with cotton, administrators incorrectly believed that the flood plains of the Bani and Niger rivers could successfully sustain an irrigation system that would support large-scale rice production along the model of the Asian rice cultivation techniques that they had seen in Indochina. Rice cultivation in the Bani River floodplains was long established in the Buguni-Sikasso region, and the ecology of the region accommodated seasonal rice cultivation by submersion, interspersed with cattle grazing and other grain production.[6] Rice was not the primary staple of the diet in the Sikasso region, but it was an important part of a diverse food system. Although efforts to develop rice-paddy production were ultimately short-lived, they reflect the colonial administration's increased desire to control local agricultural production and market flows in the 1930s.

The region of Sikasso produced a high volume of agricultural goods and did well to feed its inhabitants, but the practices and strategies of peasants in Sikasso troubled colonial administrators during the Global Depression. They wanted to see more cash flowing into the Sikasso markets and into the hands of producers so that they could pay their taxes and buy commodities from the colonial import economy. They also wanted cultivators to significantly increase production for the European markets. This was particularly the case with cotton production. Administrators were concerned that the low prices on the market, if left unmitigated, would discourage native cotton production.[7]

Although the men and women of Sikasso fared better than their neighbors in terms of food supplies and local markets, access to cash was limited, and people struggled to pay their recently increased taxes. Many households grappled with the predicament of the changing regional and transregional economy. Diversified crop production, which Sikasso peasants maintained to a relative degree despite colonial ambivalence on the topic, allowed small-scale peasants to feed themselves and their families, and produce goods for the local "African" markets. It did not, however, satisfy the demands of the increasingly cash-based economy or the European trading houses, which solicited farmers for cotton. By the mid-1930s, cash-crop production had significantly infringed on sustenance farming in the Sikasso countryside, with cotton gaining an edge in diversified fields that also grew manioc, millet, and corn.[8] This shift in crop production heralded a corresponding shift in labor relationships and the social and political world of agricultural life.

Ideally, from at least the early nineteenth century into the 1920s, Senufo farmers distributed their agricultural labor across two different types of fields, which corresponded to their membership in village residential area and a matrilineage, as well as their conjugal household.[9] Men and women worked primarily on collective labor fields of a residential area, comprised of members of a common matrilineage and managed by the village elders of established matrilineages.[10] These collective fields were viewed as the most important, as the gains from these fields were used for funerary and marriage celebrations, food for guests, as well as basic sustenance for each household belonging to the lineage. The collective fields were also important because work in the fields solidified the importance of the matrilineage, an important exercise in virilocal matrilineages. Virilocality emphasized the authority of the oldest male in the household, while matrilineal descent groups privileged kinship ties through the mother's line to a common female ancestor. Men, namely matrilineal uncles, still held tremendous authority in a matrilineage, but authority in a virilocal household that belonged to a matrilineage was diffused, as it was shared both by the father (who was the head of his household) and the mother and her brothers (who represented the matrilineages interests).

As shown in previous chapters, oral accounts and ethnographies depict marriage in the precolonial and early colonial period as a component in an organized, stable society. According to these accounts, Senufo peasants worked together in subgroups according to age-grade, sex, and status (slaves and descendants of slaves often worked in units together, for example). People strived to maintain a balance of gendered labor distribution across various fields. Ideally, men and women farmers worked on the collective fields for four days out of a six-day working week. For the remaining two days of the week, conjugal households worked together on individual fields managed by the male head of the household.[11] If a household was particularly wealthy, a husband might give his wives, or at least his senior wife, a small plot for her own garden, which she would use for condiments and other supplements for the daily meals. The yield from these fields supplemented the bare essentials that came from the collective field and might be used for market sale as well. A portion from both fields would be stored for food reserves. According to such labor schemes, men and women worked for both their matrilineage and their household, thereby ensuring some degree of balance between household heads and lineage heads, though the matrilineage and its fields always took precedence.

Thus, among Senufo farming families of the Sikasso region, labor obligations were ideally deeply embedded in larger social and cultural obligations, primarily those tied to matrilineal connections and marriage intentions.[12] Marriages were inextricably linked to land cultivation, as they served to deepen kinship ties and create pathways of connection across certain matrilineages. During the late precolonial and early colonial period, Senufo men sought to contract marriages according to one of four common processes. Through prolonged, hard work in the collective field a man might be given a "wife of the collective field" or of the larger matrilineal descent group. If a young man had a close relationship with his maternal uncle or if he worked in his uncle's personal field, the uncle might reward the nephew by brokering a marriage with a "wife of the lineage," typically a cousin. A father, who would not normally pass on inheritance or wealth to his son in a matrilineage, could also give his son a woman who had been given to him. The last arrangement was called "giving a wife for doing a good deed." It required that a young man work one day a year over the course of fifteen to twenty years in the field of another lineage, with the help of ten to twenty of his friends.[13] This last way of brokering a marriage was perfectly acceptable, but it was not the favored or common method of marriage. This was for a number of reasons. First, it required that a young man and his age-mates take their work outside the collective and the conjugal fields, thus diffusing their labor obligations. Second, the marriage brokered from such an arrangement was a marriage completely outside the lineage, thereby dividing the allegiances and the labor power of the conjugal household across lineages.

In her study of Chewa history in Nyasaland/Malawi, Megan Vaughan commented that "the near invisibility of the economic role of the matrilineage in the culture of the area contrasts strongly with the emphasis placed on the matrilineage and its more formal role as a political or ritual unit."[14] This predicament appears also to be true for Senufo families in the Sikasso region, perhaps even more so than what Vaughan observed in the matrilineal and *matrilocal* communities that she studied. As Senufo families tended to be virilocal, meaning that the location and the general makeup of the household pivoted around the husband, the economics of the household unit probably appeared to be exclusively patriarchal to the colonial officials observing work. However, inheritance and most importantly, labor obligations, and rights to determine marriage remained either squarely in the matrilineage or were a point of struggle between the conjugal household and the matrilineage.

During the late 1920s and the 1930s, there was a dramatic shift in labor demands and land use. In addition to the Global Depression, the 1930s were a time of heavy labor recruitment for the deuxième portion, a system of forced labor that existed between 1926 and 1950. The *deuxième portion de la contingent militaire* was part of the larger effort to recruit soldiers for military conscription, but the deuxième portion vetted men who were not fit enough for military conscription into forced labor projects for the colonial state.[15] In the French Sudan, the main projects associated with the deuxième portion were road construction, railway construction, and the immense irrigation projects of the Office du Niger in the Niger River Valley. Although the Office du Niger pulled workers from Sikasso region away from their home villages, the deuxième portion road projects were an even larger draw from the southern French Sudanese region. In Sikasso, deuxième portion workers primarily toiled on two road construction projects, one heading south to Côte d'Ivoire and one heading east to Bobo Dioulasso. The workers of the deuxième portion received a meager wage, clothing, and food in exchange for two or three years of hard labor. Frederick Cooper estimates that on average, 1,900 men were recruited each year in the French Sudan for the deuxième portion.[16] Although there are no reports available to this study that indicate the numbers of men recruited from the Sikasso region for the deuxième portion, all of the older men interviewed in the villages of the Sikasso region vividly recalled the work that men performed on deuxième portion projects, particularly the road to Côte d'Ivoire. Workers recalled that meals in the deuxième portion consisted of coarse millet and bad fish, but they also ate uncooked peanuts and locally produced rice that colonial officials considered too poor for the global market but acceptable for local consumption.[17] Cékoura Berté recalled the hardships of deuxième portion work:

> We carried banco [dense mudbricks] on our heads for the road. There weren't any machines, so we crushed the banco with picks. We would pile it up as high as our chests, otherwise they would hit us. They would whip you five times. We would always sing when we worked. They always had a whip with them. And the crickets ate us up for 7 years. You could go from here all the way to Kebeni without seeing any millet. . . . If God had not helped us, truly we would have died.[18]

Berté explained that the men of Sikasso region were responsible for carrying wooden planks, broken gravel, or banco, and iron rods to the road site, where four men would lay the rods, then build the road around the foundation. He explained that they were beaten often for laziness, for "incorrect" work, and for hiding. However, he indicated, "the whites themselves never hit anyone, it was always the blacks. . . . It was the power of the *jamanatigi* [canton chief]."

Men's migration to Côte d'Ivoire undermined local labor conditions and field cultivation responsibilities. Men migrated for work on cotton and rubber plantations and for work in the big cities, which were closer to Sikasso than the other colonial outposts in Senegal, Kayes in western French Sudan, or Bamako, the colonial capital. In a 1947 census and regional assessment of the canton of Folona, the colonial administrator lamented the fact that after the harvest each year, in approximately September, more and more young men left their villages to make money in Côte d'Ivoire.[19] This already occurred over the course of the early twentieth century but dramatically increased in the early 1930s. Although the young men who left often returned for the next harvest with currency for tax payment, their absence created more of an agricultural burden for those who remained. Yacouba Koné and his brother, both of whom resided in Sikasso, went to Côte d'Ivoire to earn cash working on the plantations when they were very young men. Koné recalled that at the time he was surprised to discover that there was forced labor there as well. He stated that he went there to cultivate and that a commandant came to the fields and exclaimed that "even the farmers" were required to do forced labor.[20]

Forced labor recruitment and cash-crop cultivation significantly interfered with social and cultural obligations, particularly if these practices were tied to the land or involved agrarian labor. As labor demands intensified with colonial intervention in everyday life, men's and women's agricultural labor practices shifted. As a result, marriage arrangements shifted in response to changes in labor patterns.

By 1945, the large, collective fields in Korhogo, northern Côte d'Ivoire, had dissolved.[21] Forced labor and cash-crop cultivation, the latter of which was done in the fields controlled by the jamanatigi, pulled men away from the village-based, collective fields, thereby taking authority away from matrilineal heads, who would otherwise control the labor of their sisters' sons and the balance of the collective. In Korhogo, the practice of "giving a wife for doing a good deed" became increasingly common because the collective fields had largely dissolved as a result of the decrease in workers' availability during the bulk of the week. As a result, matrilineal heads lost control over the labor of the young men of their kin group. Young men's labor became more central to their household-level production and to other matrilineages in the process of brokering marriages to "wives who were earned for doing a good deed."

In the Sikasso region to the north of Korhogo, the same dynamic appears to have taken place. In fact, control over youth was even more difficult in Sikasso as young men were not only pulled into forced labor and cash cropping, but actively participated in seasonal migrant labor to the Ivorian cotton and cocoa fields. Under such labor conditions, the power of the jamanatigi increased, the power of the matrilineal elder decreased, and young men attempted to forge alternatives that would give them access to the new cash economy and some degree of autonomy from elder male authorities. This relatively sudden shift in labor control and harvest flows created shock waves among matrilineal male elders who did not directly participate in the political hierarchies rewarded by the colonial state. Elders struggled to find avenues for harnessing the labor power of young men in a changing world. Although young men could not be urged to work regularly in the collective fields and therefore be rewarded with wives for such work, they could do field labor one day a year, thereby earning their wives. However, the labor obligations for the intended bride's family became increasingly prolonged. Furthermore, as such labor for marriage required the strength of ten to twenty men, young men were obligated not only to work the one day a year for their own wives, but a day for each of the other men who belonged to the labor collective. In addition to field cultivation, the suitor might also be expected to offer gifts to the bride's family, as well as play an important role in funerary rites and other important celebrations that honor the ancestors of his wife-to-be's matrilineage. When the intended bride comes of marriage age (around the time of puberty) the actual marriage would be brokered between an intermediary of the suitor's household or family and the head of the bride's household. The protracted quality of the marriage obligation was the cement that bound the marriage contract between the suitor and the bride's family.[22]

In interviews, elderly men in the Sikasso region recalled the details of the practice in different ways. For example, Cékoura Berté of Kaboïla recalled that a young man would approach the father of the woman he wanted to marry, and if the father agreed to the arrangement, the young man would work in the fields for more than ten years with nine or ten of his friends.[23] Berté emphasized that it was especially difficult to cultivate during the time of forced labor. Quite simply, he stated, "We suffered." Yaya Dow recalled:

> If a man was courting a girl, each year he would work in her father's field with nine of his friends or brothers. All of us [gesturing to other compounds nearby] did that for our wives. With the politics, we found that this cultivation was too difficult. You would be responsible for cultivating right up until your wife had her first child. The child had to bring the daba [hoe] with his fathers to the fields in order for you to stop.[24]

However, matrimonial arrangement through cultivation was not the only acceptable way to contract a marriage at this time. During times of increased pressure on land and labor use, other forms of contracting agreements proved to be more preferable. In addition to marrying women who were "wives for doing a good deed," men with sisters or with nieces engaged in *tyéporogo* (Siena-re) or *faaraceewe* (Supyire), which was essentially an exchange of sisters as wives. The practice of exchanging sisters or young girls between families was a form of marriage engagement practiced among Senufo matrilineages which became increasingly common as different groups placed overwhelming demands on the labor and time of young men. Holas writes that families sometimes preferred exchange, or tyéporogo, because it bypassed "certain inconveniences" associated with cultivation.[25] This type of practice did not preclude the offering of material gifts to the bride's family, but it did cut out the cultivation obligation that tied young men and their male age-mates to work on the land.

For some men, sister exchange was the preferred avenue for acquiring a wife, particularly if that young man was a migrant worker. In chapter 2 we saw that French administrators attempted to eradicate exchange-based marriage by 1912, but in 1937 an administrator remarked that "among the

Sénoufo of Kénédougou, marriages are settled by means of exchange or purchase; at least this is the custom that seems to prevail."[26] However, in the late 1950s Holas stated, "It is not accurate to call this type of marriage an exchange because it does not entirely suppress the prestations imposed on the husband-to-be, which have a ritual and sacred function."[27] However, this type of marriage is still, by its intrinsic character, an "exchange" because the balance of women in each of the respective families should remain constant. If a lineage had a number of daughters and nieces, this was an opportunity to create ties with a corresponding lineage who had daughters and nieces who could be exchanged as wives. Such exchange reinforced cross-family, matrilineal ties in a way that "earning a wife for a good deed" did not. Exchange marriages consolidated the authority of matrilineal elders and prevented the diffusion of wealth in people across different lineages that were not of the matrilineal head's choosing. Wives who were part of sister exchanges would have found it difficult to leave those marriages, as the dissolution of their marriages affected not only them but also the stability of the corresponding marriage. In response to the high rate of divorce and marriage dissolution evident during the early colonial period and World War I, this might have been a coping mechanism of male elders of matrilines who felt that they were losing control of the younger generation's marriages. Aminata Kouyaté of Sikassoville explained, "My father told me that if you did not have a sister, you could not find a wife. Marriage was like an exchange. You give me your sister, I'll give you mine. That's why if a sister talks [badly about her situation] everyone is afraid because it was with her bridewealth that we nourished the family, bought beef, and looked for wives for the other brothers."[28] Kouyaté's comments indicate that sister exchange may have occurred in conjunction with bridewealth exchange in goods, which Holas also noted in the 1950s. In fact, it is likely that young men returning from migrant labor had money and goods to spend on bridewealth. Some households may have welcomed the wealth in goods over wealth in people. Likewise, it may have been in the interest of besieged matrilineages to promote the idea that sister exchange was widespread—thus the evidence for it in ethnographic information collected from the time. In any case, sister exchange appears in the historical record. Because of the benefits accrued to elder men who brokered sister exchange marriages, matrilineal heads would have worked hard to maintain this form of marriage arrangement in Sikasso during this time.

All these changes associated with labor and Senufo marriage in the 1930s resulted in increasing control over young women and girls. Put differently, as the power of the matrilineage to control young men's labor declined over the course of the colonial period, elders worked to control the wealth in women generated from their matrilineage and their households. Colonial state projects such as military conscription and the deuxième portion relied primarily on the labor of young men. Although young women did accompany men to the deuxième portion projects in some places, particularly in the settlement villages of the Office du Niger in the Niger River Valley, the state was not trying to control the labor of young women outright. The agricultural and household labor of young women, which was always highly valued, became even more precious as matrilineal control over the everyday labor of young men's labor declined. In other words, as men in Sikasso left for migrant labor, the cash crop fields of the jamanatigi or the deuxième portion road projects, it became that much more important to control the labor of young women. Whereas Senufo men and women before the 1930s had worked together in the collective fields, now women far outnumbered men on the matrilineage's fields and were thus more responsible for the agricultural work that yielded subsistence crops. Not only were young women valued for their sheer labor power in this sense, but they were valued by matrilineal elders for the potential they represented in garnering young men from other matrilineages through marriage. This was a meaningful investment for matrilineages, for children born of such a union would work for their matrilineal uncles in the future. As the possibility of acquiring wealth in young men decreased, the importance of wealth in young women increased.

The governor-general of French West Africa at this time, Jules Brévié, championed the Office du Niger settlement and irrigation plan as well as the deuxième portion, which he viewed as examples of the potential for successful collaboration between African capacity for hard labor and European technological innovations in irrigation and cultivation schemes.[29] Brévié stressed the importance of upholding what he considered an "Africanized" legitimate chieftaincy, a group of educated and informed intermediaries who would allow for more effective colonial rule while promoting local knowledge and opinions on good governance. However, Brévié's desire to restore an "Africanized" canton chieftaincy did not necessarily yield all the results that he envisioned. Men and women who lived through these hard times in Sikasso recalled that the execution of the works projects relied on the absolute power of the canton chiefs. Canton chiefs, even those who appeared to be generally just or at least respected out of fear, such as Abderahamane Berté, knew that successful tax payment and rudimentary development of infrastructure required tremendous sacrifices in farming villages. Most of them were willing to facilitate the necessary extractions.

Canton chiefs also understood that people would find ways to use their other assets in order to pay their taxes. In regions throughout French West Africa, including Sikasso, this meant that some unfortunate villagers resorted to spending their wealth in women.

MARRIAGE IN HARD TIMES: PAWNING AND POLITICAL ACTION

Pawning is a sociohistorical practice that has attracted the attention of historians of West Africa for some time, as it was identified in a variety of contexts throughout West Africa in the precolonial period and then again with the transformations of the monetized economy in the 1930s.[30] A pawn was a person, typically a junior member of a household or lineage, transferred to another person or household outside their own as security against a loan given to the head of the pawn's household. In West African history, pawns were usually women and children. Pawning did not completely die out during the colonial period with the eradication of legal slave status—indeed, it increased in many parts of both French and British West Africa with the convergence of taxation, cash cropping, and the Global Depression. Pawning served a purpose in societies where land was not transferred between people, but where rights in individuals and their labor were transferable. Most colonial officials likely turned a blind eye to pawning, as addressing it would have created more bureaucratic struggles and logistical challenges in the way of collecting taxes. Missionaries, in contrast, did not turn away from pawning and urged the administration to deal with it head on, as missionaries saw it as akin to slavery.

Among the matrilineal Asante in Gold Coast, scholars have shown that pawning was related to the "two linked processes" of increased desire to obtain wealth in people and a decline in lineage-based authority and control over subsistence-level production.[31] Although pawning most likely did increase as a result of market changes, it was also regarded as a reasonable option for Senufo male elders who were losing their wealth in young men's labor to market forces. The pawning of a girl not only allowed the family of the girl to pay her taxes, but it allowed a man of means, who might have lost access to the men of his lineage to the demands of the colonial state, to appropriate the agricultural labor of the girl. In this sense, a man of means preferred to trade his wealth in cash for wealth in women, which was more of a long-term investment than cash and had a higher yield for the creditor and his family. A pawn was useful for her labor, which was at a premium in the 1930s, but she could also be incorporated into the household. Although a pawn was not the same as a slave (a pawn maintained kin relations, whereas a slave was seen as kinless), some pawns did end up remaining in the household of the creditor as a wife.[32] This would likely have been the case in situations where the girl's work was highly valued, she integrated well into the household, she became pregnant, or the relationship between the creditor and debtor was such that it seemed favorable for them to shift the relationship of pawnship into one of marriage.

It seems that pawning was practiced with higher frequency in areas where men left due to migrant labor forces. This was certainly the case in Sangalan, Guinée, where the most infamous case of pawning in French West Africa occurred in 1936.[33] The Sangalan case raised the ire of certain members of the administration because it involved a high number of young women pawned so that migrant laborers could pay their taxes and because in the eyes of the minister of colonies, activists in France, and missionaries, the pawning of young women to pay taxes raised the issues of forced marriage, slavery, and colonial taxation. The issue of pawning was intimately linked to metropolitan and colonial administrative interest in African marriages and the Sangalan affair represented a watershed moment in policy on marriage in French West Africa.

In recounting his work as a scribe for the canton chief, Yaya Dow described the following acts of pawn-like marriage arrangements that occurred in the 1930s. In response to a question about his own wives and the processes that he went through to pay their bridewealth, Dow suddenly began to recount transactions that he witnessed and in which he participated in the 1930s. This was a trying time for everyone in Sikasso region and stood out in his mind when he recalled the time he spent working as a scribe for the jamanatigi.

> Burrill/Sidibé: Could you explain to us how you earned your living and how you managed to pay bridewealth for your three wives?
> Dow: I was the one who wrote out the taxes for the village. At the time, they brought the young girls of the village who were fourteen, fifteen, or sixteen years old, to sell them for 150 or 200 francs. For example, there was one man who brought his daughter to exchange her for his tax payment. They called another woman in the village to show her the girl. The woman brought 200 francs to pay the tax of the man, and she brought the girl back to her home to give to her son as a wife. There were lots of cases like that. Even my brother and I, once we were in the Sikasso market. [Some people] came and called us over. . . . They were two old

men with one girl. My brother said that he had the money, but he couldn't take another wife at that time because he had just gotten married. But we still had our father with us [our father was still alive], who at the time did not have a wife. So we proposed that if the girl liked our father, we would take her home with us for our father. So we paid the money and took her home with us. Six months later, the girl became pregnant. Our father died before the baby was born, but he ordered that the girl should stay in our family and that we should take care of her. Today, it's *her* son who is the head of the family in Sikassoville [Dow's emphasis]. He's my younger brother!

During that time, life was expensive! There was nothing but exchanges of this nature [my emphasis]. That boy went to school [koranic school]; then he went directly to Côte d'Ivoire to work. There was good work over there! And it is he who now takes care of the family. Eh! *You talk of bad times. . . . We would parade the children out to sell them, with the cows and sheep* [my emphasis]. . . . We would sell cows for 25 francs, chickens for 1 centime, sheep for 3 centimes . . . really, it was hard.

Burrill/Sidibé: What was the name of the *jamanatigi* at this time?

Dow: Abderahamane Berté. It was he who gave me my second wife. . . . She was a Traoré. She was the daughter of one of Kélétigi Berté's *sofas*, and Abderahamane gave her to me in marriage.

Burrill/Sidibé: When did this hard time end?

Dow: Oh, it was a long time ago. . . . It was around the same time as the crickets, and it finished with the appearance of the bills from France. . . . They paid the soldiers' families with that money. There were wives of the soldiers, and they tried to sell the money in the *arrondissement* to the wives, and [the wives] would throw the bills on the ground saying that it wasn't really money, that it was "White Money." I saw a lot of things like that.[34]

At that time, Dow was roughly in his early twenties and worked with Abderahamane Berté in recording tax payments, which would then be given to the district commandant. Dow's memories were vivid, and he recounted his own personal experiences and observations without hesitation. Although he was unable to provide exact dates for the time when these pawn-like marriages occurred in Kaboïla canton, Dow told us that it occurred while Berté was the canton chief, and that it occurred around the time of the "crickets." Although Berté was the canton chief of Kaboïla over the long period from 1917 to 1957, the note about the crickets, or locusts, is significant. In addition to Dow, other men from Kaboïla district villages located along the main paved road to Côte d'Ivoire recalled that around the same time that men from their villages were heavily recruited to build the road, there was a serious locust infestation. Agricultural and economic reports indicate that in 1936 and 1937 there was a locust infestation in southern Mali.[35]

Dow's depiction shows how people of means, such as the men of Dow's lineage who were mostly merchants and men of prestige connected to the canton chief, took on pawns and dependents in their families almost out of a sense of duty, but also as way of increasing a family's wealth in girls. He was proud to tell us that the young woman for whom he and his brother paid for was well cared for in his family, that his father wanted her to be taken care of after his death and to remain in the family as a widow (likely because she bore him a child), and that her son, who grew to become an elder, held an important place in the family. Although Dow may have been idealizing a past experience, his story reveals the ways in which this sort of arrangement was also a way of caring for people during a time of unbelievable struggle. The time was clearly bad, in Dow's eyes. But from his perspective people tried to make the best of it and transfer family members, usually young women and girls, into situations where they would be fed and protected, possibly even absorbed into another lineage and household, in return for cash that poor households and lineages would never gain otherwise.

The 1930s witnessed the Global Depression, but the decade was also a time of legal reform. French legislative changes pertaining to codes governing marriage took the political stage in the late 1930s, both at home and in the empire abroad. These particular reforms rested on the liberal notion of consent and, more specifically, on a woman's capacity to exercise consent within a marriage. In the French case, married women were no longer required to show their husband's consent in matters pertaining to the woman's professional or financial decisions. The historian Karen Offen vividly states, "French women's demands and nationalist family politics would remain on a collision course well into the twentieth century."[36] If the status of French women under the Third Republic was debated, particularly their civil and legal rights in marriage and work, the individual rights of African women in the colonies were at least equally contested by certain politicians and activists. This often took the form of discussions over who had rights to negotiate marriage contracts on behalf of women and what complaints in marriage were considered to be valid arguments for the termination of a marriage. Reformers of the time failed to realize that there were local processes of negotiation and contestation of marriage practices taking place concurrently with their bureaucratic efforts to reform Sudanic marriage. Furthermore, they failed to see the historical and social changes taking place throughout the French Sudan, changes that affected marriage practices and access to economic and social resources. Combing through the archives of France and Mali, we discover that the voices and opinions of the very women that missionaries and state servants were so eager to analyze and uplift are conspicuously absent.

Colonial officials and European missionaries who lived in the Sikasso region but not necessarily among the households that were the object of their interests did not always understand the complexities behind the marriage practices and labor schemes that they observed. They often failed to understand the intricate balance between the matrilineage and the household, and the competing systems of authority and familial obligation that drove people to do the things they did. During the 1930s, missionaries and some colonial administrators observed that women bore the brunt of household production and subsistence labor, and they viewed this as a sign of the African woman's primordial, substandard status. "West Africans have maintained ancient customs," wrote Sister Marie-André du Sacré-Coeur of the Sisters of Notre Dame d'Afrique (also known as the White Sisters). "The native woman in particular continues to lead the same life as her distant ancestors."[37] Catholic missionaries with the White Fathers in Sikasso, who had established a church in Sikasso in the 1920s, were primarily concerned with the individual rights of women from a humanistic and spiritual standpoint.[38] In the French Sudan, particularly among polygynous societies, missionaries saw young women as the most hopeful conduit toward the religious conversion of the household, and ultimately the reconstitution of the family as a monogamous, patriarchal unit within the church community. The first task in saving the life and the soul of the African woman, from the perspective of missionary-activists such as Sister Marie-André, was to change those practices that subjugated women, namely forced marriages, pawning, and sister exchange. "For France's civilizing work in French West Africa to be completely effective," wrote Sister Marie-André, "the assistance of African women themselves is needed." So began the article published by Sister Marie-André in a 1934 issue of the journal *Outre Mer*. Her article, titled "Vers l'évolution de la femme indigène en A.O.F.," explored what she perceived to be the shackle on the leg of every African woman: marriage. A doctor of law, Sister Marie-André saw the customary legal system supported by the colonial state as the faulty tool. "In indigenous societies of Sudan and Upper Ivory Coast, a woman has no legal existence of her own," she wrote. "She is subjected to the power of the person to whom she belongs and who disposes of her as he pleases."[39] Throughout this short piece, Sister Marie-André referred to marriage as a kind of servitude, a slavery that was the destiny of every girl and woman. The subtitle that she chose for her article is the clearest example of her perception of marriage: "Can we continue to keep her in servitude?" This question was positioned between a picture of a young mother with an infant on her back and a photograph of a young boy whispering to a young girl about her marital fate. He tells her, "You know Santigi, the shopkeeper? He's more than fifty years old. . . . Yesterday he came to ask your father for your hand in marriage. Your father said you were too young for him . . . but Santigi offered him 800 francs . . . and your father accepted."[40]

Sister Marie-André's main grievances were with the transactional quality of marriage. In this sense, she was critical of both bridewealth exchange and the levirate system, whereby a widow was inherited as a wife by her husband's surviving male kin along with his material property. She argued that an African woman, "whether she be a few months old or a fifty-year-old widow," was perceived as a thing in marriage, that she was not seen as a person with sentiments or opinions of her own, let alone control over her own destiny. But Sister Marie-André's critique was not only of what she understood to be customary treatment of African wives by their African husbands but also of the civil legal system promoted by the French colonial government.

> When intelligent young girls, a little *evolved* but given in marriage to old men and lepers want to escape from odious customary servitude, they cannot always do so because the laws have not *evolved*. If some of [them] gain their *liberty*, it is due to the good sense of some colonial administrators, in whom the spirit of equity makes up for the insufficiencies of the law [my emphases].[41]

Sister Marie-André argued for the gradual adoption of "basic human rights" as they were practiced "in her civilization," namely the understanding that marriage could not exist without consent of both parties. She believed that these understandings would take time, and most importantly, should be initiated when West African women became "conscious" of themselves and found it "unacceptable" to find themselves as part of an inheritance. In short, change should come from within, through the actions of women themselves—but this could happen only if they were educated according to a Christian, French moral code. However, educational reform was ultimately not enough: it must be coupled with legislative reform. These legislative reforms should outlaw "all that is contrary to the principles of our civilization" and should determine a legally recognized age of consent for pubescent girls (she suggests fourteen years old), and should require that widows be asked for consent in levirate cases. In conclusion, Sister Marie-André expressed a hope that in the near future, a law would be enacted that granted young girls "freedom" from the confining terms of marriage, thus enabling them to better serve France with all the influence of their recovered status.[42]

Sister Marie-André's critique is thus directed at both what she sees as a natural shortcoming in African society and the colonial legal system that interpreted local practices that they deemed customary. Her description of customary marriage practice in West Africa highlights the same qualities that state officials found noteworthy, but as we will see below, their interpretations differed slightly. Whereas missionaries such as Sister Marie-André were concerned with moral uplift, colonial administrators were concerned with categorizing and codifying behavior in order to administrate more effectively. Sister Marie-André's brief but forceful opinion piece from 1934 represents the tenor of many administrative debates in the metropole and in the colonies during the 1930s in the lead-up to the ratification of the Mandel Decree in 1939.

And yet issues of marriage and family life brought out concerns over morality more than virtually any other category of civil society for administrators, despite Sister Marie-André's frustrations. A political administrator in Sikasso wrote to the governor's office via telegram in 1934:

> The legitimate trade of women and children does not exist in the district of Sikasso. However, there exists a custom in certain corners (that is a reminder) that resembles the slave trade. The Senufos practice "mise en garantie" which consists of borrowing money and in return giving a wife or child to the creditor as backing. Those given on guarantee are well treated, and returned to the head of the family when the debt is paid. The use of this practice has, under the influence of the administration, considerably diminished. However, and despite all of the precautions taken, it is certain that this "mise en garantie" continues to exist in a clandestine way.[43]

By the mid-1930s, colonial administrators on the ground were voicing their concerns, however reserved they may have been, about local practices in marriage and how they might be in conflict with the administration's position on slavery. Administrators in regions such as Sikasso and the neighboring district of Koutiala saw pawning as very closely linked to the Senufo practice of sister-exchange in marriage, and some expressed their concerns over the perceived relation between the two practices. Practices such as these raised red flags back in the offices of the minister of colonies in the metropole, where top-down legislation would take form.

ADMINISTRATION, LOCAL AUTHORITY, AND LEGISLATION ON MARRIAGE

The Mandel Decree of 1939 defines consent, verbal or written, as the basis for any marriage contracted in French West or French Equatorial Africa. It also defined the age of consent as fourteen for girls and sixteen for boys. The decree followed the February 1938 law in France, which afforded married French women their own independent civil status; before the code married women required the permission of their husbands to work outside the home and to travel.[44] The 1939 decree in French West and Equatorial Africa challenged a father's authority over his daughters and went against certain Shari'a principles of age of consent and the role of elders in determining consent (here, it is crucial to underscore that within Islamic law, consent and agreement are important components of marriage).[45] The Mandel Decree also challenged what were understood to be ethnic customary practices of arranging marriages for young girls well before adulthood, oftentimes in infancy or before they were born. The Mandel Decree also completely outlawed wife-exchange marriages. Thus whereas administrators and court assessors deemed wife-exchange marriage "contrary to French civilization" in the years leading up to the Mandel Decree, it was now outlawed by mandate from the top.

As we have seen, the 1930s in the Sikasso region was a time of significant change and transition at the household and village level. On an administrative level, shifts also occurred in personnel and policy. Jules Brévié became governor-general of French West Africa in 1931. He would be one of the longest-serving administrators in the French West African government. His tenure as the governor-general marked a shift in colonial policy with regard to chiefs, notions of local custom and law, religion, and secularism. One of the major reforms to take place in French West Africa as a result of Brévié's administrative policy changes was the Mandel Decree of 1939, which signaled a noteworthy change in the way that the French colonial administration regarded the boundaries of African marriage and colonial intervention into the affairs of African families.[46]

When Brévié was the director of the Department of Political and Administrative Affairs based in Dakar, he wrote a book that significantly affected colonial thinking on Islam and local practices of belief. *L'Islamism contre "naturisme" au Soudan Français: Essai de psychologie politique coloniale*, with a preface by Maurice Delafosse, describes Islam in sub-Saharan Africa in a largely unfavorable light, arguing that Islam had a negative effect on the psychology of Africans. He believed that "naturism," a term that he favored over fetishism, was a cosmology and a worldview that could be harnessed and turned toward the civilizing mission perhaps more easily than Islam.[47] Naturists, he argued, were highly impressionable and innocent, and because of this were easily malleable by both Muslims and colonial expansionists. Brévié argued that the French colonial government up until the 1920s had been too lenient with what was perceived to be an Islamic influence coming from the Arabian Peninsula.[48] He was highly critical of earlier French colonial regard for Algeria as a model of Islam that could be applied in "Black" Africa (a school of thought that emanated from Paul Marty). In fact, he argued that French colonial processes had allowed for increased conversion to Islam and the ascension of Muslim political and religious leaders. As an alternative, Brévié emphasized local innovation and the importance of secular education in local African languages.[49] He argued that it was the duty of the French colonial argument to restore old "naturist" traditions that had been overcome by Islam and to renew an emphasis on their customary laws.[50] The success of secular education, "naturist" customary law, and a deeper understanding of local "naturist" beliefs relied on close collaboration with chiefs. He called for a "true native administration," an administration defined by discussion and action, not to mention association between chiefs and colonial administrators.[51] As part of this reform of native administration, Brévié argued that chiefs should be compensated for good work and recognized as an integral part of the administrative hierarchy. However, he emphasized, it should not be forgotten that chiefs played a delicate role as intermediaries between the native populations, who trusted them and looked to them for guidance, and the colonial administration, who had the best interests of the natives in mind.[52] Moreover, corrupt chiefs should be punished and removed rather than tolerated, as such fraud was a disservice to the civilizing mission and the moral uplift of African men and women. Although Brévié's general concerns were in part a continuation of administrative lip service that preceded his administration, his actions showed that he was more committed to (or at least convinced of) the importance of reform at the chiefly level of colonial administration. Perhaps most important, Brévié argued for "a new

'Africanized' elite that would be an antidote to the earlier 'Frenchified' elite," who hailed from old colonial enclaves such as those in Sénégal.[53]

One of Brévié's pet projects was the formation of a coordinated research plan on customary practice based on a precise, scientific questionnaire on local practice. As Brévié himself had risen through the ranks as a colonial official in French Sudan, he placed a special emphasis on the power of locally generated knowledge, that is, knowledge generated by the commandant, the district administrators and their collaboration with canton chiefs. He counted on the expertise of administrators who had been in the bush—whom he called "broussards"—to help construct manuals, which he hoped would be useful to both administrators and their African counterparts who worked as court assessors. Brévié's efforts in the 1930s reflect the renewed focus on codifying customary behavior in French West Africa, which he and the central colonial government in Dakar believed would provide the tools for understanding and effectively ruling over the expanse of French West Africa. "For more than thirty years," wrote Brévié, "administrative activity has been oriented toward useful research." Brévié believed that district administrators on the ground had time to familiarize themselves with the diverse customary laws of which the application was under their control, to note the individual properties of each ethnic group, and to classify each type of custom.[54] Brévié's concerns reflected a larger concern among some top-ranked officials in the colonies who were frustrated with the lack of localized knowledge among officials in each district, as well as the absence of a guide for administering local civil affairs. Chief Administrator Henri Labouret was particularly concerned with understanding marriage in French West Africa. He wrote of the common colonial administrator in 1930:

> Questions of marriage are not less confused [for the administrator]. He has the notion that dowry is paid by the husband, but he knows nothing of the payments due by the son-in-law to the father-in-law, nor to the widow [dowager], nor for levirate. . . . He takes his occupation/profession to heart, making everyone unhappy and ignoring everyone.[55]

Brévié believed that there existed discernible, fundamental principles of law that should be upheld. Although Brévié wrote of the necessity to uphold local innovations and customary practice, the emphasis on championing "natural law" and the desire to eliminate the practices that were "contrary to French civilization" led to significant efforts to identify the injurious practices of African "custom" and eradicate them, all in the name of progress and uplift. Brévié's focus on the laws of human nature and social practice reflect the prevailing "colonial humanism" among French colonial administrators of the day, which was an extension of "metropolitan productivism, statism, and welfarism," which generated a "dual imperative to transform and to preserve indigenous societies."[56] This succinctly describes the political approach to practices such as marriage in the colonies. Under Brévié's direction, colonial administrators worked to support what they considered to be African institutions while eradicating those practices that they considered against human nature and, therefore, contrary to the principles of French civilization. The hazy line between "the principles of French civilization" and "inalienable human rights" is where colonial administrative policy on African marriage perched.

Immediately following his rise to the position of governor-general of French West Africa, Brévié went to work drafting a number of reforms to the judicial system that he believed would better implement the locally generated knowledge of years of colonial rule and combat ignorances such as those that Henri Labouret bemoaned. Brévié wrote in a circular to the lieutenant governors that the establishment of native custom was something that administrators had wanted to do for many years, but that the war effort sidelined those initiatives. Now was the time to take up the mantle once more. "With the assistance of the native tribunals themselves," Brévié wrote to his lieutenant governors, "it will be possible to introduce, little by little, a rational classification, a generalization of customary practices that is compatible with the social condition of the inhabitants."[57] Brévié imagined that these customs would be evaluated not in opposition to French metropolitan judicial doctrine, but against "fundamental principles of natural law" which he saw as the true source of all legislation.[58] However, he emphasized that he did not want local customs to be thrown into a crucible, "from which would come an amalgam of all African customs," but rather he wanted there to be a reference manual of sorts that administrators could refer to in moments of uncertainty or ignorance. But he warned against fixing otherwise evolving practices and customs in time and encouraged officials to consider revising codified law in the presence of evidence that practices had shifted. At the base of Brévié's grand project would be the circulation of questionnaires, the results of which would be used to draft codes of civil practice.

"For years, metropolitan public opinion has not ceased to concern itself with certain matters of droit privé for the native in French West Africa, most notably in issues of marriage," wrote Brévié in 1936, in a memo concerning native marriage to the minister of colonies. Brévié emphasized, as he had done before, that African customary law was always changing for reasons that were owing in part to religion (Christianity and Islam) and to French civilization. To Brévié, this meant that administrators and court assessors needed to be aware of the "evolutions of African custom" and apply them as law, to recognize that practices were advancing. This was particularly the case "for the fate of the woman, one of our first projects." To not recognize these innovations in customary law, Brévié, argued would be both a failure to sincerely apply native custom as well as a failure to advance the cause of higher civilization for both the individual native and the collective.[59]

Brévié's tenure as governor-general of French West Africa ended in 1936, soon after he sent this memo to the minister of colonies. His dream of a compendium of French West African civil customs was never fully realized, though his labors generated about one hundred responses and written reports on African civil customs, particularly those surrounding property, family, marriage, and inheritance practices. The Mandel Decree, which was finalized in 1939, was largely the fruit of Brévié's labor, which in turn was a response to pressures from the likes of missionaries such as Sister Marie-André du Sacré-Coeur and others. The thrust of the Mandel Decree was the standardization of a minimum age for girls and boys, to be interpreted as the age of puberty, indicating an ability to procreate and bear children on the wife's part. Furthermore, the Mandel Decree required the mutual consent of the intended husband and wife in marriage, rather than the consent of parents. By putting certain marriage practices into law, the colonial administration essentially codified those practices that the French government and the Catholic Church believed to be inalienable human rights: the right to choose a marriage partner and the right to live as a child until puberty. Administrators could also use it as a tool of intervention in cases of pawning, as the Mandel Decree was also an attempt to limit parental authority to transfer the rights in person of their children to others— through pawning or marriage. The Mandel Decree was a major effort toward centralizing marriage laws in French colonies throughout Africa. For missionaries, this was a particularly significant event: the Mandel Decree allowed them to legally intervene or influence decision making in cases where Christian girls were promised in marriage by their husbands to non-Christian boys, particularly those deemed of animist custom.

Although here we see examples of state administrators and missionary experts disagreeing on the experiences of African women in marriage, there are also links between Catholic missionary observations of indigenous marriage and administrative decision making. Indeed, the archival file containing Sister Marie-André's opinion piece exists as a result of an inquiry into the status of women in the colonies started by a French deputy in 1938.

The attached information, including the piece by Sister Marie-André, influenced the deputy to the degree that he formally inquired about the state of "native Christian girls" at the office of political affairs of the governor-general of French West Africa.[60] This inquiry was part of a larger interest in indigenous marriage that developed in the metropole during the 1930s, leading up to the signing of the Mandel Decree.

The Mandel Decree of 1939 marked a transition toward state policies in French West Africa that attempted to regulate African marriage and family life and mandate that specific marriage customs adhere to parameters of "natural law," which in practice were French civil laws. Before the 1930s and the Brévié administration, the colonial administration in French West Africa had created an avenue through which African men and women could air marriage-related grievances against one another, in the form of civil tribunals. But although the tribunals handed down rulings on such matters as abandonment of the conjugal home, divorce, child custody, and bridewealth disputes as early as 1905, it was decades before a decree was written into law that established parameters for African marriages in the way of age, consent, and the involvement of bridewealth transactions. As we have seen, marriage and family life concerned some colonial administrators when such matters appeared to intersect with slavery, particularly the enslavement of women. We saw in chapter 3 how some administrators had begun to question the "legality and morality" of African marriages, and whether customary marriage practices were in line with notions of French civilization and social mores. However, there was no top-down sanctioning of particular marriage practices or governmental intervention in how marriages could be brokered—and between whom—until the late 1930s.

In the context of a global economic crisis, competing labor demands, and consolidated chiefly authority, the men and women of Sikasso struggled to create security in their households and lineages. However, men and women of different generations struggled with how they would obtain security through marriage and work, and for whom. Colonial officials and missionaries who observed this changing landscape of marriage and practices of gaining wealth in people believed that they were witnessing the timeless subjugation of women. As a result, they worked to initiate reforms that would be implemented through state-based, legal avenues.

Earlier we saw that French colonial political philosophies and the civil courts reinforced male elder authority over marriages in the 1920s. In the 1930s, some colonial administrators such as Jules Brévié, and Catholic missionaries, such as Sister Marie-Andre du Sacré-Coeur, viewed their work as a form of gender justice: the delivery of justice expressly for women, through a reform of colonial state laws. However, these gender-justice reformers operated more out of a sense of purpose deriving from liberalism and natural law than an understanding of the socioeconomic pressures in French West Africa. Gender justice, as it was manifested through African marriage reform and customary law, rewarded different genders at different times. As French colonial state-sponsored definitions of African marriage became more and more fixed through legal decree and code, the less these definitions of marriage reflected the contours of marriages that were actually forged by African men and women, as we will see in the chapters that follow.

5 ↫ Defining the Limits and Bargains of Patriarchy
Narratives of Domestic Violence

IN THE VILLAGE OF KIGNAN, ZEGUEDUGU CANTON, on 3
November 1938, Salia Sangaré forcefully reprimanded his wife, Massara
Dembélé. It was very early in the morning—approximately four a.m.—
and Salia was upset with his wife because she was not eating. A neighbor,
Ouaraba Bagayogo, had risen and was preparing the morning meal for
her own family before she left for the fields, when she heard Salia and
Massara disputing. When Ouaraba heard Salia harshly scolding his wife,
Ouaraba walked to the wall separating their compounds, looked over into
the Sangaré compound, and told Salia to leave his wife alone. At that
point, Ouaraba heard Salia strike his wife twice; Ouaraba quickly hurdled
over the wall separating their compounds to intervene. Ouaraba saw that
Massara was sitting on the ground, with her infant at her breast. Ouaraba
attempted to restrain Salia, who took a rope to his wife, whipping her
once. Because it was still dark out, Ouaraba did not see where the rope
had hit Massara. Ouaraba took Salia by the arm, pulling him outside of his
hut to calm him down. She then returned to her own compound to finish
preparing the morning meal. When she entered her own compound she
heard Salia's mother "crying the death cry." At that moment Ouaraba realized that Massara was dead.[1]

When Ouaraba was questioned at the tribunal she asserted that the blows inflicted by Salia "had not been violent." To her knowledge, he had only "beaten" Massara twice in their three years of marriage. This coincided with Salia's own testimony, and that of Massara's co-wife, who was in her own hut throughout the dispute, emerging only when she heard Salia's mother announcing the death of Massara. Because Salia allegedly did not intend to beat his wife to death, and because of Ouaraba's testimony that the blows had not been excessively violent, Salia was tried for involuntary homicide. Furthermore, an autopsy performed by the French doctor assigned to the commandant's post in Sikasso found that Massara was suffering from a severe and recurring case of malaria.[2] Her illness curbed her appetite and enlarged her spleen, which ruptured as a result of the blows she received. Given this evidence, Salia was convicted of inflicting "death without intention" and sent to prison for two years.[3]

This brief chapter accompanies chapter 4 in an exploration of 1930s Sikasso, but here we see the intimate details of domestic violence cases as they emerge from the civil and criminal tribunals. Gender-based violence in the household represented a particular category of behavior that was deemed "contrary to French civilization," and the types of cases on which these are based—largely criminal—are different from the civil cases examined in other chapters. The willingness of the court to enter into the intimate goings-on of the household via witness testimony, as well as the use of new forms of medical and legal tools of inquiry, signals the development of new forms of surveillance and measurement of African marriage practices. Furthermore, the depth of the testimony from these types of cases allows us to look at the anatomy of the cases and explore new ways of thinking about gender, generation, and patriarchy that enhance our understanding of gender justice in the context of marital violence. Here, gender justice took the form of prison sentences for men who killed their wives: that is, gender justice for dead women. However, we see another form of gender justice taking shape through the court testimony. Witness testimony that provided a narrative of "just action" on the part of husbands who physically punished their wives worked to exonerate men who had killed their wives. Both forms of gender justice help us see, in stark ways, how violence upholds patriarchy.

This chapter on domestic violence in Sikasso is based primarily on marriage and divorce cases from the subdivisional courts in Sikasso, as well as involuntary homicide cases heard before the criminal tribunal of Sikasso in the 1930s. Its purposes are threefold: First, I use the testimony of litigants and witnesses in an attempt to understand the mundane world in which physical punishment of wives occurred at the hands of their husbands.[4] I argue that the actions of individuals that come to the surface in court testimony help us understand the meaning of physical control and abuse in domestic relationships. The testimony from cases where abuse—and in some of these cases, death—occurred gives us insight into the expected roles and behavior of husbands and wives toward each other and within society. These behavioral obligations did not exist within a vacuum and were significantly affected by demands placed on husbands and wives from outside the conjugal home. I argue that mundane acts of physical punishment committed by husbands against their wives were seen as appropriate corrections that maintained the balance of a marriage. However, punishment—often slapping, hitting, or whipping—was a dangerous instrument, and could potentially exceed the limits of acceptability. What constituted these limits was open for debate not only between a husband and a wife, but neighbors, other compound members, court assessors, and colonial adjudicators. It is here where the role and meaning of proof becomes important in the form of testimony from witnesses and in the form of medical examination.

Second, I argue that the context of the 1930s is important for understanding these involuntary homicide and divorce cases in which women were physically punished or killed by their husbands. As we saw in chapter 4, the 1930s in the French Sudan was a time of increased labor obligations for the men and women of Sikasso, particularly among Senufo families, as well as a period of increased colonial interest in African families and the status of African women. New labor demands brought on by both lineage elders and chiefs working for the colonial state placed pressures on conjugal relationships in the way of work obligations, distribution of wealth in people, wealth in commodities, and figures of familial authority. Most of these pressures fell onto the shoulders of young men and women, as they worked to forge marriages and create their own households. At this same time, the colonial government as well as missionaries became more invested in the relationships between male figures of parental and marital authority and their wives and daughters. During the 1930s administrative decrees clearly outlined parameters of acceptable behavior in the context of marriage and control over girls in a way that clarified the well-established but vague distinction between "that which is according to local custom" and "that which is contrary to French civilization." In short, the 1930s was a time of competition between young men, lineage and village elders, canton chiefs, missionaries, and colonial administrators over African marriages and especially the place of African women in those marriages. Investigations into domestic abuse and its acceptability and relevance to criminal and civil law are an example of this struggle.

Third, rather than propose an essentialist assessment of the fact that husbands beat their wives and therefore subjugated them, this chapter examines the ways in which compounds and households interacted—as units and as individuals within a unit—to support a patriarchal system in which wives were physically punished and controlled. I apply Deniz Kandiyoti's notion of the "patriarchal bargain," which asserts that women are also active agents in the implementation of patriarchal systems even as they are subjected to them, to the study of domestic violence cases in 1930s Sikasso.[5] Women who participate in the subjugation of other women were rewarded with certain protections and benefits at the hands of men. In the case of co-wife abuse or abuse of female lovers, wives directly benefited from the physical subjugation of other women, vis-à-vis their relationship with the male perpetrator. However, I take this notion of the patriarchal bargain further by arguing that in a context such as a village compound in the rural region of Sikasso, women had the potential to form an informal system of observation of male behavior, which held men to their part of the bargain. This enforced not only a certain code of behavior within a marriage itself (in which physical punishment was acceptable, but within limits), but also the place of the conjugal compound within the larger village. This comes to the fore in the role that mothers and other women played as witnesses or alleged provocateurs in homicide and divorce cases.

Although criminal cases involving death were uncommon, the involuntary homicide cases are rich for the simple fact that the claims rest on the notion that husbands were otherwise behaving *normally* (in other words, acting in ways where death was an unexpected outcome), that physical punishment was common and even expected at the hands of husbands, and it was in those atypical cases that this everyday form of subjugation resulted in death. By contrast, divorce cases were fairly common in the civil level courts at the tribunal in the 1930s, and while it appears that the courts were not as commonly used to regulate marriage crises as they were in the earlier years of the colonial period, the fact that the divorce cases remained the most common type of case reveals the persistence of marriage-related problems that women may have found difficult to resolve at the household or village level.[6] Court cases from civil-level cases on marriage and divorce as well as criminal cases on homicide are rich sources for understanding gendered corporal punishment and domestic violence in a historical context. Although physical punishment as correction of a wife's bad behavior was legally acceptable in the French Sudan and therefore not punishable by law as such, I find that evidence of abuse and physical punishment in marriage appears in testimony where women are arguing for divorce in the colonial tribunals, as well as involuntary homicide cases.

Although very little of the existing research on African marriage and gender specifically examines domestic violence as a historical element of marriage and society, scholars are beginning to turn their attention to domestic violence as an element of family and gender history in Africa.[7] This and attendant scholarship on the history of marriage disputes, divorce, and other family-related conflicts sheds light on issues related to power and control in marriage, often examining how the management of marriage on the part of new states and local authorities changed during the colonial period.[8] In addition to this developing body of literature on domestic and gender-based violence in African contexts, there is scholarship that examines the role of flogging and corporal punishment in the subjugation of African men in colonial history.[9] This work is of a different kind of violence, however, not only because it was primarily inflicted on male bodies, but because it was inflicted as punishment for crimes and misdemeanors committed by African men against the colonial state. What set these forms of gendered violence apart are not only the perpetrators and the victims, but the conditions of the punishment itself. While the flogging of African men by agents of the colonial state was sanctioned, it was an infrequent occurrence in the life of an African man. Corporal punishment of wives at the hands of their husbands in this context was mundane and routine, and served to uphold a code of conduct within the marriage. Furthermore, flogging was deliberately framed as an exceptional act of violent punishment by those who carried out the act, whereas corporal punishment of wives was seen as a form of quotidian correction embedded in the very fiber of the marriage. However, the cases examined here show the ways in which everyday acts of violence could become exceptional and break the ties of marriage. In cases where men unintentionally killed their wives in Sikasso of the 1930s, husbands and witnesses stressed the conventional quality of physical punishment. In civil-level divorce cases, I find that wives worked to demonstrate how they were victims of unusual, unacceptable punishment. In both types of cases, we see the emergence of colonial, medico-legal tools used to examine the bodies of African women in order to show evidence of exceptional abuse. The autopsy and the physical exam play a significant role in building a body of evidence in these cases and were incorporated with the testimony of African witnesses. As a result, we see some of the ways that testimony and physical evidence were used in the colonial legal system. These two categories of proof rely on different systems of knowledge:

one is colonial and scientific, whereas the court sees the other as evidence of local, African customary behavior. Both rely significantly on the expertise of men, though witness testimony provided a space for female voices.

Work on domestic violence, where female bodies are the object of violent acts, is historically useful not only because it helps scholars understand the role of power and authority in relationships between African men and women but also because it reveals the central role of women and control over female bodies and sexuality in the debates on customary law between colonial administrators and African male leaders.[10] In studies of the Middle East and India, work on *sati* (self-immolation of widows at the death of a husband) and honor killing is useful to Africanists because it provides a theoretical framework for understanding gendered acts of violence upon the female body relative to a woman's relationship with men and her place in society at large. Whereas the cases examined here are examples of unintended death, the examples of sati and honor killing are sanctioned acts of the murder of women, including wives. However, the research on these forms of gender violence remains instructive because it highlights the debates that occurred (often between local men deemed customary experts and colonial authorities) over the place of physical subjugation of female bodies in the colonial and even postcolonial state. While French colonial authorities wanted to delegate authority to local court authorities who were assumed to be experts on local custom, they continued to be concerned with crimes that they determined "contrary to French civilization," such as corporal punishment of wives. The involuntary homicide cases were clear examples of acts that were "contrary to French civilization" in the eyes of the administrator presiding over the criminal court, but the divorce cases where women pleaded abuse tended to more ambiguous.[11]

Furthermore, justification, or at the very least, explanations of these acute forms of violence against women bring to the fore societal notions of a woman's place in her household and society, and the prevailing sense of propriety surrounding a woman's behavior, particularly toward men. They are examples of the role that men played as the keepers of a young woman's or a widow's virtue and the central role of subjugation of the actual, physical embodiment of womanhood (i.e., abuse of a female body) in maintaining normative gender roles for females. Historical examples of debates over sati and honor killing also highlight acute fears of transgressive gender behavior. Recent research on these forms of gender violence remind us that because acts of domestic violence are ultimately political in nature and linked to larger sociocultural values, we should look more closely at the links between brutality directed toward women in their conjugal relationships and families, social and economic strife, challenges to local political authorities, and disputes about state power.[12] Such conclusions and observations are suggestive of new directions that Africanist scholars can take in understanding domestic violence in the colonial period.

COURT TESTIMONY AS HISTORICAL RECORD: LIMITATIONS AND POSSIBILITIES

Only the Jula know how to speak to the Whites.[13]

As we have seen throughout the chapters in this book, court cases are useful for gleaning information about everyday life in African society, but they are not without their pitfalls. The court experience in Sikasso (and elsewhere in the French Sudan) usually required the work of a translator, who mediated the communication between litigants and judges, and as a result, between subject and historian.[14] Roland Colin, the former deputy commandant of Sikasso from 1952 to 1954, tells us in his memoirs of the problematic quality of court testimony in a colonial setting prior to his term of service:

> In the time of my predecessor, the stature of the great interpreter significantly affected the decisions of justice. Bakary Doucouré explained to me that there existed, in fact, two episodes in the course of the trial. The first took place at the residence of the chef de canton, between all of the African actors, and the decision's outcome was a function of force, primarily between the chieftaincy and the peasants. At the time of the administrative hearing the great interpreter recapitulated the state of the debate in front of the concerned parties, in [Jula language], and fixed his own opinion. . . . The great art was to give [the colonial administrator] the illusion of having settled the matter and having declared the law himself.[15]

Bakary Doucouré outlined a process for Roland Colin which reveals the basic problem with using court testimony from particular periods such as the 1930s to understand social history: the testimony comes from the "second episode" of justice, and represents to some degree the intervention of the "great interpreter" in the original case. Translators and court interpreters wielded tremendous power, affecting not only the court experience and outcome, but the interaction between stewards of the colonial state and local Africans. Colin eradicated the role of the translator during his tenure, preferring litigants to speak freely in Jula, but this also caused problems.

The court assessors, often chosen by the canton chiefs and appointed by the deputy commandant to assist with rulings according to certain customary laws, were typically implicated in the power structure described by Colin and his assistant, Bakary Doucouré. Assessors were interested in maintaining the power base of the canton chiefs and were potentially threatened by unmediated testimony where litigants could speak directly to the court, voicing their issues to the colonial administration.[16] And although Jula, or Bamana, was the lingua franca of most colonial intermediaries and administrators (in addition to French), it was one of many languages spoken in the Sikasso region, and it was associated with the precolonial dynamics of empire that subjugated many people in the countryside of the Sikasso region. The quote at the beginning of this section highlights a common belief that Jula, or Bamanankan, was not only the one language that was useful with the French colonial government, but that Jula or Bambara *people* (as opposed to Senufo, Fulbe, Samogho, or Gana, for example) were the only possible intermediaries between local Africans in Sikasso and the French colonial administration. It may be that this affected Senufo-speaking litigants' decisions to appear before the provincial tribunal, despite the fact that Senufo customary authorities were appointed to the tribunal as assessors as a reflection of the fact that Senufo was the most commonly spoken language and claimed ethnic identity among the people of Sikasso region throughout the colonial period.

In divorce cases by the 1930s, litigants had previously appeared before the canton chief for a required attempt at reconciliation. It is unclear how many of these reconciliation attempts were successful, but we can assume that fewer cases made it to the provincial tribunal level as divorce cases. Thus, by the time a case reached the level of the tribunal, the grounds on which a woman requested divorce were heard by her husband, who was in turn able to secure a core of witnesses who could attest to the qualities of their marriage. Equally, a woman could hear her husband's argument as to why a divorce was not a desirable outcome, develop an argument, find witnesses, and amass proof of her claims. As we will see here, some women proved adept at working within the colonial legal system, while others did not.

Criminal cases were tried at the highest level of the native court system. The criminal tribunal was composed of four to five court assessors: the president of the tribunal, a European assessor, who was typically another official European in residence, and two African court assessors, chosen from among the canton chiefs and court assessors presiding over the lower-level tribunal. At times a third European assessor served at the criminal tribunal, in addition to the four assessors, though it is not clear how it was determined that a fifth assessor was needed. The president of the tribunal was responsible for assigning defense counsel from among the European staff of the cercle administration. This person was not a defense attorney but was someone trained in colonial law.[17] In involuntary homicide cases, the colonial state constructed a case against the accused. The canton chief gave the commandant and his office permission to investigate the conditions of the homicide in the village.[18] The deputy commandant represented the defendant in the few Sikasso cases of the 1930s. In both the involuntary homicide cases and the divorce cases, each witness was asked to give his or her name, age, place of birth, place of residence, marital status, occupation, and the names of his or her parents. The witnesses issued written testimony through the translation and assistance of a letter writer, but could also be asked to provide verbal testimony under some circumstances, such as in the involuntary homicide cases. Mediated testimony such as this, then, particularly from illiterate men and women in a colonial context, is a source rife with challenges.[19] However, it remains useful and instructive because though mediated through translation, transcription, and the gendered authority of the colonial tribunal, testimony provides an indication of the role and meaning of violence in conjugal relationships. At the very least, mediated testimony reveals what canton chiefs and interpreters may have deemed "acceptable" ways of claiming abuse and talking about the role of corporal punishment in African marriages in Sikasso. At the most, the testimony reveals the voices of women who claimed abuse in their marriages and who were willing to reconstruct proof of abuse according to the demands of the court.

PUNISHMENT, DISOBEDIENCE, AND THE MORAL ECONOMY OF MARRIAGE IN SIKASSO, 1930S

In this chapter, two different sets of cases are examined: divorce cases heard at the provincial tribunal level, in which women requested divorce based on claims of abuse and mistreatment, and involuntary homicide cases heard at the *tribunal de cercle*, or district level, in which husbands were tried for causing the death of their wives through physical abuse. These latter cases of "death without intention" examined here are valuable not because of their quantity; in fact, there were only sixteen criminal cases heard in the district tribunal in Sikasso between 1932 and 1944. What is valuable about these criminal tribunals is their depth of testimony and what they reveal about the "patriarchal bargain" at work, but it also helps us understand the moral economy of marriage, the ways in which this code could be broken, and responses to an imbalance.

The first case of Salia Sangaré and Massara Dembélé reveals a number of components that help us understand both the moral economy of marriage and the role of evidence of abuse. The case supporting Salia's claims of involuntary homicide rests on the autopsy performed by the colonial doctor assigned to the cercle of Sikasso and the testimony of Ouaraba Bayogo and Salia's first wife, Kadidja Traoré. In this case, the neighbor and the co-wife were the important witnesses who helped construct a moral sketch of the defendant in light of the charges against him. Ouaraba Bayogo's testimony is powerful both because she did intervene, even going so far as crossing the compound wall to physically separate the couple. However, while her calls to Salia to leave his wife alone and her intervention indicate that perhaps she perceived the dispute to be either unwarranted or excessive, her testimony asserted that Salia's physical punishment was not extreme. Ouaraba's testimony indicates that she did not find Salia's strikes to be violent; that she could not determine the subject of their dispute because they were talking too fast; that the couple did not often fight; that she was surprised that the blow she heard had killed Massara. Similarly, Kadidja, Salia's first wife, stated in her testimony that she knew of no quarrel between her husband and his co-wife; that Massara had not been eating for some time; and that the morning that Massara died, Kadidja was in her own hut, and only heard Salia hit his second wife twice. After that, Kadidja heard her husband's mother "announcing" the death of Massara.

Both women who were called as witnesses are deeply embedded in a patriarchal bargain at play, both within Salia's compound and in the larger village. For Kadidja, it was in her best interest to maintain that Salia was a model husband. Kadidja relied on Salia's support as the *fama*, or head of her household; if she were implicated negatively in his punishment for the death of her co-wife, then she would suffer as well as an abandoned woman with an imprisoned husband. Similarly, if Ouaraba testified that her neighbor beat his wife excessively and caused her death, she could be ostracized in her village. Thus we can see how these two women in particular participated in the patriarchal bargain and that Ouaraba in particular performed a sort of surveillance, through the monitoring of Salia's physical treatment of his wives.

The science of the medical exam clarified the conditions of abuse of the victim's body; in cases of involuntary homicide, the concern moved between determining if the beating was seen as "excessive," and if it was the cause of death. Massara Dembélé suffered from recurring malaria, as many in southern French Sudan likely did at the time; although the blow to her midsection was the ultimate cause of death, Massara's preexisting medical conditions indicated that she was in an already fragile state of physical health. The autopsy was, by the 1930s, an established practice in cases resulting in death. Although the witness testimony was powerful in establishing the qualities of Salia as a husband, the autopsy presented facts that accounted for Massara's inability to eat as well as her physical fragility.

The involuntary homicide case of Salia Sangaré also indicates the role of the patriarch in enforcing good behavior in his compound—in this case, of a younger, second wife who chooses not to eat and was seen perhaps as ungrateful or sullen. Massara's older co-wife testified that at times she left her conjugal home to visit her mother. In younger co-wives, this could have been interpreted as a sign of homesickness and a rejection of the conjugal home and her role as second wife. As we have previously seen, in polygynous communities, such as the village of Kignan, second wives were expected to bear the brunt of the housework, particularly the preparation of the early morning meal before the women departed for the fields. As most agricultural villages in Sikasso in the 1930s experienced an increase in duties and responsibilities for women in subsistence as well as cash-crop fieldwork, this was an essential component to one's contribution to the working of the household. In Kignan, where there was a high number of male migrant laborers compared to neighboring areas, household and field labor pressures on young women, particularly junior wives, were high.

Let us turn now to another case of involuntary homicide with slightly different elements at play. On 26 July 1934, Lamoussa Traoré was tried in the criminal court of Sikasso for causing the unintentional death of his wife, Sikanga Berété. In this case, there was no autopsy performed on the body, though it is not indicated in the records why this would have been omitted from the process. Testimony from five witnesses was taken in this case: a neighbor, the father of the accused, the mother of the accused, the second wife of the father of the accused, and a maternal relative of the deceased. The neighbor, Babou Sanogo, did not witness the act of violence that contributed to Sikanga's death, but he asserted that Lamoussa often "disciplined" his wife, who was very disobedient. On 9 June 1934, Lamoussa had asked his wife to bring him his water pot so that he could perform the ablutions necessary for Muslim prayer. According to the testimony of Lamoussa's father, Sikanga, the wife, "seemed to make fun of [her husband]" and either refused to bring the water or took her time doing so. He saw Lamoussa punch his wife in the neck with a closed fist, knocking her to the ground and killing her. Lamoussa's mother, who also lived in the compound with her son and husband, offered her testimony. Her account is basically similar to that of her husband, but with one notable exception. According to her testimony, she heard two loud "blows." She believed that it was her son beating his wife, so she immediately went to where they were in order to intervene. She left them, and a bit later she heard more blows and cries. She went back to her son and his wife, and it was then that she saw Sikanga on the ground, dead. Her testimony concludes with the sentence: "My son was in the habit of hitting his wife." Finally, the testimony of a female relative of the deceased, by the name of Kamissa Dembélé, confirmed that Sikanga did not react when her husband asked her to get him water to prepare for his prayers. Lamoussa began to beat his wife, until his mother came and intervened. A bit later, he resumed beating his wife. Sikanga fell on the ground, dead. Kamissa's testimony ends with her stating, "I don't think Lamoussa intended to kill his wife, but she often needed to be disciplined."[20] In the tribunal records for Lamoussa's testimony, the interrogation of the accused was recorded as follows:

Q. Were you in the habit of beating your wife often?
A. Yes, she didn't obey me—I was even obliged to do her work myself.
Q. How did you kill her on 9 June 1934?
A. I disputed with her because she did not want to bring me water for my ablutions. The first time, my mother came and separated us. A little later, after she refused once more to serve me, I became very angry. I hit her in the neck with a closed fist. She fell to the ground. She was dead. I only wanted to discipline her, not kill her. I've been unhappy because of it.[21]

Lamoussa's defense counsel argued in his closing statement that his client was following the behavior of local custom when he beat his wife, but that the tribunal should enforce certain punishments. Punishment should be enforced not because he beat his wife, but because he beat her about the head. The defense counsel attempted to minimize the severity of the beating by adding that "he hit her about the head the same way you might punish a child, but too hard." Although he had hit her forcefully about the head, he did not intend to kill his wife. In the end, Lamoussa was convicted of causing unintentional death and was sentenced to five years in prison.

While Lamoussa was described as a man who beat his wife often, all witnesses were quick to add that his wife was "disobedient" and that she required "correction" and discipline. Her ultimate act of disobedience was to disrespect him by abusing a particular religious idiom, in this case the "water pot," or *selidaga* as it is called in Bamanakan or *sèrècwòo* in Senufo. The water pot is an important part of maintaining Muslim practices of cleansing the body before prayer, to be performed up to five times a day. In this particular scenario, Sikanga "insulted" or "made fun of" her husband's authority as the head of household by refusing to serve as an interlocutor in the maintenance of his role as a proper Muslim man. As a result, she showed that she was a very improper wife and was subsequently beaten about the head, an uncommon and unacceptable way to reprimand a wife. In this way, both Sikanga the wife and Lamoussa the husband broke the code of behavior governing their marriage and the place of the marriage in the compound, requiring the intervention of others in their conjugal affairs.

The fundamental physical layout of a village compound in southern Mali at this time would have been relatively open, with permeable boundaries between domestic compound space and village space. Within the compound, co-wives were separated and had distinct domiciles, and family interactions were almost always observed and known by others. In the involuntary homicide cases I am highlighting here, we see that other women outside the marriage—in one case an elder mother, in another, a neighbor of the same age-grade as the husband and the wife—intervened when they believed that the physical punishment was outside the realm of what was normal or safe punishment. The outside women attempted to facilitate reconciliation or at least serve as intervening forces. When in both cases highlighted here the acts of punishment resulted in the death of the victim, the court solicited the opinions of the intervening women, relying upon their informed knowledge of the frequency and severity of the punishments that the husband in question meted out. In this way, the testimony of the intervening women contributed to the sentencing of the accused men.

These women were participants in the patriarchal bargain that operated in the village compound, as they bore witness to the beating and death of other women, but justified to some degree the beating (in the first case, Ouaraba underscores the fact that although Massara received a blow strong enough to rupture her spleen and kill her, the hit wasn't that hard and that "it was difficult to believe that one blow could kill a person; Salia was not in the habit of seriously reprimanding his wife"). In the second case, the role of the patriarchal bargain is much clearer—Lamoussa was simultaneously described as someone who frequently beat his wife, and as someone who endured the hardship of a disobedient wife. His beatings of his wife are justified by the women of the compound—one who is even a direct relative of the deceased—because she, the wife, did not uphold her responsibility in marriage and therefore upset the moral economy of the marriage.

In divorce cases, claims of abuse in Sikasso were more ambiguous, in part because the husband and wife could debate the conditions of alleged abuse and call witnesses. Divorce on grounds of abuse was a common complaint of women, yet it was not considered a "customary" practice according to the ethnographic studies sanctioned by the colonial government at the time.[22] In 1932, A. Aubert published a study of "judicial custom" in the French Sudan. Included in this multivolume study is a section on the ethnic groups that the colonial administration deemed most important. It is worthwhile to note that there is no study included of the Senufo or Minianka in this study. Aubert conducted a study of Buguni Bambara custom, in consultation with regional "experts" on customary practice, including village and canton chiefs. According to the counsel Aubert received, divorce could be granted in seven cases: if either the husband or wife were sterile; if the wife committed adultery; if the woman offered in wife exchange is refused; if a husband repudiated a wife for bad behavior or a sour disposition; if a wife aborted a pregnancy; if the husband abandoned his wife; if the wife died.[23] Nowhere here is abuse listed as grounds for divorce, yet it was a common complaint. In fact, the study observes that a wife must obey her husband, and that in cases where she is disobedient, "correction is sanctioned—and often inflicted with rigor. Necessary rigor, they say."[24] As a result, divorce cases on grounds of abuse were contentious, in the court and, one would imagine, also in the compound or village. In these cases, the burden of proof of abuse lay squarely on the wife, and women approached this in different ways. On 20 January 1936, Tenin Diakité appeared before the civil tribunal at the provincial level of Sikasso, where she asked for divorce on the grounds of physical abuse. Both Tenin and her husband, Karamoko Traoré, claimed Senufo-Muslim status. Tenin and her husband had attempted an unsuccessful reconciliation before the canton chief of Bugula, and thus appeared before the tribunal. Tenin argued that in the ten months that they were married, her husband treated her poorly and hit her. Furthermore, she argued, he still owed her family bridewealth payments. Her husband claimed that he had never hit her in their ten months of marriage. Furthermore, he pointed out that there would be no good motivation to beat her, since she had already given birth to a child and his first wife seemed to be sterile. He argued that it was her mother who pressured her daughter into asking for a divorce, coming to their village and telling Tenin to claim that Karamoko beat her. Karamoko brought three male witnesses to back his testimony; one of them was Tenin's uncle who was responsible for arranging the marriage between them. He stated that Tenin's mother had wanted to dissolve her daughter's marriage six months after it began, but that the allegations of abuse were unfounded. All three of the witnesses argued that the mother regretted agreeing to the union and wanted her daughter to divorce. Since Tenin could provide no physical proof or witness testimony to back her claims, the divorce was not granted, and Tenin was ordered by the court to return to her husband's home.[25]

Tenin Diakité's divorce request was the only divorce case brought on claims of abuse that was rejected by the tribunal between 1935 and 1940. On the same day as Tenin Diakité's case, Assitan Coulibaly appeared before the court and asked for divorce on grounds of abuse. She claimed that a few months before, she had attempted to chase her husband's lover out of their compound. Her husband interceded and brutally beat her with a whip and a stick. At the time, the couple was living in Bouake, Côte d'Ivoire, where Malick Coulibaly, the husband, was working as a merchant; Assitan promptly left her husband and returned to her parents' home in Sikasso. Upon her arrival in Sikasso, Assitan went to the colonial doctor to have her injuries certified and have him attest to their severity. Her husband responded by letter but was absent from the court. He acknowledged that he had beaten his wife after she attempted to turn a "stranger" away from their home; however, he refused divorce on the grounds that his wife would never be able to repay the bridewealth that he had paid to her parents for their marriage. In this particular case, the judgment rested on the medical exam that Assitan received when she arrived in Sikasso. The medical exam was performed two days after the beating occurred, and the certificate stated, "The characteristics of the lesions allow for the conclusion that they were caused by a whip and/or a stick, applied with extreme violence." Even in the absence of witnesses, the certificate was proof enough of excessive abuse. The court found in favor of Assitan, and because of the conditions of the abuse and the medico-legal documentation, the court ordered that no bridewealth was to be reimbursed to Malick Coulibaly.[26] The medical exam here is noteworthy; it indicates that Assitan was savvy with regards to the procedures involved in making a claim for abuse when she did not have available witnesses. It is not clear whether this was common practice for women at this time, or how a woman like Assitan would have known that such services were available to her as a woman seeking divorce. What is clear is that she turned directly to colonial avenues for solving her problem of domestic abuse and request for divorce.

A third divorce case taken from this time period shows the importance that was placed on witness testimony. On 24 July 1937, Fanta N'Diaye appeared before the tribunal as the plaintiff in a divorce case. Fanta's husband, Oumar N'Diaye, was assigned to Sikasso as a teacher, though both were from Senegal. According to the tribunal records, Fanta made a verbal request rather than a written request to the court to have her case heard. She claimed that her husband did not love her, and she knew this because he beat her frequently. The notes on her case indicate that she had first appeared the day before at the *"tribunal repressif"* where she lodged a complaint of assault against her husband. This tribunal directed her to the civil tribunal, where Fanta filed for divorce. Fanta brought to the tribunal three male witnesses to back her claims of abuse: her uncle and former guardian, Mamadou Diallo of Sikasso, and two neighbors who were also colleagues of her husband. In the tribunal record, the court then turned to Oumar N'Diaye, who declared:

> It is completely natural that I would hit my wife every time she provokes me. For a slap or two—never more—she comes immediately to the administration to lodge a complaint. As I am a functionary of the state, and in order to avoid any associated prejudices regarding the difficulties between my wife and me, I do not ask for special treatment. I ask that divorce be pronounced between me and my wife, Fanta N'Diaye.[27]

Despite the fact that Oumar N'Diaye agreed to the divorce, the tribunal proceeded to question both parties in the case.

> Q. What were the conditions of your marriage to Fanta N'Diaye?
> A. I married her in Bamako on 20 July 1929, in accordance with a bridewealth price of 1,500 francs, of which 750 francs were paid. There is a marriage certificate, certified and on record with the district administrator of Bamako. I should also add that we have four children, two of whom are very young: Oumou N'Diaye and Kadiyatou N'Diaye.

The witnesses then took their oath to tell the truth and were warned of the consequences of lying in the tribunal. The first to speak was Mamadou Diallo, thirty-nine years of age, uncle of the plaintiff, chauffeur, and resident of Sikasso. Diallo stated:

> It is I who gave my ward in marriage to Oumar N'Diaye, so that he could treat her however he wanted. . . . Regretfully, I can attest to the incompatibility of the spouses, and above all to the serious injuries

that have been inflicted by the husband upon the wife. My work as her guardian is to request that the court separate them, in order to avoid a more serious incident.

The next testimony was offered by the two neighbors and colleagues of Oumar N'Diaye. These two men had witnessed the abuse and recounted it in vivid detail. The first to speak was Dadie Traoré, thirty years old and a teacher in the service of Sikasso. Dadie claimed:

> Two months ago, I was called around 7 or 8 in the evening by my colleague, Mamadou Diakité (who now lives in Luluni), to come and help intervene between Oumar N'Diaye and his wife, Fanta N'Diaye. Upon my arrival at their home, I found that my colleague was already there, and that the door to the home had been thrown to the ground. Diakité was inside and had the inanimate body of Fanta in his arms. Together, we poured water over her head. She eventually came to her senses. We sat on the bed and listened to her. After setting aside what she had said, we made amends with the husband, and the two of us left.

The second friend and colleague, also a teacher in the service of Sikasso, was Fakourou Coulibaly. Coulibaly added:

> I have intervened twice in the affairs of Oumar N'Diaye and his wife. The first time I was in the company of Mamadou Diakité and Dadie Traoré. The wife had been beaten to the point where she was disoriented the second time, which was last July 23, I was in my house and I heard the couple arguing. N'Diaye asked his wife, "Why do you slap the iron on the table when you are ironing?" to which she responded, "This is not the first time that I've ironed the laundry [like this]." Suspecting a quarrel, I went over to their compound. On my way there, I found the wife on the ground, and her husband next to her. I picked up the wife and brought her to my home for a time, because Oumar was still very angry.

In the resume of the case that followed the testimony, the tribunal president and assessors were interested in three things: the fact that Fanta N'Diaye had first attempted to lodge a complaint at the tribunal for assault, which indicated the seriousness of the matter from her view; the narratives of abuse offered by the defendant's own colleagues; and the fact that Oumar N'Diaye claimed that he only corrected his wife "in accordance with customary practices of disciplining a wife." Rather than immediately grant divorce in this case, however, the court granted a separation, during which time Fanta N'Diaye would live with her uncle. The reasons for this are unclear, but given the circumstances, it is likely that divorce was not initially granted because Fanta did not first go through a reconciliation attempt through the canton chief and because there was an outstanding case of assault initiated by the wife against the husband in the tribunal. Furthermore, since Oumar N'Diaye was a functionary of the state in his role as a teacher, it may be that the court did see "special circumstances" at play, and decided to postpone deliberation. This case is notable for several reasons. First, Fanta N'Diaye, as someone who was connected to the colonial administration through her husband, relied directly on the tribunals of the colonial state to rectify her situation, as opposed to village or canton chiefs. Fanta secured the testimony of three notable men, which strengthened her case significantly. Furthermore, all parties involved, with the exception of the wife, were servants of the state in some way. Although we do not know whom Mamadou Diallo worked for, we can assume that it was either a European or a wealthy African working for the state, as he was a chauffeur. Oumar N'Diaye notes that their marriage is legitimate in the eyes of the state, citing the existence of a marriage certificate, which many African colonial subjects in French Sudan did not have in the 1930s.

All of the observers and intervening parties in this particular case were men. This indicates the ways in which men and women were both part of a community social network that enforced the proper boundaries of discipline at work in a marriage. The three men who were witnesses in Fanta N'Diaye's case, in addition to the intervening women in the other involuntary homicide cases, all attempted to facilitate reconciliation as a first move toward rectifying the marital disputes based on corporal punishment of the wives. However, I would suggest that men were considered more valuable and reliable in cases of divorce: men were the ones who were best equipped to determine whether or not corporal punishment went beyond the limits of acceptable correction, because men were often the ones who were considered to have knowledge about "customary" practice.

The cases examined in this chapter further highlight the place of legal custom in the liminal space between "acceptable customary practice" and "practices contrary to French civilization," a dynamic outlined in earlier chapters. Correction or punishment of wives challenged administrators and activists to consider this hazy line. Here, I have drawn out intimate case-study examples of corporal punishment of women resulting in unintentional death as well as divorce cases brought on grounds of abuse as a means for looking at a few ways in which the social dynamics at the household and village level contribute to a system that upholds the physical subjugation of women. However, in order to understand these dynamics, we must look to the role of other women in the maintenance of such a system. I have provided a glimpse of the seemingly conflicting ways that women in southern French Sudan could both uphold and constrain efforts to physically subjugate women. Further explorations of this complex dynamic can help us better understand marriage and the meaning of local, everyday authority at the village level.

The detailed narratives from civil and criminal tribunals allow us to look closely at the story embedded in testimony. The narratives reveal how village and compound-level systems of observation act as deterrents to men who overstep boundaries in corporal punishment, just as they can curtail women from accusing men of unwarranted abuses. By the 1930s, medico-legal tools, such as autopsy and medical examination were used not only in colonial criminal courts, but by litigants in civil-level courts seeking to authenticate the physical proof of abuse to their bodies. This warrants further research in French colonial medicine and the intersections between colonial legal systems and medical practice. Although the testimony reveals social practice, it may also reflect the actions of particular culture experts, such as assessors, canton chiefs, and interpreters. However mediated, testimony provides a view of the justification of violence against women in their homes in colonial Sikasso, as well as the overall ethical world of the compound that either accepts or rejects such corporal punishment and abuse. These cases help us understand more about how patriarchal authority was upheld within marriages and families, and how the courts, for their part, also upheld patriarchal authority. Justice for dead women—and for the colonial state—was perceived as prison time for guilty husbands, but we also see different articulations of what it mean to act "justly"—for husbands, who were called upon to correct and punish their wives, and for wives, who argued that their abusive husbands behaved in unjust ways, breaking the moral economy of the family.

6 ~ Gender Justice and Marriage Legibility Projects in Late Colonial French Sudan

Recently, the Senufo woman has become conscious of the rights afforded her by French laws on marriage, and it is more and more common for a Senufo girl to refuse her marriage and that she turns to the tribunal de premier degré in her area. She is certain, since the 1939 decree, to win her case.

—Bohumil Holas, *Les Sénoufo*

When my marriage was arranged, I didn't love my husband, the marriage was forced. No way! But my uncle threatened me: "If you refuse . . . !" And my father was even on my side! So my uncle said to my father that he would split me in two and give one half of my body to my husband, and my father could give my other half to anyone; he didn't care. So, I reconciled with my uncle. I went to see him, and I told him that I was okay with his decision. That's how you arrange a marriage!

—Aminata Kouyaté, Sikassoville, 2009

IN 1951, THE FRENCH COLONIAL ADMINISTRATION passed the Jacquinot Decree, named after Louis Jacquinot, the minister of overseas France.[1] The Jacquinot Decree built on the Mandel Decree's emphasis on consent and the rights of the individual in new ways. The 1951 act stated that any woman who had achieved the age of twenty-one or who was legally divorced had the right to freely choose her own spouse without interference from anyone who might profit from her marriage. It further stated that parents and family members could not interfere in the marriage of a woman under the age of twenty, particularly in cases where the parents disapproved of a young woman's marital choice. The Jacquinot Decree empowered the *tribunal de premier degré* (the entry-level civil tribunal for all litigants) to determine whether or not these protections from familial interference were upheld in questionable marriage cases. Bridewealth limits were to be established by the chief official of a given territory, in accordance with what was determined to be locally acceptable. The Jacquinot Decree also authorized the official registration of marriages in civil records, and required that men indicate whether or not they were entering into a polygynous or monogamous marriage at the time that their marriages were registered with the state. Women were not given this choice.

In many ways, the Jacquinot Decree was intended to reinforce the sovereignty of the individual in the contracting of his or her marriage. The reforms introduced by state actors in the name of delivering gender-specific forms of justice for women and men emphasized the rights of the individual to make decisions, consent to contract, and be unencumbered by tremendous financial debt and obligation to others. Although the Jacquinot Decree contained a number of provisions that were intended to serve the interests of African women, the decree's limitations on bridewealth garnered the most attention and consideration from colonial administrators and chiefs. This was because the limitations on bridewealth mitigated the power of fathers and male elders. The Jacquinot Decree was a reflection of local consideration for pressures that young men and women experienced in the marriage contract, but it was also a reflection of the larger postwar context and the formation of an international community engaged in discussion over rights and universal categories, namely the United Nations. And yet, though the Jacquinot Decree emerged out of a context of colonial self-consciousness regarding its membership in a rights-driven international community and out of a desire to create cross-colony uniformity in rule and law, the deployment of the Jacquinot Decree depended on emphasizing local innovation and interpretation of bridewealth. In this context, marriage certificates, or marriage validations, created an administrative trail documenting the legitimacy of a marriage. For some men, these were important insurances that protected bridewealth they had paid in marriage. Not all men and women used such avenues to document their marriage, however, and sought alternative approaches to the brokering of marriage arrangements that did not adhere to state pathways.

In chapter 4, we saw how the Mandel Decree sought to protect girls from forced child marriages and to decrease the control that fathers and other males with patriarchal authority wielded over marriage. This was because by the 1930s, amidst colonial intervention due to fears of girl pawning, as well as the rising tide of sentiment for the condition of African women in

France among missionaries in the colonies, the administration in Paris and Dakar was prepared to intervene boldly in customary legal affairs. In theory, the Mandel Decree allowed women to appeal decisions such as levirate transfers in civil courts. Marriages of any girls under the age of fourteen were deemed invalid by the colonial administration. However, in practice, these effects were rarely realized. The Mandel Decree could be enforced only if men and women brought their cases before the state in a court of law or if colonial administrators witnessed practices that went against the Mandel Decree and decided to act on them.

Many marriages forged in the French Sudan did not have certificates to prove their legitimacy, as this was a practice followed almost exclusively by African men and women who worked for the colonial government. In fact, records from 1956 in Sikasso show that only 109 marriages were registered with the commandant's office for that year.[2] Even when men and women did obtain marriage certificates, this did not mean that the marriage was exempt from the power struggles that had driven marriage arrangements before the late 1930s. Marriages without certificates were still considered legitimate marriages if multiple parties attested to the marriage's existence, if the parties involved had engaged in the contractual practice of bridewealth, if the bride had consented, and if the bride was at least fourteen and the groom at least sixteen at the time of marriage.

As we have seen in previous chapters, elder men increasingly attempted to gain control over the direction of marriage arrangements in the 1920s and the 1930s. Young women felt the heightened pressure of marriage arrangements and the increased value placed on wealth in people through marriage. Some reacted by approaching the civil tribunal and demanding divorces on grounds of abuse or neglect. Some women were able to use arguments such as unpaid bridewealth to win their cases for divorce or to support their reasons for abandoning the conjugal home. Others, emboldened by the Mandel Decree, approached the civil courts to seek the dissolution of marriages to which they had not consented, as Holas observed in the epigraph at the beginning of this chapter. Still others chose to leave their conjugal homes without legal recourse. A number of these women were brought to the civil tribunal as runaway wives in abandonment cases. Young men who wanted to protect their marriage interests could often rely on the courts to support their interests and claims in such "runaway wife" cases.

Cases from the tribunal de premier degré in Sikasso reveal that some men in Sikasso sought to validate their marriages through the colonial tribunals in the 1940s and 1950s, partially as a precautionary act against wives who might leave the conjugal home. If a marriage certificate existed, a husband had a better chance of proving that his wife had abandoned the home without reason, thereby securing his entitlement to bridewealth reimbursement or custody of children. At the same time, the definition of marriage was increasingly limited by state regulations. For their part, elder men worked to limit young women's abilities to leave their marital households and forge multiple relationships. Men and women who appeared before the civil tribunal in Sikasso articulated marriage-related grievances against one another that showed their dissatisfaction with increasing intergenerational pressures on them in marriage. In some cases, women responded by refusing to abide by expectations of conjugal life articulated by male lineage heads, fathers, and husbands. Young men decried the bridewealth payment and labor expectations that were placed upon them by male elders.

In this chapter we see how, at the local level, some of the claims that young men and women made in court reflected their desire to break with the older generation in the management of their marriages. Exceptional cases stand out as examples of what was possible, but these did not necessarily represent the rule. Still, the 1940s and 1950s were a time when young people, returned veterans, and workers tested the hierarchies that had been propped up by the colonial administration in the past, such as the canton chieftaincy and the authority of household heads.

The pervasive discontent of the 1940s and 1950s throughout French West Africa—and French Sudan in particular—was largely fed by returned soldiers from World War II and labor activists. Military and civil servants, who were predominantly men, experienced the shortcomings and the failures of the colonial administration to support their claims and interests, despite the fact that most colonial projects and state infrastructure were built on the backs of these men. However, not all discontent or acts of resistance were part of a "seamless pattern of struggle," as Frederick Cooper reminds us in his work on the period that preceded decolonization and independence from colonial rule.[3] Furthermore, many of the struggles of the post–World War II period were localized and intimate, despite our postindependence vantage point that tends to privilege "movements" and organized resistance.[4] This is not to de-emphasize the effectiveness of organized movements nor their place in West African history, but rather to assert that not all who tested the boundaries of power in the post–World War II period were part of such large-scale struggles—or did not perceive themselves to be, at the very least.

Notably, the records from the tribunal de premier degré are relatively silent on the matter of returned soldiers from World War II. Unlike their predecessors who fought in World War I, World War II veterans in Sikasso do not seem to have approached the court with the same frequency. This could be for a number of reasons. Gregory Mann observes that on their return from the Second World War, many veterans ascertained that their interests were different from those of the generation that preceded them. World War I veterans, some of whom, decades after their war, found themselves to be older men of some prestige, were more likely to align themselves with the politically conservative canton chiefs in the French Sudan.[5] This division was felt in organized politics as well; the veterans of World War I were more likely to be members of the Parti Progressiste Soudanais (PSP), the conservative party of canton chiefs which was supported by the colonial administration, than of the Union Soudanaise-Rassemblement Démocratique Africain (US-RDA), the socialist party that broke with conservative forms of authority. World War II veterans, on their return from France, were, by and large, more likely to be skeptical of local forms of governance than their predecessors. This often translated into an unwillingness to participate as litigants in the civil tribunals, which were headed by the deputy commandant and court assessors drawn from the ranks of the canton chiefs.

The 1940s and 1950s were characterized by a heightened reliance on written records, and attempts to create "paper trails" for marriages. James Scott argues that such projects as decrees and legal record keeping were often attempts on the part of modern colonial state actors to make social practices legible.[6] Legibility, in this sense, has both a literal and a figurative meaning. Complex practices and identities were actually written down and codified for bureaucratic purposes, thus rendering them readable, but they were also cognitively repackaged and stripped of their local meanings in order for them to be broadly understood within the bureaucratic system. Although Scott is primarily concerned with modern, authoritarian political regimes grounded in leftist ideologies, such as Soviet Russia or Nyerere's policies of *ujaama*, his ideas are useful for colonial French West Africa. The large-scale forced labor and agricultural projects of the Office du Niger and the deuxième portion were precisely the types of agricultural and economic "high-modernism" that Scott describes.

Attempts to enforce principles of the Mandel and Jacquinot Decrees, the use of marriage certificates, and the civil litigation process were part of this "legibility project" in French West Africa. But this is not to say that the process of writing down the definition of marriage and other customary practices was done in a world separate from the reality on the ground, as scholars such as Sean Hawkins seem to suggest.[7] The "world on paper", that Hawkins describes as bound within centers of colonial knowledge and power in Northern Ghana, such as the legal courts and Christian missions, was very much the "world of experience" for African men and women. However, Hawkins is right to urge historians to examine the central role of writing in colonial projects. Writing did shape the form of knowledge in colonial Sikasso. When knowledge was written down, it became portable. The written word—in the form of marriage certificates, receipts, and transcripts of legal testimony—existed in the material world and affected the strategies used by men and women in negotiating their marriages.

Men and women throughout the Sikasso region knowingly used tools from both the bureaucratic world of the colonial administration and the experiential world of everyday life. Conversely, certain administrators, particularly during the stirrings of nationalism and decolonization, willingly threw themselves into the "illegible" everyday in the Sikasso region, worked closely with African court assessors, chiefs, and intermediaries, and in doing so realized the limits of many of their colonial projects. Many administrators on the ground were wary of reforms such as the Mandel Decree because they did not believe that they would have any meaning in rural settings away from colonial urban centers, especially outside of the Senegalese coast. The state provided possibilities for marriage reform through decrees and the civil legal system, but there were limitations to what the state could enforce in the way of marriage reform, as marriage was a crucial alliance between families and corresponded to agricultural practices as well as social and gendered obligations. Men and women endeavored to use avenues such as the civil tribunals to serve their interests, or they worked to avoid state avenues and colonial intermediaries when such elements might thwart their goals. However, these pathways were not always diametrically opposed. As Meredith McKittrick has said, "Colonial and traditional spheres were not distinct worlds; the vicissitudes of everyday life constantly entangled them with one another."[8] When it came to brokering marriages or settling marriage-related disputes in colonial Sikasso, this was certainly the case. Men and women in Sikasso consistently used the tools of the colonial state to solve their disputes, but not necessarily in the ways intended by those who drafted decrees and presided over tribunals. If anything, efforts to make African marriage more legible, and therefore more manageable and streamlined, in fact revealed that marriage was a messy engagement and could not be excised from other social obligations, labor and kin relationships, and political interests.

IMPOSTORS AND SWINDLERS:
THE CASE OF THE FALSE MARRIAGE CONTRACT

Allah kana nafigiw don aw cè [may swindlers not interfere].

—Bamanankan marriage benediction

Koniba was promised in marriage to Daouda from the time that she was two years old, in approximately 1931.[9] Both of them were from the village Daoulasso, in the canton of Kaboïla. Daouda, like so many men of his region and generation, turned to labor over the border in Côte d'Ivoire in order to earn more money than he would have by remaining in Sikasso. Over the years, Daouda and his family were able to complete bridewealth payments for his marriage to Koniba in installments, which were made to her male guardian. In addition to monetary and material gifts, Daouda's family members worked in the fields of Koniba's guardian on Daouda's behalf. An intermediary between the two families, who was a farmer also from Daoulasso, brokered the marriage arrangement, which had percolated over some seventeen years. In 1949 the families of Koniba and Daouda arrived at the agreement that the payments and farm labor were adequate for the marriage. It was time for Koniba to join Daouda as his wife. The intermediary, who was traveling at the time the marriage was to be finalized, sent his son on his behalf to escort Koniba to the home of Daouda's father and brothers. Despite Daouda's absence from Daoulasso, 15 July was to be the marriage day, a day of celebration and festivities that signaled the transfer of Koniba from her home to the family of Daouda. After the marriage celebrations, Makan, Daouda's brother, would travel to Côte d'Ivoire with Koniba and escort her directly to Daouda's Ivorian residence.

However, Koniba would have none of this. She was not interested in marrying Daouda; furthermore, she had a boyfriend in Sikassoville, Zeke, with whom she spent most evenings and with whom she wanted to maintain a relationship. Her relationship with Zeke was acceptable and widely known according to testimony from many people in the village of Daoulasso, including the village chief. However, it did not preclude her marriage to Daouda, in the eyes of either family. Koniba refused to go with the intermediary's son on the day of her marriage. She did not attend the marriage celebrations in her village of Daoulasso, and she refused to go with Makan when he approached her in order to deliver her to Daouda.

Koniba's refusal of a marriage promise, which involved so many individuals in a tightly knit village in Kaboïla and which had been sealed through bridewealth payments and fieldwork, caused tremendous consternation for all the parties involved. Koniba's guardian and Koniba's mother escorted Koniba to the home of Abderahamane Berté, the venerable canton chief who was known for his close relationship to the colonial administration and his integral role with the civil tribunal in Sikasso. The guardian and the mother questioned Koniba's refusal and implored her to accept Daouda as a husband, hoping that Berté would intervene and force Koniba to join Daouda. Koniba continued to adamantly refuse marriage ties with any of the men of Daouda's household. It turns out that she had initially been promised to Daouda's father, but it was only after some time that the marriage agreement was shifted to Daouda. In light of Koniba's refusal, Abderahamane Berté informed her guardian and mother that they could not force her to marry Daouda, that he would not facilitate her coercion into marriage, and that Daouda should make a formal request for bridewealth reimbursement.

At this point, the affairs related to the marriage arrangement between Koniba and Daouda took a complicated and bitter turn. Zeke, fearing that Koniba's family would abuse her or force her to marry Daouda despite Berté's advice, employed the services of an *agent d'affaires*, or a business agent, in Sikasso, by the name of Amara. Amara submitted, in Koniba's name, a complaint at the justice of the peace against Koniba's parents on 4 August 1948. Amara collected 2,000 francs on this occasion from Koniba and Zeke for his work as a legal assistant and intermediary. Some days later, Amara demanded another deposit from Zeke and explained that the families of Koniba and Daouda would secure the help of his esteemed colleague, a man of great influence. It would be difficult, Amara argued, for him to convince the court of Zeke and Koniba's grievances in light of his colleague's tremendous skill. Therefore, Amara explained, Zeke should give him another 2,000 francs, which would be given as a "gift" to the esteemed colleague, who would then throw the case in their favor. Zeke, desperate to clear the situation and not knowing how such legal processes operated, gave the sum to Amara, who was supposed to have given the money to his colleague on Zeke's behalf. Amara then asked Zeke for another sum of money, but Zeke refused, saying he had no more to give.

Makan, who wanted to solve this problem and defend the interests of his brother, employed both Amara and Amara's esteemed colleague as agents d'affaires. Amara requested 10,000 francs from Makan, arguing that Zeke had already given him 7,500 francs to file a complaint against Koniba's guardian and mother. They arrived at a compromise: Makan gave him 8.500 francs, telling him that if things worked out in his favor, he would give Makan 1,500 francs more. Makan also approached Amara's colleague and gave him 2,000 francs to file a countercomplaint against Zeke. In the midst of such intrigue and double-crossing, Amara devised a plan that he believed would yield him a tremendous sum of money. He would procure for Makan a marriage certificate attesting to the civil marriage of Koniba and Daouda. The existence of the marriage certificate would then allow Makan to take Koniba to court on Daouda's behalf for abandonment of the conjugal home.

On the morning of 9 August, Amara, Makan, Koniba's guardian, and Koniba's mother appeared before the office of the commandant of Sikasso with a paper attesting to the existence of a civil marriage between Daouda and Koniba. All of the employees at the commandant's office assumed, or were led to believe, that Makan was Daouda, the husband. One of the commandant's assistants advised the parties that in accordance with the Mandel Decree, the wife must be present to give her consent to marriage in the presence of an employee of the cercle. Only then would a marriage certificate be signed and validated. The party of four left the office and returned in the afternoon with a young woman whom they claimed to be Koniba. The commandant's assistant accompanied all five of them into the commandant's office, where Makan claimed to be Daouda, and Koniba's impostor claimed to be Koniba, both stating that they consented to marriage in the presence of the real Koniba's guardian and mother. Amara, as the agent d'affaires and mastermind, observed the entire charade in silence. What is more, at some point, upon learning that Koniba was in Sikassoville and planned on appearing before the commandant to pursue her complaint against her parents (which Amara had since abandoned), Amara told Koniba that if she did not marry Daouda, the commandant would most likely throw her in prison. Knowing that Koniba was a village girl with no education or real understanding of legal procedure, Amara thought that she would be naïve enough to believe him.

However, the commandant's assistant observed all of the parties involved in the civil marriage declaration with great skepticism. Just prior to the afternoon session at the commandant's office, his afternoon nap had been interrupted by a young man he knew from town named Youssouf. Youssouf said that he was visiting on behalf of his father, who wanted to deliver one thousand francs as a gift to the commandant's assistant, who did not understand why he would be the recipient of such a monetary gift. Youssouf explained that his father was the *jatigi*, or host, to three strangers from nearby Daoulasso who were in Sikassoville to settle a marriage-related conflict. In fact, Youssouf went on, they had visited the commandant's office that very morning—perhaps he had seen them there. The strangers were having a difficult time convincing the young woman in question to carry through with a prearranged marriage that had been already been properly brokered through bridewealth payments and labor obligations, and they feared that neither the commandant nor the civil court would rule in their favor. As their local host, Youssouf's father decided to send one thousand francs to the commandant's assistant in the hopes that he would help facilitate their request for a marriage certificate. Youssouf explained that the girl had a lover and that it would be very difficult to convince her to appear before the commandant. The commandant's assistant explained to Youssouf that she must appear and reiterated that there was a law in place now that required a woman to consent to marriage. With this, Youssouf silently returned home with the money still in his pocket. Later that afternoon, upon returning to work, the commandant's assistant saw exactly what Youssouf had said would take place that afternoon. The only difference is that there *was* a young woman with them, who claimed to be Koniba and who appeared to be quite docile and compliant. In fact, this unknown young woman was Makan's sister, whom he had forced to come to the tribunal and pretend to be Koniba. The commandant's assistant knew immediately that something was amiss. After the party left the commandant's office, believing that they had secured a civil marriage certificate, the assistant intervened and told the commandant not to notarize the certificate and to stop the process. He believed it was an affair of lies, swindling, double-crossing, and impostors. All parties involved were promptly brought back to the commandant's office and questioned. The scandal was thus revealed. Amara, Makan, Koniba's guardian, her mother, and Makan's younger sister were charged with the serious crimes of swindling, assuming false identities, falsifying official documentation, and, most important, forcing a woman into a marriage without her consent. Throughout the entire charade, Daouda remained in Côte d'Ivoire. It is unknown whether he was ever aware of the goings-on up north in Sikasso.

This case stands out for many reasons. It leaps from the pages of correspondence between the commandant of Sikasso and the attorney-general in Bamako as if it were a theater production, filled with lies and manipulation and a full cast of characters. But the seemingly extraordinary story of the ill-fated marriage between Daouda and Koniba has a narrative arc that, one can imagine, was all too common in Sikasso at the time: a young woman promised in marriage refused her suitor, fled her home, and attempted to maintain a relationship with a preexisting boyfriend. Her choice was often met with threats or beatings, exacted by a range of people from the head of her own household to the village and canton chiefs. The husband-to-be, having committed himself to cash bridewealth payments or labor in the fields of the guardian of his intended bride, fought to get his bridewealth back from the woman's family, who had most likely already consumed the payment.

In the case of Koniba and Daouda, Amara's role highlights that the colonial and traditional spheres were not distinct worlds. As an agent d'affaires, Amara actively traversed the so-called world of paper and the world of experience, pushing what he and Koniba's family perceived to be the failures of the state to protect their customary interests. Amara was the intermediary (and perhaps instigator) of a plan whereby Makan and Koniba's guardian manipulated the court's tools and rules to support the very positions of authority that were undermined by the Mandel Decree. Koniba's willingness to state her refusal of marriage not only to her guardian, her mother, and Makan, but to the canton chief, revealed the possibility of a power shift that undermined a hierarchy that rewarded men such as Makan, the guardian, and the canton chief himself. Amara, the agent d'affaires, was able to harness the fears of the men involved and convince them that they could use the very system that threatened to destabilize them to put Koniba in her place.

The testimony from the case shows that those individuals implicated in forging a marriage certificate, impersonating others, and attempting to force Koniba into marriage argued that they were fulfilling their societal and familial obligations and roles and that it was Koniba who was transgressive. In a similar case taken from Tanzania in the 1990s, Dorothy Hodgson has argued that when women defied dominant representations of what it meant to be such things as an obedient daughter or a duty-bound bride, they were subject to ostracization as "wicked women."[10] To maintain control over such women, the men who benefit from patriarchal authority position themselves as morally superior and normative, and they portray the women in question as abnormal troublemakers.

When the tribunal asked Makan why he falsely assumed his brother's identity, coerced his younger sister into assuming Koniba's identity, willingly participated in the falsification of official documents, and attempted to force a woman into a marriage, his explanation was simple: "I am Daouda's brother," Makan's testimony states. "I am obligated by custom to represent him and his interests. Koniba has been promised in marriage to him for seventeen years, and all the expenses have been paid. Koniba already had sexual relations with Daouda last year before he left for Côte d'Ivoire."

In chapter 4 we saw how competitions between colonial projects and Senufo lineage heads over access to young men resulted in increased pressures on young women in the realm of women's work and availability in marriage. The agricultural labor of wives replaced the labor of departed young men, and the bridewealth gained from marrying off daughters and nieces provided material security in a time of economic hardship. The desire to marry off daughters and develop secure relationships with other households through sister-exchange placed a premium on wealth in girls. Some women responded to these pressures by rejecting marriage claims and turning to relationships with lovers. Relationships that were not bound by marriage released young women from certain expectations, but they also came at a tremendous risk. If a woman had a child with a lover outside of marriage, she would be more apt to secure custody of her children if the relationship dissolved. Although the matrilineal, patrilocal practices of Senufo society gave Senufo women more control over their children than their Jula or Bambara counterparts, the act of rendering marriage practices legible in customary courts virtually erased this dynamic from civil legal practice in the eyes of the state. Throughout the French Sudan, if a woman sought a divorce from her husband in the tribunals, she would more than likely lose her children to him because he was recognized as the patriarch according to customary law. In turn, young men in Sikasso may have preferred lovers to wives as well. Although they would have had less control over a woman's labor than if married, men who did not marry were not responsible for completing the exorbitant bridewealth payments or labor obligations that were expected of fiancés. To some young men in the Sikasso region, this might have been preferable.

As we saw in chapter 1, intimate relationships between girls and slightly older boys or young men were acceptable and even encouraged in Senufo society. These premarital ties could secure a girl's honor and physical safety, as she was permitted to be physically intimate with her boyfriend but not engage in sexual intercourse. However, these relationships were not expected to turn into marriages and were rather seen as unions that would usher a girl through adolescence into adulthood.[11] Whether these relationships developed into longer-term conjugal relationships is more complicated than the idealized and prescriptive notion of how they were expected to be conducted. These relationships could endure over a number of years, allowing the couple to develop a long-standing bond. In cases where young women were promised in marriage to men who were not even physically located in their home village, such as in the case of Daouda and Koniba, a girl might be more likely to turn to her sanctioned boyfriend. During times of increased pressure on young girls in Sikasso, a Senufo girl might have turned to her boyfriend as an outlet from the demands being placed upon her by a fiancé and her family's expectations of her to marry. After the 1930s, some young women in Sikasso also knew that if they had developed security with their boyfriends, then they might also take the next step and appeal to the civil tribunals if their families still pressured them to marry. This secondary option was not without risks, but it was a possibility and an increasingly viable one after the Mandel Decree.

THE JACQUINOT DECREE, GENDER JUSTICE, AND POSTWAR POLITICS

By the mid-1940s and the 1950s, the state had become increasingly interventionist in the arena of African marriage throughout the French Sudan. In fact, the colonial state had become more interventionist in most aspects of everyday life for Africans. The 1940s and 1950s are often referred to as the "second colonial occupation" throughout Africa, and this was certainly the case in the French Sudan. Surveillance of Muslim community leaders, intervention in school programming, particularly Islamic education, labor monitoring and extraction, and the actual presence of colonial administrators in villages and remote parts of the colony all increased.[12] In addition, two important laws were passed in 1946 that improved the legal status of African subjects and contained certain basic elements to better the quality of life. The Houphouët-Boigny Law of 1946, named after the socialist union leader and former village chief (and future president) of Côte d'Ivoire, abolished forced labor throughout French West Africa and French Equatorial Africa. The Lamine Gueye Law, also passed in 1946, abolished the distinction between subject and citizen in Africa, but it also effectively ended the punitive and violent code de l'indigénat. These changes were part of a larger shift in what Frederick Cooper has called "the developmentalist" state in French colonial Africa.[13] Whereas decentralized government and colony-by-colony reforms characterized the British imperial government after World War II, French colonial policy in Africa was centralized, largely in an effort to create a federated and unified territory, which would be unified through its common experience of French colonial rule. African delegates would have a seat at the assembly table in Paris, but as a minority representation, really operating from a place of political weakness and tokenism. And yet change was under way. West African political leaders and activists pushed back and artfully negotiated the terms of representational government within the empire, and ultimately without it.

In addition to these shifts that were specific to the French colonial context, the dynamics of the post–World War II world significantly shaped the process that lead to the Jacquinot Decree—specifically, the formation of the United Nations and the Universal Declaration Human Rights in 1948. The Declaration of Human Rights was drafted over two years of collaborative work initiated by an eight-member committee, headed by Eleanor Roosevelt, the US delegate to the United Nations General Assembly and the Chair of the UN Commission on Human Rights. The original intent behind the document was to respond, in a preventive way, to the dynamics and conditions that contributed to the massive human turmoil unleashed by two world wars. The declaration was not originally imagined to be a framework directed at liberating colonized peoples, but was largely interpreted by imperial nations involved in the process of drafting the document as a mandate for uplift within the framework of empire.[14] Still, members of the United Nations involved in drafting the Universal Declaration of Human Rights spoke directly to the issue of marriage as a human right in article 16, which states that "men and women of full age, without any limitation due to race, nationality or religion, have the right to marry and to found a family. . . . The family is the natural and fundamental group unit of society and is entitled to protection by society and the State."[15]

It was from within this context that the Jacquinot Decree emerged. In many ways, this investment in the "natural" connection between the family and the state that we see in the 1948 declaration echoes the words and thoughts of Maurice Delafosse in 1912. The Jacquinot Decree reflected the colonial state commitment to increased state intervention and increased emphasis on the rights of the individual. But just as it also seems to indicate a turn away from reliance of custom in colonial decree and law, a transformation that began in earnest with the Mandel Decree, the Jacquinot Decree's limits on bridewealth depended on local expert knowledge and male authority.[16]

The Jacquinot Decree was also embedded in the post–World War II developmentalist state in Africa. In July 1955 the colonial administration of Sikasso met with a council of notables, a practice that had become familiar throughout the colony. This council of notables included canton chiefs—in particular, the canton chiefs of Folona, Bougoula, Natie, Kaboïla, Fama, and Ganadugu—but it also included African merchants, African civil servants, and nonchiefly political leaders such as Sidi Diallo and Jean-Marie Koné. Jean-Marie Koné, a native of Sikasso, was an influential member of the US-RDA and would later become the minister of the interior of the Independent Republic of Mali. His role as an important power broker in post–World War II Sikasso and the French Sudan more broadly was significant to both local discussions of bridewealth and marriage as well as colony-wide reformation of marriage under the Jacquinot Decree and its political ramifications.

The July 1955 meeting began with a lengthy discussion of local agricultural strategies and the need for tractors and other materials to "ameliorate the life of the peasant."[17] Cement deliveries and the paving of roads were discussed, as was the creation of a new athletics field (presumably for football). The agenda shifted to a discussion of trypanosomiasis (sleeping sickness) and the possibilities of increased infection opportunity as a result of migrant workers moving between Côte d'Ivoire and Sikasso. After a break, the meeting was devoted to the topic of bridewealth. Those present expressed concern over the fact that the high numbers of those emigrating to Côte d'Ivoire were the result of high bridewealth prices—that is, that young men left Sikasso for work that paid more cash. "This question of bridewealth is serious, as it is a cause of unease. . . . [It is the cause of] brutal ruptures between the young and old that weaken the family and society, an exodus of young men to Côte d'Ivoire, and imbalances in the households of old men. . . . The only way to make this unease disappear is to set a maximum cap on bridewealth."[18] The discussion of bridewealth with the council of notables was a response to a request sent to all districts from the governor of the French Sudan, asking that each commandant meet with local experts and men of authority to determine appropriate bridewealth standards for the cantons and regions within their districts. "I want to be clear that the bridewealth rate proposed should be set in such a way as to permit the *evolution* of the custom in moderating what is in certain regions an excessive course, and which creates social problems that are very serious for young men [my emphasis]."[19] The concern of the colonial government office continued to be one of transforming local practice in accordance with what the colonial administration believed was reasonable or civilized.

To be sure, many people complained about bridewealth, and not only members of the colonial administration. Since the 1930s, bridewealth rates had risen, even during World War II. In the Sikasso administration's response to the governor outlining bridewealth rates throughout the district, the overwhelming burden of bridewealth expectations is clear. As well, the disparity between *cercles*, between town and countryside, and between different ethnic groups was also evident. In Bugula, 1955 bridewealth practices seemed to adhere to what most of the council of notables considered to be reasonable: for a young woman in Sikassoville, bridewealth consisted of 20 grams of gold or 6,000 francs, one *pagne*, or wrap, one *boubou*, one blouse, one handkerchief, one pair of shoes, one scarf, one father's *boubou*, one mother's *pagne*, one father's gift, one mother's gift, and kola nuts. Total expenses typically rounded out at 31,000 francs. For the more rural villages of Bugula, predominantly Senufo, and one of the cantons with a town center in one of the quarters of Sikassoville, twenty days of cultivation over the course of ten to fourteen years plus the cost of genital excision (10,000 francs) was expected. By contrast, in N'Golasso, also a Senufo majority canton, a man was expected to cultivate in his wife's father's field for thirty to thirty-five years.[20] Jean-Marie Koné expressed a concern that the varied approach to bridewealth throughout Sikasso district would make it impossible to establish a uniform bridewealth rate, despite his desire to reform bridewealth and do so expediently. The commandant suggested that the same lines used to establish taxation rates be applied to the bridewealth standard: the town of Sikasso would adhere to one rate, all Senufo villages would adhere to their own cultivation standard, and Ganadugu and Folona, made up of more recently settled Fulani communities, would have their own bridewealth standard to be established at a later time. This solution reflects the state's reliance on an ethnic essentialism (the development of which was addressed in chapter 1) to maintain a vision of colonial order: despite the fact that communities claiming Senufo identity adhered to a variety of different practices based on regional practice and other variables, ethnicity would be the ultimate determining characteristic of bridewealth rate. In many ways, such an approach to the bridewealth conundrum reflected the colonial state's interest in moderately turning away from custom and creating a statewide standardization of practice, a project that was in line with the developmentalist colonial state.

Much of the emphasis on the standardization of bridewealth was framed as being rooted in a desire to liberate young men from the oppression of older men. In this sense, the Jacquinot Decree was a form of gender justice for men: liberating young men from the labor constraints and material demands of their wives' fathers in an age of labor reform and the rising tide of nationalism. It also reflected the universal language seen in the Universal Declaration of Human Rights regarding marriage as a basic human right: men and women have the right to marry and to be free from the interests of others in planning their marriages. Such decisions to cap bridewealth were not shifts that members of the administration close to the ground took lightly. "We must also imagine the political aspects of this change," wrote Commandant Touze of Sikasso to the governor of French Sudan in 1955. "A decision of such importance, which will diminish the profits that the elders are accustomed to receiving from the marriage of their daughters, and which will, furthermore, facilitate the marriages of the youth, will have great consequences." He added, "To the elders [the bridewealth cap] will seem revolutionary, but to the youth it will be very popular."[21] Touze was wary of the interest that Koné and Diallo took in the bridewealth stipulations of the Jacquinot Decree. "The part taken by the two general counselors, Mr. Sidi Diallo and more particularly, Jean-Marie Koné, who, at the end of the meeting asked that we act without hesitation on the matter of circumscription, without waiting for an executive order on the maximum bridewealth rate, leads one to think that he is trying to take all the advantage that he might out of this situation."[22] Thus the Jacquinot Decree could be a lever for other matters pertaining to labor and the agenda of the socialist US-RDA. The Jacquinot Decree ultimately undermined the wealth of those who were likely to support the PSP, the party loyal to colonialists and which supported a moderate restructuring Sudan's place in the empire, as opposed to decolonization, which was what US-RDA members were calling for. Although the colonial administration framed the Jacquinot Decree carefully as an effort to eradicate—with moderation—those practices that were contrary to French civilization and bring about the so-called evolution of custom, they were not interested in subverting structures of hierarchy that propped up the colonial state. Still, the postwar global context of universal categories, discussions of human rights as embedded in social and economic justice, as well as localized demands for representational government and the eradication of forms of tyranny concerning labor and taxation—all made it impossible for the colonial administration to continue on its path. The Jacquinot Decree reforms were interpreted by members of the US-RDA as serving their interests in creating a more equitable society. However, although the Jacquinot Decree's cap on bridewealth had an impact in a political sense and in terms of its effect on redistribution of labor and material wealth through marriage, its influence on consent and its goal of restricting the interests of third parties in the marriages of young women is another matter. As scholars of other parts of French West Africa have argued, there was a high degree of noncompliance in the application of the Jacquinot Decree, precisely because it challenged elder male authority and went against prevailing cultural norms.[23] As we see in the case of Koniba and Douda at the beginning of this chapter, pulling marriage apart from other kin relations and relationships of obligation and dependence was, perhaps, an exercise in futility. If we turn to the cases that made their way to the tribunal de premier degré—the source of arbitration on which the administration relied to apply the Jacquinot Decree, particularly when it came to enforcing the protections from familial interference—we see a variety of outcomes.

"Once a month," Roland Colin wrote, "the 'little white Commandant' became the 'little judge' and presided over the *Tribunal de premier degré*."[24] Roland Colin presided as the deputy administrator of Sikasso in the mid-1950s and later authored *Kènèdougou*, a detailed memoir of his time in Sikasso.[25] Colin was an exceptional administrator in that he believed that decolonization was a necessary step. He was committed to collaboration with local politicians and officials, and he was critical of the workings of the colonial administration. Before arriving in Sikasso, Colin attended l'École Nationale de la France d'Outre Mer, where he studied under Léopold Senghor (who would later become the first president of Senegal), and took up the study of African languages. After his tenure as deputy administrator in the colonial administration, Colin went on to teach at the University of Paris and at l'École des Hautes Études in Paris. In many ways an inheritor of the scholar-administrator cloak in the French tradition, Colin devoted himself to becoming a scholar of Africa, but was also critical of the power and authority of colonial rule. Colin's 2004 memoir paints a vivid picture of the tribunal de premier degré in the 1950s and the centrality of marriage-related disputes in the court.

In his memoir, we can see the tribunal de premier degré through Colin's eyes. In Sikasso, the tribunal convened at the top of the mamelon, or hillock, at the center of the town. The mamelon had symbolic and historical significance as the former center of Kenedugu's power. At the top of the mamelon stood a small stone structure, which contained a table, a few chairs, and three benches.[26] Between the table and the bench was the space in which plaintiffs and defendants provided their testimony to the court. The colonial administrator sat at the table facing the litigants, with the stenographer sitting immediately next to him. The assessors sat on either side of the tribunal president and the stenographer. Colin admitted that his relationship with the assessors was tense; he knew many of them well from his visits throughout Sikasso. He admired their experience and wisdom, but he noted, "Wisdom does not automatically translate into parity." In the memoir, Colin expressed his wariness of the close ties between court assessors and canton chiefs and the effects that these relationships of authority might have had on the cases themselves. The reality of this power dynamic is that it rested on the colonial apparatus itself. Colin was intimately implicated as a steward of the colonial government in Sikasso.

Cases from tribunal de premier degré in Sikasso for the years 1950 to 1953 provide detailed accounts of marriage-related cases. All of the cases were contained within one bound registry at the Sikasso tribunal, marked by a handwritten label stating simply "Registre de Divorce." Certainly, not all of the cases contained within were divorce cases—not even a majority were divorce cases. However, this is an indicator of what the court had become a symbol of—marital rupture. Inside the registry, a note explains that the contents of the registry were the cases heard before the tribunal de premier degré of Sikasso, headed by the deputy administrator and president of the tribunal, who was assisted by two assessors, assigned because of their expertise in a particular custom (this varied according to the litigants and apparently the availability of certain assessors), two interpreters, and a court stenographer. Taken as a whole, the seventy-two cases recovered from the unclassified Sikasso archives make up an irregular pattern that is difficult to interpret. But like the cases examined in chapter 3, they do constitute a useful sample for possible trends in cases brought before the tribunal during the period, and their detail provides a glimpse of how Sikasso women and men engaged with the tribunal process.

Although in 1951 and 1953 there were apparently only nine cases heard before the civil tribunal, there were thirty cases heard in 1952, with eleven of them falling under the category of inheritance disputes. There were also no divorce cases recorded for that year. There is one consistency in the relative frequency with which men approached the civil tribunal to force the return of their wives to the conjugal home. Increasingly, men took their wives to court for abandoning the conjugal home. But the majority of these cases of abandonment in Sikasso show that women maintained relationships with men outside of marriage. These cases, like the one of Koniba and Daouda, seem to indicate that young men and women worked to broker their own arrangements outside the terms of the bridewealth contract between a fiancé and the male lineage head of the intended bride.

Although the legal avenues and the decrees that were attached to them had limited, real effects on how people went about arranging marriages in Sikasso, these cases indicate that the courts at least supported a path of nonmarital cohabitation in situations where women and their lovers were brought to court by the men who wanted to contract "correct" marriages that were grounded in bridewealth exchanges and labor or material obligations to a woman's male elder. This was because by the 1950s, the courts were interested in supporting consent. These relationships were outside the purview of elder male authority and were therefore threatening and subversive. Although in some ways they were also outside the reach of the state, the state supported claims of extramarital relationships on occasions when a woman's consent lay squarely with the relationship that was outside of marriage. However, if she had given consent first to a marriage and simply left the home because she was unhappy, she would have to file for divorce. Notions of consent and acceptable relationships were debated through the cases that appeared at the tribunal.

On 7 August 1950, Samba, a man of roughly forty-five years, brought his wife, Konimba, thirty years old, to court for abandoning the conjugal home.[27] They resided in the canton of Bugula, in the village of Finkolo, where both of them had been raised. Samba explained to the court that they had been married according to Senufo custom. One day when he was away, Konimba took advantage of his absence and left the home for that of her lover, Lansina, who also lived in Finkolo. "I approached her father, Zie, and explained to him that if she did not return that I was going to take my children or demand that I be reimbursed bridewealth," he stated before the court. In this particular case, Samba and Zie appeared before the canton chief of Bugula and sought his help to retrieve Konimba. Through questioning, it was revealed that Konimba had spent only three nights with Samba and that she had three children by her lover. Koniba provided testimony where she declared, "I am not married to Samba, I did not give my consent, and it has been seven years since I was at his home." Konimba had spent the past seven years with Lassina, her boyfriend and the father of her three children. Following Konimba, Zie declared through his testimony that Samba had paid 600 francs in bridewealth, but he made a point of telling the court that Samba had never cultivated for the marriage contract. The tribunal quickly ruled in Konimba's favor, in light of her clear refusal of the marriage, but also because of the amount of time that had passed between the time that Konimba had left Samba's home and the moment that Samba had filed his complaint.

A very different case of abandonment of the conjugal home appeared before the court on 18 September 1950. Kouloutelou, a Senufo man of roughly thirty years of age from the canton of Bugula, appeared before the court asking for the return of his wife, Koro.[28] Kouloutelou explained to the court that he had cultivated in her father's fields over the course of fifteen years for their marriage and that Koro had given birth to two children by him, one of whom was still living. One day, she left the home, and although he claimed that he was not sure of the circumstances, he claimed that she had been "taken" by N'Golo, another man of their village. Kouloutelou sent a close friend on his behalf to N'Golo's home who asked to have Koro returned to Kouloutelou. N'Golo, according to Kouloutelou's testimony, refused and stated that Koro would never go back. When the court questioned Koro, she explained, "I had a fight with my husband.

He told me that had no more use for me, and that I should return to my father's compound. So, I left." The court then asked if there had been witnesses to this exchange, to which she replied that there had not. The court also asked her if she acknowledged that her marriage to Kouloutelou was valid. Koro affirmed that he had worked for fifteen years in the fields of her matrilineage for the marriage, and they had two children together. In light of the validity of the marriage arrangement, the fact that Koro had initially consented to marriage, and that there were no witnesses to his repudiation of her, Koro was told by the court to return to Kouloutelou, and that there was no valid reason for her to have left the conjugal home.

Both of these cases from 1950 involve marriages for which there was no certificate in place, but for which there was bridewealth exchanged. They are distinct in the ways that the women involved applied consent. In the first case, it was very clear to the court that Konimba never consented to her marriage and that she was never a willing participant, although she did spend a few nights at her husband's home. In the second case, Koro initially consented to her marriage, but made the choice to leave her husband for a lover. These cases are examples of how the court consistently upheld the existence of a marriage provided there was evidence of some form of contractual agreement as well as consent by the bride. However, a marriage was dissolved in the absence of consent after the Mandel Decree. A woman who initially consented to her marriage would have to go through the process of arguing for divorce through the tribunal. With all of this, and in light of the pressures of bridewealth payment and coerced marriages that implicated outside family members, young men and women may have been more inclined to turn to relationships that were outside the bounds of marriage.

Many cases constituting abandonment of the conjugal home resulted in women being ordered to return. On occasion, women would enter the case as defendants and argue that they were never actually married to the man bringing them to court in the first place, for example in two cases from 21 July 1952 in Sikasso: the cases of *Fatoumata Koné v. Amadou Traoré, and Bakary Diarra v. Siritio Bengali*. When the husband could produce a marriage certificate in the face of his wife's claim that the marriage was void, he was certain to win his case. However, even if he could not, the witness testimony of patriarchal figures weighed heavily in the eyes of the court.

On 21 July 1952, Fatoumata Koné, Muslim, Senufo, and residing in Bugula, requested a divorce from her husband, Amadou Traoré, also Muslim, Senufo, and residing in Bugula. Despite the fact that Koné was the plaintiff and this was her claim, the Sikasso tribunal labeled this case as a "reintegration of conjugal home" case. Koné sent the following information to the court in a written letter: "I was married to Amadou Traoré, a jewelry maker from Bugula in Sikasso. As I didn't want any part of him, the justice of the peace of Sikasso condemned me and my mother, Kadidia Coulibaly, to three months in prison. When I left prison, Amadou Traoré filed another complaint against me. The tribunal decided that I should rejoin him in the conjugal home. I did not want to do so. The justice decided to condemn me to one more month of prison. Amadou Traoré told the justice of the peace not to condemn me, and he excused me. At this time, I ask the tribunal for a divorce."

Amadou Traoré responded, "I do not want a divorce. My wife was put in prison because she lied and said that she was not married to me. Her mother was also condemned to prison for false testimony. It was she who started this. Here are my copies of the marriage certificate." Amadou Traoré gave the president of the tribunal a copy of his *jugement suppletif*, his marriage certificate, number 590, dated 25 June 1951. This certificate declared that Amadou Traoré had contracted marriage with Fatoumata Koné in 1949. The tribunal found that Fatoumata Koné had no valid reason for divorce, and ordered her to immediately return to the conjugal home.[29] Here again, we see the comingling of the bureaucratic and the experiential world—Koné's letter to the tribunal, almost certainly drafted by a letter writer versed in the language and processes of the court, and the jugement suppletif itself—powerful and legible proof of the marriage, which no testimony or sentiment could deny. But given the story that emerges from the false marriage contract scandal at the beginning of this chapter, we see the social complexities and corruptible power that could potentially undergird something seemingly definitive and clear, such as a paper contract. In addition, cases such as *Koné v. Traoré* point to the ambiguities of consent. How was Fatoumata Koné's consent issued or measured in the first place, and what do we know of those who may have "benefited from the marriage," to use the language of the Jacquinot Decree? Although the tribunal de premier degré cases are rich with testimony, the "world of the court" does not capture the kin obligations and social demands that we only begin to glimpse through other types of sources that capture the world "outside the court."[30] What we do know is that Fatoumata Koné was willing to approach the court again, even after serving jail time, to get a divorce: in doing so, she was hedging her bets, and perhaps indicating that the court was her best option, in the face of local patriarchs, such as chiefs, fathers, and uncles.

Patriarchal and masculine political authority emerges as a significant factor in the case of *Bakary Diarra v. Siritio Bengali*. On 21 July 1952,

Bakary Diarra, seventy years old, Muslim, and a resident of Kignan village in Zeguedugu canton, brought his wife, Siritio Bengali, approximately forty years old, Muslim, and also of Kignan, to the Sikasso tribunal requesting that she return to the conjugal home. Diarra had previously attempted to reconcile with Bengali before the village chief of Kignan, as well as the canton chief of Zeguedugu. Diarra approached the tribunal with a written request, addressed to the president of the tribunal, explaining that he had married Siritio Bengali in 1938, and approximately five years ago she had left him, abandoning the conjugal home. He found her again in April 1952, but she refused to rejoin him. Diarra stated that despite the council of the village elders and canton chiefs, Bengali refused to come home. At the tribunal, Bengali stated, "I am not married to Bakary Diarra. It was Datigui Ballo who gave me to Bakary for 200 francs." The president of the tribunal called for the witness testimony of one Souleymane Bengali, brother of Siritio, approximately thirty years old, Muslim, and a farmer residing in Kignan. Souleymane Bengali offered the following testimony under oath: "My sister was married to N'Zie Ballo. Ballo left the village without leaving an address. The brother of N'Zie, Datigui Ballo, gave Siritio to Bakary Diarra." The president of the tribunal then read aloud from a letter sent to the court from the canton chief of Zeguedugu, Adama Coulibaly. "I have the honor of informing you that Siritio is the wife of Bakary Diarra of Kignan. Bakary Diarra, having 'satisfied the customs of the land' [paid bridewealth], is seen as having been abandoned by his wife with no valid reason. All of the village notables witnessed this marriage." Considering the testimony from the canton chief, in addition to the information that the village council of elders had attempted to reconcile the couple, to no avail, the Sikasso tribunal ruled that Bakary Diarra and Siritio Bengaly were legitimately married and that Seritio should immediately return to the conjugal home.[31] This case reveals the limits of the Jacquinot Decree, as far as its capacity to affect the influence of family members on the marriages of adult women. The tribunal accepted the testimony and authority of the village and canton chiefs over the woman in question, Siritio Bengali, and her brother, in determining the legitimacy of the marriage. In this particular case, there was no marriage certificate introduced as evidence.

At times, however, women and men wanted to marry on their own terms and sought out the tribunal's help in doing so. The following case shows both the possibilities that the state provided for women and men seeking to forge their own marriages and the limits of the state in enforcing the rule of consent outside the courts.

On 25 August 1952, a young woman named Fata, twenty-five years old and a resident of Kaboïla canton, brought a dispute against her father, Nampaya. Both parties were listed as Senufo-Muslim. Her testimony was noted as follows:

> I was raised by my aunt, Sadio, not by my father or in my father's household. Recently, a man by the name of Lansine came to me with my father, and explained that he wanted to marry me, with my father's consent. I said that I would not marry Lansine. I told my father that I wanted to marry Sinaly. My father declared that he would never allow me to marry Sinaly. But I love Sinaly, and I have a child with him. I therefore ask the court to intervene between me and my father so I can marry Sinaly.[32]

Sinaly was then called before the tribunal. He stated before the court that he was thirty-five years old, Senufo, and a farmer. According to the record, he stated that he was the father of Fata's son, an infant named Abdoulaye. He also declared that he wanted to marry Fata and that he was prepared to pay bridewealth for a marriage. The court ruled in Fata's favor, arguing that her father could not force her to marry against her consent, and all parties signed a written statement in the court agreeing to honor the marriage contract between Fata and Sinaly.

This case is extraordinary for a number of reasons. It exemplifies the rare possibility that a young woman could make a marriage claim against her father in the native courts. Marriage for a young woman at twenty-five was also rare. By local standards of the time, Fata was an old bride and was certainly was not behaving as a dutiful daughter by bringing her father to court. Yet her point that she was not raised in her father's household can be interpreted as an explanation of why she felt it particularly acceptable for her to bring her father to court. She was raised by her aunt and not in her father's household; thus, although she was making a claim against her father, she was also making it known that she was a not a dependent of his household. Still, Fata's case is notable. While some women experienced the pressure and marital obligation described by Aminata Kouyaté at the opening of this chapter, in the 1940s and 1950s women had the legal option of breaking away and forging their own marriages. Fata's case at least shows the possibilities available to women and men who sought to break away from the authority of their fathers.

However, the question remains how such developments, such as the Mandel Decree and the Jacquinot Decree, affected the everyday lives of men and women and how people actually approached marriage. It is debatable what these mandates truly meant to people in their everyday worlds, as they were applied in various ways to their conjugal unions through the tribunal system, as we have seen in this chapter. Although mandates in principle protected girls and young women, they did so only when a union interfaced with the colonial state in some fashion—and even then, there was inconsistency in how the tribunal applied the decrees, depending on the details of the case. In the period when the marriage legibility project was at its height—1939 through 1952—it seems that both men and women may have increasingly arranged relationships that brought them farther away from the legal definition of marriage under colonial civil law, and away from how male elders preferred to contract marriages according to customary notions of conjugality. If we use the tribunal registries as an indicator of the frequency with which women and men brought their marriage-related cases before the court, then we see a withdrawal from the courts in managing marriage conflict.

As in the early years of colonial rule—but under different circumstances—young men and women tested the possibilities in the civil tribunal's litigation of marriage-related matters in the 1940s and 1950s. Likewise, male elders and those who felt threatened by new state interventions in marriage devised their own strategies for using state avenues for contracting marriages. Some attempted to go around state processes of marriage control, or they devised ways of using the state-sanctioned tools to support their control over young women. Some young women and men forged their own conjugal arrangements outside the scope of both the family hierarchy and the civil state. Still, some young women and men sought out the civil tribunals to assist them in breaking with patriarchal ties in order to form conjugal unions that were recognized by the state, if not by their families. All of the examples from this chapter show the myriad ways in which women and men in Sikasso tested both the limits and the possibilities of state intervention in forging marriages.

The Jacquinot Decree of 1951 was embedded in the politics of nationalism and, ultimately, of decolonization. It emerged at a time when young men sought to break free from the constraints of male elders and traditional forms of masculine authority. Indeed, here we see how agitation for bridewealth reform and the Jacquinot Decree were part of a political agenda imagined by members of the US-RDA in Sikasso, such as Jean-Marie Koné. Although the Jacquinot Decree was intended to adhere to categories of justice that served both women and men, its amelioration of exploitative bridewealth was its most influential and controversial point. This was interpreted largely as gender justice for young men seeking to marry and forge their own marriage-based households in a new age at the end of the colonial period. However, as we see from some of the Sikasso tribunal cases presented here, the Jacquinot Decree's ability to actually restrain the influence of family members on the marriage arrangements and, ultimately, the issuing of consent by young women is debatable. The Jacquinot Decree emerged from a global and a local context of calls for justice in the form of marriage reform. The period after World War II was a time when a self-conscious human rights community began to emerge, but it was entirely unclear how top-down notions of rights and universality would translate in local contexts, such as Sikasso. As well, what remained in question was what it meant to be an individual within a marriage, and the role that a marriage might play in the formation of communities and, ultimately, states. Here we see that marriage was integral to state making and political claims within a larger context of nationalism and redefining the late colonial state. However, what marriage should look like—and to whom—remained an unresolved question.

Conclusion

"There Are Always Laws That Are Not Practiced"

IN THIS BOOK, REFORMS IN MARRIAGE LAW and the political significance of the institution of marriage to colonial rule are analyzed as central components of change in the French Sudan. Many of these shifts can be traced by studying the transformations of the court, but marriage's place in debates over state making and colonial rule extended well beyond the courtroom. These changes reflected the political culture of the colonial administration as well as the sociohistorical transformations of everyday life for men and women living in the region of Sikasso and throughout the colony of the French Sudan.

The story of Momo Traoré opens this book. As the namesake of a woman whose marriage solidified kinship lines between local households and an emerging empire, she represents many things: the rise of the Traoré family and its ethnic complexity, as well as the possibility of women's political effectiveness in Kenedugu. With the fall of Sikasso to the French army, histories of Momo and what she represented faded, as the French colonial administration sought out particular men of influence from the ranks of Kenedugu's political and military hierarchy. These men became important to the formation of a corpus of information that colonial administrators used to develop ethnographic sketches of the Sikasso region. This information also served as the basis for customary law, which framed administrative dealings in local marriages.

In the first few years of the twentieth century, women seeking to rene-
gotiate their bonds with men—namely, husbands and former masters—
inundated the colonial courts in Sikasso. More often than not, the courts
granted these women divorces or otherwise supported their claims against
men. The historical record shows that there were close linkages between
marriage contestations and slavery in the early years of colonial rule. Men
and women argued in court over the transactional quality of marriage contracts. These debates, and the administrative correspondence regarding the
debates, reveal that the colonial administration had yet to work out what
appeared to be fine distinctions between women in bondage and women
in marriage in southern Mali. Cases from these early years of the colonial
civil courts reveal a period when men and women tested local forms of authority by resolving their conflicts in civil court rather than at the village
level. Although the court cases on marriage from this period may seem at
first glance to indicate women's desire to break ties, in many situations this
was not the reason. Women did not always work toward their liberation, but
rather they worked to gain control over their options and to decrease their
vulnerability. These were crucial strategies for survival in Sikasso, as villages rebuilt after the devastating wars of conquest at the turn of the century
and the resulting massive enslavement that plagued the countryside.

Reforms in marriage law after 1912 were part of Governor-General Ponty's
politique des races, a political philosophy that, in theory, emphasized the
diversity of local practices and ethnic identities. In practice, post-1912 legal
reforms did not necessarily stress local diversity and instead reinforced patriarchal authority in ways that the 1905–12 legal system did not. Court cases
from this period reveal intergenerational struggles between older men and
young men, particularly young men who went to fight in World War I.
Young men relied on older men to protect their marriage interests, but this
did not always happen. Younger women were often caught in the midst of
these intergenerational struggles.

As in many other parts of colonial Africa, generational tension continued to reveal itself as a contributor to marriage-related troubles in the
1930s. The Global Depression and labor and military recruitment drove
many young men from rural villages to participate in migrant labor to Côte
d'Ivoire. As a result, family heads began to lose control over young men's
labor, while canton and village chiefs consolidated their control and authority as intermediaries of the colonial state. Matrilineal heads of Senufo
families attempted to combat this loss of power by increasing demands on
young men in the way of marriage prestations and field labor. At the same
time, young Senufo women bore the burden of agricultural labor in new

ways, as a result of the absence of young men. Some families under tremendous hardship pawned their daughters in an attempt to gain material wealth during the Global Depression, in the face of relentless taxation by the colonial state. These shifts represented a transformation in an emphasis on wealth in men to wealth in women. Women represented access to material wealth and labor through marriage promises to young men, but they were also workers themselves.

Missionaries and administrators perceived the changes around them as a sign of African women's subservient status, and worked to reform the laws governing African marriage and family life in French West Africa. This period culminated in the Mandel Decree, which required consent on the part of the woman and man entering into a marriage, and established minimum age requirements for marriage. These reforms signaled an effort to protect the individual rights of young women. As a result, they diminished the rights of fathers and patriarchal authorities before the state. In effect, the political pendulum had swung from supporting the entrenchment of patriarchal authority in marriages in the 1920s, to the maintenance of young women's autonomy in the forging of their marriages in the 1930s.

If the period from the late nineteenth century through the 1920s was a context in which colonial administrators attempted to render certain Sikasso marital practices legible according to customary law, the 1930s heralded a period in which the state attempted more forceful interventions in African marriages. Thus, in the 1930s, ideas about gender justice were based on a shift in the marriage legibility project: a move from efforts to establish marriage legibility to the enforcement of restrictions and definitions of acceptable practice in African marriage. The Mandel Decree of 1939 is illustrative of this shift.

During the 1930s administrative decrees clearly outlined parameters of acceptable behavior in the context of marriage and control over girls in a way that clarified the well-established but vague distinction between "that which is according to local custom" and "that which is contrary to French civilization." However, cases of domestic violence or the physical punishment of wives by husbands tested judicial categories of "acceptable" African customary practice. That is, administrators believed that mundane, physical punishment of wives was acceptable according to local practice in Sikasso, but they struggled to define the limits of acceptability. Domestic violence cases from the 1930s reveal how some women were implicated in the abuse of other women. The "patriarchal bargain" asserts that some women, when they support the actions of men who commit abuses, are implicated in the very acts of physical violence that subjugate other women. Moreover, this is a culturally grounded survival strategy. This conceptual tool, taken from Deniz Kandiyoti, illustrates the generational hierarchy embedded in many patriarchal systems: older women were often the ones who participated in the bargain at the expense of younger women. However, as we see in the cases highlighted in this book, older women who bargained were also in a position to surveil, and ultimately challenge, gendered hierarchy gone awry, pressing men to hold up their part of "the bargain." The patriarchal bargain shows us both the limits and the possibilities of gendered agency within oppressive social systems, in colonial West Africa and elsewhere. Gendered violence and oppression occurred, but the conditions of its acceptability were always contested.

Although increased state involvement in the management of African marriages occurred in the 1930s, it remained to be seen if these initiatives would be successful. Indeed, African men and women used tools of the state and processes approved by the colonial administration to get what they wanted out of marriages. Examples from the 1950s show the ways in which senior men and younger men who benefited from traditional lines of authority devised ways to use state avenues to serve their own interests. Men engaged with the state to further their interests in marriage even when their goals were not in line with what the colonial administration believed was in accordance with "French civilization."

And yet cases from this period also show that despite the limitations of the state, civil courts and state decrees created a legal space for young women and young men who wanted to break away from family elders and forge their own conjugal relationships. Mandates such as the Mandel Decree and the Jacquinot Decree, protected women in principle, but this worked only when a union was recognized by the colonial state in some fashion. Both men and women increasingly arranged relationships that brought them farther away from the legal definition of marriage under colonial law, and away from how male elders preferred to contract marriages according to customary notions of conjugality. To be sure, laws may exist but there are always "laws that are not practiced," as one informant noted in 2005.

If, as legal theorist Robert Cover once stated, "Law is the imagined future projected onto reality," then French colonial administrators imagined a future in which the individual had control over her or his choices in marriage and, perhaps more important, a future in which individuals saw the state as a significant and relevant overstructure to their marriages.[1] So much of the later colonial effort to render African marriage practices legible in the French Sudan, and Sikasso in particular, rested on establishing and recognizing consent. What does it mean to indicate consent—signifying oneself as a liberal and sovereign body—when one is a colonial subject, particularly a female colonial subject? It is at least a fiction; at most, a signifier of complex relationships that reveal the limitations of using a liberal frame for understanding agency and choice in modern colonial and postcolonial worlds. The implicit and explicit violence of colonial state power, wherein a subject is necessarily less than a citizen in the eyes of the state, and in the ways in which the subject has the capacity to marshal rights and obligations of the state, renders the liberal idea of consent in this context fairly meaningless.[2] The political theorist Carole Pateman goes so far as to argue that consent is not truly possible within the institutions of any liberal democratic state, because the liberal democratic state is a patriarchal structure. "In the relationship between the sexes," Pateman writes, "it is always women who are held to consent to men. The naturally superior makes an initiative, offers a contract, to which the subordinate, who is inherently passive, 'consents.'"[3]

While the Third Republic of France was a democracy in transition, its colonies certainly were not representational democracies.[4] In France, women were not considered full citizens with voting rights until 1944; in the colonies, after the fall of Vichy, the Lamine Gueye Law of 1946 was passed, extending French citizenship to all colonial subjects, and in 1956 the Loi Cadre (or Framework Law, or Overseas Reform Act) granted a significant measure of self-governing capacities to government in the colonies. Sudanese women won the right to vote in 1956 with the Loi Cadre. Consent, as a legal tool, within this ever-changing and undulating context of imperial democratic process, was precarious at best.

But this does not mean that consent is meaningless; indeed, consent is deeply meaningful and signifies a relationship in play. In a post–Mandel Decree French Sudanese context, to participate in the colonial project of consent was about forsaking kin-tie obligation and privilege—the "weight of custom and tradition," according to Mahmood—for a bond to the colonial state.[5] "Consent," in a legal sense, and in many cases also a practical and experiential sense, did not mean that one was sovereign and capable of exercising free will and agency, but rather that one was a necessary participant in the French colonial project of a civilizing mission, a mission that was based on the application of a political and legal apparatus that reflected the French Republican model (importantly, a commitment to secularism and anticlericalism) and that promoted the idea of social uplift in a socially and politically liberal fashion. To signal consent and to participate in the performance of giving consent or not giving consent, under the Mandel and Jacquinot Decrees, was to become a participant in this project. In this regard, African women were essential to the liberal project of the civilizing mission.

The reality is that we know that many colonial subjects chose not to participate in this liberal colonial project of consent-manufacturing, and that the Mandel Decree and, later, the Jacquinot Decree were perceived as being at least fraught and at the most failures by colonial administrators on the ground. That is to say, the vast majority of marriages forged in the French Sudan were not registered with the state through a marriage contract. The reasons for not participating in consent were many. Participating in consent (i.e., asserting yourself as a sovereign body unencumbered by the will of others) could mean the abandonment of kin or ethnic ties and values; it might mean forgoing future familial support during times of strife and celebration; it could potentially mean the loss of bridewealth for the family of a betrothed woman. Most important, it could mean that marriage decisions—which were so important to the maintenance of cross-familial bonds of obligation, service, and support—would be untethered from the structures of gendered authority and obligation that ordered social, political and cultural worlds. In short, signaling consent was potentially a way of unmaking the world.

The fact is that the colonial state needed marriage. This was because marriage ordered colonial subjects into categories and household units recognizable to the state. That is, marriage became a mechanism of control and ordering. In this book, "the marriage legibility project" is used to illustrate this element. But the state also needed marriage because it could be used as a platform to deliver the imagined realities made possible through colonial rule. In this way, marriage was not so much a chimera—a metaphor often used by scholars of colonial Africa to describe the improbabilities of colonial realities—but a Trojan horse of gender justice. Gender justice in the form of colonial marriage reform purported to be a gift for all, bestowed in order to make lives easier and more livable. Instead, it frequently exacerbated generational tensions and could be fashioned as a tool for suppressing and alienating young women and men from elders as well as the colonial state.

Perhaps all of this risks giving colonial renderings of African marriage too much weight in our consideration of the recent African past. The way in which African women and men lived their conjugal lives is a different story. To be sure, what we learn through the stories that unfold throughout this book is that, over time, there was a distance between marriage on the ground and "the state's marriage." Yet what is striking is the fact that marriage continues to hold such a place in political discussion not only in colonial and postcolonial contexts, but in modern states throughout the world. The 1948 Universal Declaration of Human Rights defined the right to marry and found a family as a universal human right—a right that has been denied slaves, interracial, cross-caste, homosexual, and cross-religion couples throughout history and the present in different societies. It is not a coincidence that the United Nations Convention on Consent to Marriage was ratified in 1962 and put into law in 1964, on the heels of widespread de-colonization throughout the Global South. If we return to the introduction of this book, we are reminded of Mali's ongoing struggles with its marriage and family code in the postcolonial period. As I write this, it remains un-clear what the marriage code will look like in a newly restored Mali, after the 2012 coup and the democratic elections of 2013. Yet I feel certain that discussion of the marriage code and the types of gender justice and rights it may deliver will emerge once again as a topic of political debate as Malians continue to refashion their democratic state. And once again, our attention will be drawn to the great divide between marital practice and marital law. We can only hope that an increasing diversity of participation in what is Mali's new "marriage legibility project" will result in a body of laws that are more relevant and more favorable to the people whose lives are governed by them. There are always laws that are not practiced, to be sure. But may the imagined reality be a bit closer to what is possible—and desirable—in the world in which people live.

Notes

INTRODUCTION

1. Dorothea Schultz, "Political Factions, Ideological Fictions: The Controversy over Family Law Reform in Democratic Mali," *Islamic Law and Society* 10, no. 1 (2003): 132–64. This is part of a trend of political reform in different parts of former French West Africa. See Jeanne Maddox Toungara, "Changing the Meaning of Marriage: Women and Family Law in Côte d'Ivoire," in *African Feminism: The Politics of Survival in Sub-Saharan Africa*, ed. Gwendolyn Mikell (Philadelphia: University of Pennsylvania Press, 1997), 53–76; Abd-el Kadr Boye et al., "Marriage Law and Practice in the Sahel," *Studies in Family Planning* 22, no. 6 (1991): 343–49.

2. For example, the BBC misleadingly referred to the Personal Status and Family Code as "Mali's women's rights bill" in the days following its ratification by the National Assembly and President Touré's decision not to ratify it. Martin Vogl, "Mali Women's Rights Bill Blocked," http://news.bbc.co.uk/2/hi/8223736.stm.

3. Nancy Cott, *Public Vows: A History of Marriage and the Nation* (Cambridge, MA: Harvard University Press, 2002).

4. Suzanne Desan, *The Family on Trial in Revolutionary France* (Berkeley: University of California Press, 2004).

5. Rochona Majumdar, *Marriage and Modernity: Family Values in Colonial Bengal* (Durham, NC: Duke University Press, 2009).

6. Gender justice is a term used widely in legal rights and human rights circles; a simple internet search will yield hundreds of instances of its use. For example, in 2010 Oxfam International held the "Oxfam International Gender Justice Summit." http://www.oxfam.org/en/about/issues/gender.

7. Dorothy Hodgson's work has had a significant impact on my reading and critical interpretation of gender justice. Personal communication with Hodgson, but see also Dorothy Hodgson, ed., *Gender and Culture at the Limit of Rights* (Philadelphia: University of Pennsylvania Press, 2010); Dorothy Hodgson, "My Daughter . . . Belongs to the Government Now: Marriage, Maasai, and the Tanzanian State," *Canadian Journal of African Studies* 30, no. 1 (1996): 106–23; Dorothy Hodgson, ed., *Gendered Modernities: Ethnographic Perspectives* (New York: Palgrave), 2001. Hodgson was also the convener of the February 2012 conference "Gender Justice in Africa: Historical and Comparative Perspectives" hosted by Rutgers University–New Brunswick.

8. This definition comes from my reading of distributive justice philosophy, which informs much of the work on human rights. John Rawls, *A Theory of Justice* (Cambridge, MA: Belknap Press of Harvard University Press, 1971).

9. On legibility, see James Scott, *Seeing Like a State: How Certain Schemes to Improve the Human Condition Have Failed* (New Haven, CT: Yale University Press, 1998. Pamela Scully makes a similar argument for legible behavior in Pamela Scully, "Should We Give Up on the State? Feminist Theory, African Gender History, and Transitional Justice," *African Journal on Conflict Resolution* 9, no. 2 (2009).

10. Scott, *Seeing.*

11. Alice Conklin, "Colonialism and Human Rights: A Contradiction in Terms? The Case of France and West Africa, 1895–1914," *American Historical Review* 103, no. 2 (1998): 420.

12. Thanks to Dorothy Hodgson for helping me work through this concept as it changed over time.

13. Conklin, "Colonialism," 422.

14. Barbara Cooper, *Marriage in Maradi: Gender and Culture in a Hausa Society in Niger* (Portsmouth, NH: Heinemann, 1997), xxvii.

15. Suzanne Miers and Igor Kopytoff, eds., *Slavery in Africa: Historical and Anthropological Perspectives* (Madison: University of Wisconsin Press, 1977); Jane Guyer, "Wealth in People and Self-Realization in Equatorial Africa," *Man* 28, no. 2 (1993): 243–65.

16. Joseph Miller, *Way of Death: Merchant Capitalism and the Angolan Slave Trade, 1730–1830* (Madison: University of Wisconsin Press, 1988).

17. Jane Guyer argues that Paul Bohannan's research on "spheres of exchange" among the Tiv is one of the most formative works in this particular vein. Paul Bohannan, "Some Principles of Exchange and Investment among the Tiv," *American Anthropologist* 57, no. 1 (1955): 60–70.

18. Wealth in people derives much of its inspiration from Marcel Mauss and, later, Marilyn Strathern's gift-and-exchange economy analysis. However, like Jean-François Bayart's argument for the "politics of the belly," this theoretical argument of exchange is rooted very squarely in African contexts of accumulation, commodity value, and sociocultural capital. Marcel Mauss, *The Gift: The Form and Reason for Exchange in Archaic Societies* (London: Cohen and West, 1954); Marilyn Strathern, *The Gender of the Gift: Problems with Women and Problems with Society in Melanesia* (Berkeley: University of California Press, 1990); Jean-François Bayart, *L'état en Afrique: La politique du ventre* (Paris: Fayard, 1989).

19. Jan Vansina, *Paths in the Rainforest: Toward a History of Political Tradition in Equatorial Africa* (Madison: University of Wisconsin Press, 1990); Jan Vansina, *How Societies Are Born: Governance in West Central Africa before 1600* (Charlottesville: University of Virginia Press, 2004); Jane Guyer and Samuel Eno Belinga, "Wealth in People as Wealth in Knowledge: Accumulation and Composition in Equatorial Africa," *Journal of African History* 36, no. 1 (1995): 91–120.

20. See in particular Caroline Bledsoe, *Women and Marriage in Kpelle Society* (Stanford: Stanford University Press, 1980); John Comaroff, ed., *The Meaning of Marriage Payments* (London: Academic Press, 1980); Barbara Cooper, "Women's Worth and Wedding Gift Exchange in Maradi, Niger: 1907–1989," *Journal of African History* 36 (1995): 121–40.

21. For example, Emily Osborn ably invokes wealth in people as a way of framing precolonial household formation and political strategy in the West African context of

Kankan-Bate, Guinee. Emily Lynn Osborn, *Our New Husbands Are Here: Households, Gender, and Politics in a West African State from the Slave Trade to Colonial Rule* (Athens: Ohio University Press, 2011).

22. For a similar argument on bridewealth in Mali, see Maria Grosz-Ngaté, "Monetization of Bridewealth and the Abandonment of 'Kin Roads' to Marriage in Sana, Mali," *American Ethnologist* 15, no. 3 (1988): 501–14.

23. Brian Peterson, *Islamization from Below: The Making of Muslim Communities in Rural French Sudan, 1880–1960* (New Haven, CT: Yale University Press, 2011), 170–75.

24. Influential anthropologists in this area include Max Gluckman, Lloyd Fallers, Sally Falk Moore, among others. For ground-breaking historical work, see Margaret Jean Hay and Marcia Wright, eds., *African Women and the Law: Historical Perspectives* (Boston: Boston University African Studies Center, 1982); Terence Ranger, "The Invention of Tradition in Modern Africa," in *The Invention of Tradition*, ed. Eric Hobsbawm and Terence Ranger (Cambridge: Cambridge University Press, 1983); Martin Chanock, *Law, Custom, and Social Order: The Colonial Experience in Malawi and Zambia* (Cambridge: Cambridge University Press, 1985).

25. Kristin Mann and Richard Roberts, eds., *Law in Colonial Africa* (Portsmouth, NH: Heinemann, 1991).

26. See, in particular, Cooper, *Marriage*; Kristin Mann, *Marrying Well: Marriage, Status, and Social Change among the Educated Elite in Colonial Lagos* (Cambridge: Cambridge University Press, 1985); Richard Roberts, *Litigants and Households: African Disputes and Colonial Courts in the French Soudan, 1905–1912* (Portsmouth, NH: Heinemann, 2005); Judith Byfield, "Women, Marriage, Divorce, and the Emerging Colonial State in Abeokuta (Nigeria), 1892–1904," *Canadian Journal of African Studies* 30 (1996): 32–51, reprinted in *"Wicked" Women and the Reconfiguration of Gender in Africa*, ed. Dorothy Hodgson and Sheryl McCurdy (Portsmouth, NH: Heinemann, 2001), 27–46; Sean Hawkins, "'The Woman in Question': Marriage and Identity in the Colonial Courts of Northern Ghana, 1907–1954," in *Women in African Colonial Histories*, ed. Jean Allman, Susan Geiger, and Nakanyike Musisi (Bloomington: University of Indiana Press, 2002).

27. H. F. Morris, "Native Courts: A Corner-Stone of Indirect Rule," in *Indirect Rule and the Search for Justice: Essays in East African Legal History*, ed. H. F. Morris and James Read (Oxford: Oxford University Press, 1972).

28. Philip Nord, *The Republican Moment: Struggles for Democracy in Nineteenth-Century France* (Cambridge, MA: Harvard University Press, 1995), 136–37.

29. Meredith McKittrick, "Faithful Daughter, Murdering Mother: Transgression and Social Control in Northern Namibia," *Journal of African History* 40, no. 2 (1999): 265–83.

30. The question of sources and methodology in the historiography on African women is rigorously attended to in a number of fine works. For edited volumes and synthetic overviews, see Nancy Rose Hunt, "Placing African History and Locating Gender," *Social History* 14 (1989): 359–79; Catherine Coquery-Vidrovitch, *African Women: A Modern History* (Boulder, CO: Westview Press, 1996); Iris Berger and E. Francis White, *Women in Sub-Saharan Africa: Restoring Women to History* (Bloomington: Indiana University Press, 1999); Jean Allman, Susan Geiger, and Nakanyike Musisi, eds., *Women in African Colonial Histories* (Bloomington: Indiana University Press, 2002); Dorothy Hodgson and Sheryl McCurdy, eds., *"Wicked" Women and the Reconfiguration of Gender in Africa* (Portsmouth, NH: Heinemann, 2001).

31. For recent work on Saharan women involved in trans-Saharan trade and their use of Islamic law in engaging with trade networks, see Ghislaine Lydon, *On Trans-Saharan Trails: Islamic Law, Trade Networks, and Cross-Cultural Exchange in Nineteenth-Century Western Africa* (Cambridge: Cambridge University Press, 2010).

32. Gregory Mann, "What Was the *Indigénat?* The 'Empire of Law' in French West Africa," *Journal of African History* 50 (2009): 331–53.

33. Steven Pierce and Anapuma Rao, eds., *Discipline and the Other Body: Correction, Corporeality, Colonialism* (Durham, NC: Duke University Press, 2006); Florence Bernault, ed., *Enfermement, prison et châtiment en Afrique du 19e siècle à nos jours* (Paris: Karthala, 1999); Michael Crowder, *The Flogging of Phinehas McIntosh: A Tale of Colonial Folly and Injustice: Bechuanaland, 1933* (New Haven, CT: Yale University Press, 1988).

34. Laura Nader, *Harmony Ideology: Justice and Control in a Zapotec Mountain Village* (Stanford: Stanford University Press, 1991).

35. James Clifford, "Identity in Mashpee," in *The Predicament of Culture: Twentieth-Century Ethnography, Literature, and Art* (Cambridge, MA: Harvard University Press, 1988), 179–205.

36. Gary Wilder, *H-France Forum* 1, 3 (2006), no. 5.

37. Harri Englund, *Prisoners of Freedom: Human Rights and the African Poor* (Berkeley: University of California Press, 2006).

38. On the *indigénat*, see Mann, "What Was the *Indigénat?*"; Bernault, *Enfermement*; Isabelle Merle, "Retour sur le régime de l'indigénat: Genèse et contradictions des principes répressifs de l'empire français," *French Politics, Culture, and Society* 20, no. 2 (2002): 77–97.

39. On domestic violence, see Emily Burrill, "Disputing Wife Abuse: Tribunal Narratives of the Corporal Punishment of Wives in Colonial Sikasso, 1930s," *Cahiers d'études africaines* 187–88 (2007): 603–22.

40. Deniz Kandiyoti, "Bargaining with Patriarchy," *Gender and Society* 2, no. 3 (1988): 274–90.

41. Roberts, *Litigants*.

42. This is different from an examination of households and family history, which center on different units of analysis, albeit units of analysis that might include marriage. Osborn, *Our New Husbands*; Jane Guyer, "Household and Community in African Studies," *African Studies Review* 24, no. 2/3 (1981): 87–137; Pamela Scully, *Liberating the Family?: Gender and British Slave Emancipation in the Rural Western Cape, South Africa, 1823–1853* (Portsmouth, NH: Heinemann, 1997).

43. This historical scholarship is emerging in new and exciting ways. See, for example, Kenneth Cmiel, "The Recent History of Human Rights," *American Historical Review* 109, no. 1 (2004): 117–35; Lynn Hunt, *Inventing Human Rights: A History* (New York: W. W. Norton, 2008); Samuel Moyn, *The Last Utopia: Human Rights in History* (Cambridge, MA: Harvard University Press, 2010); Michael Barnett, *Empire of Humanity: A History of Humanitarianism* (Ithaca, NY: Cornell University Press, 2011); Pamela Scully, "Gender, History, and Human Rights," in *Gender*, ed. Hodgson, 17–31.

44. Alice Conklin, *A Mission to Civilize: The Republican Idea of Empire in France and West Africa, 1895–1930* (Stanford: Stanford University Press, 1997).

45. Scully, "Gender."

46. Scully, *Liberating*.

47. The Universal Declaration of Human Rights, http://www.un.org/en/documents/udhr/.

48. Many of these works examine precolonial history through the lens of centralized Muslim societies and Islamic states or West African empires. This literature is vast, but the most influential works include Amadou Hampaté Bâ and Jacques Daget, *L'Empire Peul de Macina* (Koulouba: Institut Français d'Afrique Noire, Centre du Soudan, 1955); Jean Bazin, "Guerre et servitude à Ségou," in *L'Esclavage en Afrique précoloniale*, ed. Claude Meillassoux (Paris: François Maspero, 1975), 135–81; David C. Conrad, ed., *A State of Intrigue: The Epic of Bamana Segu according to Tayiru Banbera*, trans. Soumaila Diakité (Oxford: British Academy, 1990); John Hanson, *Migration, Jihad, and Muslim Authority in West Africa: The Futanke Colonies in Karta* (Bloomington: Indiana University Press, 1996); John Hunwick, *Shari'a in Songhay: The Replies of al-Maghili to the Questions of Askia al-Hajj Muhammad* (Oxford: Oxford University Press, 1985); John Hunwick, *Timbuktu and the Songhay Empire: Al-Sadi's "Tarikh al-Sudan" down to 1613 and Other Contemporary Documents* (Leiden: Brill, 1999); Nehemia Levtzion, *Ancient Ghana and Mali* (New York: Africana, 1980); Roderick McIntosh, *Ancient Middle Niger: Urbanism and the Self-Organizing Landscape* (Cambridge: Cambridge University Press, 2005); Charles Monteil, *Les Bambaras de Ségou et du Kaarta* (Paris: Maisonneuve, 1924); Richard L. Roberts, *Warriors, Merchants, and Slaves: The State and the Economy in the Middle Niger Valley, 1700–1914* (Stanford: Stanford University Press, 1987); David Robinson, *The Holy War of Umar Tal: The Western Sudan in the Mid-Nineteenth Century* (Oxford: Clarendon Press, 1985).

49. The exception to this is work on Kayes, which was a colonial outpost and railroad town. Located on the Senegal River, Kayes was the capital of the French Sudan from 1892 to 1899, and served as an administrative outpost throughout the colonial period. In particular, see Louis Brenner, *Controlling Knowledge: Religion, Power and Schooling in a West African Muslim Society* (Bloomington: Indiana University Press, 2001). Brenner's study is concerned with Mali as a whole, but his main case studies are Bamako, Kayes, and Segu. B. Marie Perinbam, *Family Identity and the State in the Bamako Kafu, c. 1800– c. 1900* (Boulder, CO: Westview Press, 1997); Richard Roberts, *Two Worlds of Cotton: Colonialism and the Regional Economy in the French Soudan, 1800–1946* (Stanford: Stanford University Press, 1996). The studies by Perinbam and Roberts straddle the pre-colonial and colonial periods. Monica M. van Beusekom, *Negotiating Development: African Farmers and Colonial Experts at the Office du Niger, 1920–1960* (Portsmouth, NH: Heinemann, 2001); Eric Silla, *People Are Not the Same: Leprosy and Identity in Twentieth-Century Mali* (Portsmouth, NH: Heinemann, 1998).

50. Many recent works on border towns and centers outside of the Niger beltway in modern-day Mali concern northern Mali, and focus on the trans-Saharan and West African–Maghreb connections. These works are emerging. See, for example, Benjamin Soares, *Islam and the Prayer Economy: History and Authority in a Malian Town* (Ann Arbor: University of Michigan Press, 2005); Ghislaine Lydon, "Writing Trans-Saharan History: Methods, Sources, and Interpretations across the African Divide," *Journal of North African Studies* 10, no. 3–4 (2005): 293–324; and Lydon, *On Trans-Saharan Trails*. For new work on southern Mali and the border region with Guinea and Ivory Coast, see Peterson, *Islamization*.

51. Anna Loenhaupt Tsing, *In the Realm of the Diamond Queen: Marginality in an Out-of-the-Way Place* (Princeton, NJ: Princeton University Press, 1993); Charles Piot,

Remotely Global: Village Modernity in West Africa (Chicago: University of Chicago Press, 1999).

52. This is much more of an Ivorian issue than a Malian issue. Mike McGovern, *Making War in Côte d'Ivoire* (Chicago: University of Chicago Press, 2011).

53. Notions of the "Mande world" and Mande studies predominate in West African studies. This is for good reason: Mande languages make up the languages of the majority of the West African population in former French colonies, and there is a rich history of oral tradition and accounts of precolonial states and Mande society.

54. For monographs on marriage, see Mann, *Marrying*, and Cooper, *Marriage*. Legal anthropology has significantly influenced the recent growth in historical writing based on court records. Relevant book-length historical studies are Chanock, *Law, Custom, and Social Order*; Allen Christelow, *Muslim Law Courts and the French Colonial State in Algeria* (Princeton, NJ: Princeton University Press, 1985); Mann and Roberts, *Law*; Lauren Benton, *Law and Colonial Cultures: Legal Regimes in World History, 1400–1900* (Cambridge: Cambridge University Press, 2002); Thomas McClendon, *Genders and Generations Apart: Labor Tenants and Customary Law in Segregation Era South Africa, 1920s–1940s* (Portsmouth, NH: Heinemann, 2002); Roberts, *Litigants*; Marie Rodet, *Les migrantes ignorées du Haut-Sénégal, 1900–1946* (Paris: Karthala, 2009).

CHAPTER 1: LOCATING GENDERED KNOWLEDGE AND AUTHORITY AT THE TURN OF THE CENTURY

1. This is the generally accepted narrative that most people recount in oral histories, but it is also cited as such in Quiquandon, "Histoire de la puissance Mandinque d'après la legende et la tradition," *Bulletin de la Société de géographie commerciale de Bordeaux* 15 (1892): 305–18.

2. Edna Bay, *Wives of the Leopard* (Charlottesville: University of Virginia Press, 1998). This is likely apocryphal, but in the cases of Momo, the Dahomian female soldiers, and the legendary Amazons, such stories point to the possibility of body modification as an element of gender modification.

3. This dynamic has been noted elsewhere by other historians. Of note to this book, see Elizabeth Schmidt, *Peasants, Traders, and Wives: Shona Women in the History of Zimbabwe, 1870–1939* (Portsmouth, NH: Heinemann, 1992); Jean Allman and Victoria Tashjian, *"I Will Not Eat Stone": A Women's History of Colonial Asante* (Portsmouth, NH: Heinemann, 2000); Emily Lynn Osborn, *Our New Husbands Are Here: Households, Gender, and Politics in a West African State from the Slave Trade to Colonial Rule* (Athens: Ohio University Press, 2011); Lorelle D. Semley, *Mother Is Gold, Father Is Glass: Gender and Colonialism in a Yoruba Town* (Bloomington: Indiana University Press, 2011).

4. As Bruce Hall aptly states, "There are African histories of race that do not obey colonial logics." Bruce S. Hall, *A History of Race in Muslim West Africa, 1600–1960* (Cambridge: Cambridge University Press, 2011), 2.

5. Osborn, *Our New Husbands*, esp. 23–24.

6. David William Cohen, Stephan F. Miescher, and Luise White, "Introduction: Voices, Words, and African History," in *African Words, African Voices: Critical Practices*

in Oral History, ed. Luise White, Stephan F. Miescher, and David William Cohen (Bloomington: Indiana University Press, 2001), 1–27.

7. Liisa Malkki, *Purity and Exile* (Chicago: University of Chicago Press, 1995), 54.

8. Ibid., 52.

9. William H. McNeill, *Mythistory and Other Essays* (Chicago: University of Chicago Press, 1986); Joseph Mali, *Mythistory: The Making of a Modern Historiography* (Chicago: University of Chicago Press, 2003).

10. David Henige, *The Chronology of Oral Tradition* (Oxford: Oxford University Press, 1974); Jan Vansina, *Oral Tradition as History* (Madison: University of Wisconsin Press, 1985); White, Miescher, and Cohen, *African Words.*

11. David William Cohen, "Doing Social History from Pim's Doorway," in *Reliving the Past: The Worlds of Social History*, ed. Olivier Zunz and David William Cohen (Chapel Hill: University of North Carolina Press, 1985), 191–236.

12. Ibid. To underscore the importance of intergenerational knowledge transfer between grandmothers and granddaughters, we can look to Jan Bender Shetler's work in the interior Mara region of Tanzania. Shetler discovered in 2010 that many women had lost their sense of family and local history, due to the fact that they did not sleep with their grandmothers because they had moved into their husbands' compounds as child brides. Jan Bender Shetler, "Restriction of Women's Networks and the Rise of Domestic Violence in Interior Areas of Colonial Mara Region, Tanzania, 1930s–40s." African Studies Association Conference, Philadelphia, 30 November 2012.

13. Anita Glaze, *Art and Death in a Senufo Village* (Bloomington: Indiana University Press, 1981), 12.

14. Anita Glaze, "Women and Power in a Senufo Village," *African Arts* 8, no. 3 (1975): 28.

15. The literature on *jeliw*, also called *griots* or *griottes* (feminine) is extensive and rich; however, it is outside the scope of this book to fully revisit this scholarship. See, for example, Lucy Duran, "Ngaraya: Women and Musical Mastery in Mali," *Bulletin of the School of Oriental and African Studies, University of London* 70, no. 3 (2007): 569–602; Ralph Austen, ed., *In Search of Sunjata: The Mande Epic as History, Literature, and Performance* (Bloomington: Indiana University Press, 1999); Thomas Hale, "Griottes: Female Voices from West Africa," *Research in African Literatures* 25, no. 3 (1994): 71–91.

16. Weybi Karma, "Stop Crying Bride," in *Women's Voices from West Africa*, ed. Aissata G. Sidikou and Thomas A. Hale (Bloomington: Indiana University Press, 2012), 47.

17. Adama Traoré and Fousseyni Traoré, Madubugu, 21 March 2005; Coumba Traoré Coulibaly, Sikasso, 12 February 2005; Salimata Dembélé, Sikasso, 5 February 2005.

18. Adama Traoré and Fousseyni Traoré, 21 March 2005.

19. Patrick R. McNaughton, *The Mande Blacksmiths: Knowledge, Power, and Art in West Africa* (Bloomington: Indiana University Press, 1988); Viviana Paques, "Bouffons Sacres du Cercle de Bougouni (Soudan Français)," *Journal de la Société des Africanistes* 24, no. 1 (1954): 63–110; Glaze, *Art and Death*, 11–12, 92–99.

20. Glaze, *Art and Death*, 11.

21. Zanga Koné, Kafoziela, 14 February 2005.

22. Salimata Dembélé, 5 February 2005.

23. Bohumil Holas, *Les Sénoufo (y compris les Minianka)* (Paris: Universitaires Presses de France, 1966), 93–94.

24. Ibid.

25. Ibid., 96; L. Tautain, "Le Dioula-dougou et le Sénéfo," *Revue d'ethnographie* 6 (1887): 395.

26. John Comaroff, ed., *The Meaning of Marriage Payments* (London: Academic Press, 1980).

27. Not to be confused or conflated with W. E. B. Du Bois's notion of "twoness" in African American identity consciousness and philosophy. "Thirdness" is a similar but different notion of relationality and subject-position that appears in different African societies. See Mariane Ferme, *The Underneath of Things: Violence, History, and the Everyday in Sierra Leone* (Berkeley: University of California Press, 2001); Mike McGovern, *Making War in Côte d'Ivoire* (Chicago: University of Chicago Press, 2011).

28. Anita Glaze, "Dialectics of Gender in Senufo Masquerades," *African Arts* 19, no. 3 (1986): 30.

29. Théodore André, "Le Droit Privé des Sénéfo du Kénédougou (Cercle de Sikasso)" (doctoral thesis, University of Bordeaux, 1913), 53.

30. Ibid., 54.

31. Glaze, *Art and Death*, 54

32. Ibid., 60.

33. René Caillié, *Voyage à Tombouctou* (Paris: François Maspero, 1979), 2:30.

34. Jean-Loup Amselle and Emmanuelle Sibeud, eds., *Maurice Delafosse: Entre orientalisme et ethnographie: L'itinéraire d'un africaniste, 1870–1926* (Paris: Maisonneuve et Larose, 1998).

35. Louis Gustave Binger, *Une vie d'explorateur: Souvenirs extraits des carnets de route* (Paris: F. Sorlot, 1938).

36. Mary Louise Pratt, *Imperial Eyes: Travel Writing and Transculturation*, 2nd ed. (New York: Routledge, 2008), 7–9, 200.

37. Caillié, *Voyage*, 2:50.

38. French Lieutenant Louis Binger was probably the first to officially use the term "Senufo" in print to describe the Siena-speaking people of the region, circa 1888. Louis Binger, *Du Niger au Golfe de Guinée par le pays de Kong et le Mossi*, 2 vols. (1887–89) (Paris: Hachette, 1892). Also see Jean-Loup Amselle, *Mestizo Logics: Anthropology of Identity in Africa and Elsewhere* (Stanford: Stanford University Press, 1998), 49n37.

39. Maurice Delafosse, *Haut-Sénégal-Niger* (Paris: Maisonneuve, 1972), 1:300.

40. Today the name Minyanka is used to describe the people native to the area of Koutiala, which is to the north of Sikasso.

41. Delafosse, *Haut-Sénégal-Niger*, 1:300–301.

42. See Jean-Paul Collyn and Danielle Jonckers, "Ceux qui refusent le maître: La conception du pouvoir chez les Minyanka du Mali," *Africa: Journal of the International African Institute* 53, no. 4 (1983): 43–58.

43. Robert Launay, *Beyond the Stream: Islam and Society in a West African Town* (Berkeley: University of California Press, 1992), 55.

44. Richard Warms, "Continuity and Change in Patterns of Trade in Southern Mali" (PhD diss., Syracuse University, 1987), 68–69; Holas, *Les Sénoufo*; Sinali

Coulibaly, *Le paysan Sénoufo* (Abidjan-Dakar: Nouvelles Éditions Africaines, 1978); Colleyn and Jonckers, "Ceux qui refusent le maître."

45. Warms, "Continuity"; Holas, *Les Sénoufo*.

46. Binger, *Du Niger*, 1:114.

47. This is not to suggest a harmonious precolonial past; as George Brooks reminds us, landlords and strangers created reciprocal relationships, but they were not necessarily egalitarian and were often hierarchical. George Brooks, *Landlords and Strangers: Ecology, Society, and Trade in Western Africa, 1000–1630* (Boulder, CO: Westview Press, 1993).

48. Yves Person, *Samori: Une révolution dyula*, vol. 1 (Paris: IFAN, 1970), 75.

49. Nehemia Levtzion, *Ancient Ghana and Mali* (London: Methuen, 1973); Jean-Loup Amselle, *Negoçiants de la Savanne: Histoire et organisation sociale des Kooroko (Mali)* (Paris: Editions Anthropos, 1977).

50. *Jula* is a term that has come to demarcate ethnicity (particularly in contemporary Cote d'Ivoire), language (Mande), or a trade (merchant) in various parts of West Africa, particularly Guinea, Mali, Cote d'Ivoire, and Burkina Faso.

51. René Caillié, *Voyage*, 2:4, 6. Caillié traveled with Jula traders through northern Ivory Coast and southern Mali in the 1820s. Robert Launay, "Landlords, Hosts, and Strangers among the Dyula," *Ethnology* 18, no. 1 (1979): 71–83.

52. Marie-Joseph Vendeix, "Nouvel essai de monographie du pays Senoufo," *Bulletin du Comité d'études historiques et scientifiques de l'Afrique occidentale française* (1934): 578–652; L. Tautain, "Le Dioula-dougou et le Sénéfo," *Revue d'ethnographie* 6 (1887): 395, Delafosse, *Haut-Sénégal-Niger*, 1:300–301.

53. Caillié, *Voyage*; Binger, *Du Niger*. There is a difference of sixty years between Caillié's and Binger's travels, but both observed similar layouts of Senufo farming villages, despite the political differences in the region between the 1820s and the 1880s.

54. Robert Launay, *Traders without Trade: Responses to Change in Two Dyula Communities* (Cambridge: Cambridge University Press, 1982), 15.

55. Caillié, *Voyage*, 1:57–58.

56. "Sarakole" usually means Soninke-speaking, from northwest of Sikasso. Interview with Drissa Dembélé, M'Pegnesso, 2 March 2005.

57. Drissa Dembélé and M'Pegnesso men's discussion group, M'Pegnesso, 2 March 2005. Brian Peterson clearly illustrates the intertwined processes of slave emancipation, return to natal villages, and self-identification as a Muslim in the region of Buguni to the west of Sikasso. Brian Peterson, "Slave Emancipation, Trans-Local Social Processes and the Spread of Islam in French Colonial Buguni (Southern Mali), 1893–1914," *Journal of African History* 45, no. 3 (2004): 421–44; Brian Peterson, *Islamization from Below: The Making of Muslim Communities in Rural French Sudan, 1880–1960* (New Haven, CT: Yale University Press, 2011).

58. John O'Sullivan, "Slavery in the Malinke Kingdom of Kabadougou (Ivory Coast)," *International Journal of African Studies* 13, no. 4 (1980): 633–50; Notice sur la Côte d'Ivoire, 1908, ANM (Archives Nationales du Mali), FA (Fonds Anciens), 1D 179.

59. Martin Klein, "Defensive Strategies: Wasulu, Masina, and the Slave Trade," in *Fighting the Slave Trade: West African Strategies*, ed. Sylviane Diouf (Athens: Ohio University Press, 2003). Paul E. Lovejoy, *Transformations in Slavery: A History of Slavery in Africa*, 2nd ed., (Cambridge: Cambridge University Press, 2000); A. Grodet, "Étude sur la captivité au Soudan," 1895, ANM, FA, 1D 2.

60. Drissa Dembélé, M'Pegnesso, 2 March 2005.

61. Seydou Diamoutene, M'Pegnesso, 2 March 2005.

62. The interviews and discussions that generated this information were all conducted in Jula/Bamanankan with the assistance of Oumou Sidibé.

63. Amselle, *Negoçiants*.

64. Launay, "Landlords, Hosts, and Strangers," 73.

65. Ibid., 78.

66. Ibid., 80.

67. Bakary Koné, Sikassoville, 1 May 2005.

68. This last point is central to Emily Osborn's recent history of Kankan-Baté, Guinée Française. Osborn, *Our New Husbands*.

69. Quiquandon, *Renseignements sur la situation des colonies: Rapport adressé à M. Le Lieutenant-Colonel Commandant Supérieur de Sudan Française sur la Mission Auprès de Tíeba, Roi du Kénédougou* (Paris: s.n., 1891), 371, 313.

70. LeVell Holmes, "Tieba Traore, Fama of Kenedougou: Two Decades of Political Development, 1873–1893" (PhD diss., University of California, Berkeley, 1972). In 1975, Holmes conducted countless oral histories with the descendants of Tiéba and Babemba Traoré, as well as the descendants of Kélétigi Berté, their highest-ranking soldier. Kélétigi became a powerful canton chief under colonial rule and will be discussed further in the book.

71. Binger, *Du Niger*, 1:214.

72. Monographie du cercle de Sikasso, n.d., ANM, FA, 1G 322; Alpha Oumar Konaré, *Sikasso Tata* (Bamako: Jamana, 1983).

73. Bakary Koné, Sikasso, 1 May 2005.

74. Jacques Méniaud, *Sikasso, ou, l'histoire dramatique d'un royaume noir au XIXe siècle* (Paris: Bouchy, 1935), 19.

75. Holmes, "Tieba Traore," 150.

76. Quiquandon, *Renseignements*, 12; Person, *Samori*, 2:876.

77. Holmes, "Tieba Traore," 135–36.

78. Moussa Niakate, "Quatre Royaume au Soudan Français," unpublished manuscript, 1982. Thanks to Abdoulaye Traoré of Sikasso for sharing the manuscript from the Traoré family archive.

79. For another example of the relationship between enslavement and Sudanic state expansion, see Richard L. Roberts, *Warriors, Merchants, and Slaves: The State and the Economy in the Middle Niger Valley, 1700–1914* (Stanford: Stanford University Press, 1987).

80. Holmes, "Tieba Traore," 251–52.

81. Konaré, *Sikasso Tata*; Bakary Koné, Sikasso, 1 May 2005; Fousseyni and Adama Traoré, Madubugu, 21 March 2005.

82. Mamadou Traoré, Sikasso, 26 April 2005.

83. Roberts, *Warriors*; William Cohen, *Rulers of Empire: The French Colonial Service in Africa* (Stanford: Hoover Institution Press, 1971).

84. Interview with Fousseyni and Adama Traoré, Madubugu, 21 March 2005; Holmes, "Tieba Traore."

85. Fousseyni Traoré and Adama Traoré, Madubugu, 21 March 2005; Yaya Dow, Kaboïla, 22 March 2005.

86. Oumar Berté, "Memorial de Kélétigui Berté," in Roland Colin, *Kènèdougou au crépuscule de l'Afrique coloniale: Mémoires des années cinquantes* (Paris: Présence Africaine, 2004), 359–83.

87. Ibid.

88. Many scholars have addressed the civilizing mission, but the authoritative text is Alice Conklin, *A Mission to Civilize: The Republican Idea of Empire in France and West Africa, 1895–1930* (Stanford: Stanford University Press, 1997).

89. Monographie du cercle de Sikasso, ANM, FA, 1G 322.

90. Méniaud, *Sikasso*; Colin, *Kènèdougou*, 104.

91. Carnet du chef, Samba Tiémoko Traoré, 1D series, Sikasso cercle archives, unclassified. "Fiches de renseignements des chefs des cantons, Bougoula: Fatoroma Traoré, 1908–1955," ANM, Fonds Récents (FR), 2E 59.

92. "Fiches de renseignements des chefs des cantons, Bougoula: Fatoroma Traoré, 1908–1955," ANM, FR, 2E 59. Interviews with Fousseyni Traoré and Adama Traoré, Madubugu, 6 April 2005. Fousseyni and Adama Traoré are the direct descendants of Madou Traoré, and Madou settled Madoubougou (literally, "Madou's village") upon his return to Sikasso years after French conquest. According to interviews and family histories in Madubugu, Madou never felt safe resettling in Bugula.

93. "Fiches de renseignements des chefs des cantons, Bougoula: Samba Tiémoko Traoré, 1904–1955," ANM, FR, 2E 59; "Fiches de renseignements des chefs des cantons, Fama: Bembatieni Traoré, 1916–1955," ANM, FR, 2E 59; "Fiches de renseignements des chefs des cantons, Natie: Kondiougou Sanogo, 1916–1955," ANM, FR, 2E 59; "Fiches de renseignements des chefs des cantons, Kaboïla: Keletigui Berté, 1908–1955," ANM, FR, 2E 59.

94. "Fiches de renseignements des chefs des cantons, Bougoula: Samba Tiémoko Traoré," 1908–1955, ANM, FR, 2E 59.

95. "Fiches de renseignements des chefs des cantons, Fama: Bembatieni Traoré," 1916–1955, ANM, FR, 2E 59.

96. Roberts, *Litigants*, 47. Rapport Politique Général, 1900, ANM, FA, 1E 73.

97. Monographie, ANM, FA, 1G 322.

98. Ibid.

99. Ibid.

100. Archinard, rapport de campagne, 1892–93, November 1893, Paris, ANS-AOF, 1D 137.

CHAPTER 2: CONTESTING SLAVERY AND
MARRIAGE IN EARLY COLONIAL SIKASSO

1. In the political report the French word "traite" was used, which translates as "trafficking" or "trade." "Rapports politique" (hereinafter RP), Cercle de Sikasso, June 1908, Archives Nationales du Mali (hereinafter ANM) Fonds Anciens (hereinafter FA), 1E 73.

2. It is important to note the language in the original document. Though no bridewealth was paid or marriage agreement negotiated, Ma Sidibé was called a wife and not a slave. This is in part because she had children with the deceased Sountara, but the ambiguity also highlights the difficulty with which the colonial administration determined people's status in the aftermath of war and enslavement in Sikasso, as well as the fact that people often contested their own—as well as each other's—status.

3. The report states that Sidibé's father "la racheta," which literally means that he bought her back or redeemed her.

4. RP, Cercle de Sikasso, June 1908, ANM, FA, 1E 73.

5. Julia Clancy-Smith develops the concept of "bet hedging" as a form of quotidian but complex engagement with new forms of North African authority under French colonial rule in *Rebel and Saint: Muslim Notables, Populist Protest, Colonial Encounters (Algeria and Tunisia, 1800–1914)* (Berkeley: University of California Press, 1997).

6. Richard L. Roberts, *Litigants and Households: African Disputes and Colonial Courts in the French Soudan, 1895–1912* (Portsmouth, NH: Heinemann, 2005), 99.

7. Ernest Roume, "Rapport au Ministre des Colonies" (1905), 109, in *Slavery and Its Abolition in French West Africa: The Official Reports of G. Poulet, E. Roume, and G. Deherme*, ed. Paul E. Lovejoy and A. S. Kanya-Forstner (Madison: University of Wisconsin Press, 1994), 93–110. Richard Roberts, "The End of Slavery in French Soudan, 1905–1914," in *The End of Slavery in Africa*, ed. Suzanne Miers and Richard Roberts (Madison: University of Wisconsin Press, 1988), 282.

8. RP, Cercle de Sikasso, June 1906, ANM, FA, IE 73.

9. RP, Cercle de Sikasso, March 1908, ANM, FA, IE 73.

10. Roberts, *Litigants*.

11. Ibid., 49; Alice Conklin, *A Mission to Civilize: The Republican Idea of Empire in France and West Africa, 1895–1930* (Stanford: Stanford University Press, 1997).

12. C. W. Newbury, "The Formation of the Government General in French West Africa," *Journal of African History* 1, no. 1 (1960): 111–28.

13. Emmanuelle Saada, "The Empire of Law: Dignity, Prestige, and Domination in the 'Colonial Situation,'" *French Politics, Culture, and Society* 20, no. 2 (2002): 98–120.

14. Roberts, *Litigants*, 60–61; Conklin, *Mission*, 202.

15. Isabelle Merle, "Retour sur le régime de l'indigénat: Genèse et contradictions des principes répresssifs dans l'empire français," *French Politics, Culture, and Society* 20, no. 2 (2002): 77–97; Gregory Mann, "What Was the *Indigénat*? The 'Empire of Law' in French West Africa," *Journal of African History* 50 (2009): 331–53.

16. Conklin, *Mission*, 87.

17. Ernest Roume, *Justice indigène: Instructions aux administrateurs sur l'application du Décret du 10 novembre 1903 portant réorganisation du service de la justice dans les colonies relevant du gouvernement général de l'AOF* (Gorée: Imprimerie du Gouvernement General, 1905); François Renault, *L'abolition de l'esclavage au Senegal: L'attitude de l'administration française, 1848–1905* (Paris: Société française d'histoire d'outre-mer, P. Geuthner, 1972), 58.

18. Roume, *Justice*, 29. The passage containing this statement is also quoted at length in Roberts, *Litigants*, 83–84.

19. John Finnis, *Natural Law and Natural Rights* (New York: Oxford University Press, 1980).

20. Roume, *Justice*.

21. Arrete no. 12, "Promulguant dans les Colonies et les Territoires du Gouvernement General de l'A.O.F. le decret du 12 decembre 1905, relatif a la repression de la traite en AOF et au Congo français," 4 January 1906, *Journal officiel de l'Afrique Occidentale Française*, 17. As quoted in Conklin, *Mission*, 88.

22. "Rapport sur le fonctionnement de la justice indigène," Cercle de Sikasso, June 1905, ANM, FA, 2M 93.

23. "Justice indigène," Cercle de Sikasso, 1905, ANM, FA, 2M 93.

24. "Notice sur la justice indigène et la justice musulmane au Soudan, Kayes, 1897," ANM, FA, 1D 15.

25. Ibid.

26. Ibid.

27. Colonel Trentinian, "Droits de commandant de région, de cercle et poste en matière de justice," 16 December 1896, ANM, FA, 2D 155.

28. "Fiches de renseignements des chefs de canton, canton de Fama, 1916–1955," ANM, FR, 2E 143.

29. Richard Roberts makes a similar observation in *Litigants*, 90–91. Allen Christelow, *Muslim Law Courts and the French Colonial State in Algeria* (Princeton, NJ: Princeton University Press, 1985); Shamil Jeppie, Ebrahim Moosa, and Richard Roberts, Introduction to *Muslim Family Law in Sub-Saharan Africa: Colonial Legacies and Post-Colonial Challenges*, ed. Shamil Jeppie, Ebrahim Moosa, and Richard Roberts (Amsterdam: Amsterdam University Press, 2010), 29–31.

30. Khalil ibn Ishaq al-Jundi, *Maliki Law: Being a Summary from French Translations of the Mukhtasar of Sidi Khalil: With Notes and Bibliography* (Westport, CT: Hyperion Press, 1980).

31. "*Dot*" is a misnomer, as it translates as "dowry" in French. A dowry is what a woman brings into her marriage, the opposite of bridewealth.

32. Robert Launay, "Tying the Cola: Dyula Marriage and Social Change" (PhD diss., Cambridge University, 1975), 165–67.

33. Maria Grosz-Ngate, "Monetization of Bridewealth and the Abandonment of 'Kin Roads' to Marriage in Sana, Mali," *American Ethnologist* 15, no. 3 (1988): 501–14.

34. Launay, "Tying," 167.

35. Mirjam de Bruijn, "The Hearthhold in Pastoral Fulbe Society, Central Mali: Social Relations, Milk, and Drought," *Africa: Journal of the International African Institute* 67, no. 4 (1997): 625–51.

36. Khalil, *Maliki Law*; Ghislaine Lydon, "Obtaining Freedom at the Muslims' Tribunal: Colonial Kadijustiz and Women's Divorce Litigation in Ndar (Senegal)," in *Muslim Family Law in Sub-Saharan Africa: Colonial Legacies and Post-Colonial Challenges*, ed. Shamil Jeppie, Ibrahim Moosa, and Richard Roberts (Amsterdam: Amsterdam University Press, 2010), 145.

37. Anita Glaze, *Art and Death in a Senufo Village* (Bloomington: Indiana University Press, 1981), 54.

38. "Justice indigène, troisième trimestre," Cercle de Sikasso, 1905, ANM, FA, 2M 93.

39. Kananbe v. Norobe, 6 September 1905, "État mensuel des jugements rendus en matière civile et commerciale par le tribunal de province," Cercle de Sikasso, September 1905, ANM, FA, 2M 144.

40. Fanse v. Mori, 5 January 1912, "État des jugements rendus en matière civile et commerciale par le tribunal de province," Cercle de Sikasso, January 1912, ANM, FA, 2M 144.

41. Roberts, *Litigants*, 72–73.

42. The third most common were requests for debt repayment; the fourth were inheritance disputes. RP, Cercle de Sikasso, April 1905, ANM, FA, 1E 73.

43. Bele v. Hama, 14 November 1905, "États des jugements rendus en matière civile et commerciale par le tribunal de province," Cercle de Sikasso, 1905, ANM, FA, 2M 144.

44. Batouli v. Fadio, 14 February 1908, "État des jugements rendus en matière civile et commerciale par le tribunal de province," Cercle de Sikasso, 1908, ANM, FA, 2M 144.

45. Diaara v. Mamadou, 15 February 1907, "État des jugements rendus en matieres civiles et commerciale par le tribunal de province," Cercle de Sikasso, February 1907, ANM, FA, 2M 144.

46. No name v. no name, March 1907, "État des jugements rendus en matière civile et commerciale par le tribunal de province," Cercle de Sikasso, 1907, ANM, FA, 2M 144.

47. Dio v. Traoré, 3 May 1907, "État des jugements rendus en matière civile et commerciale par le tribunal de province," Cercle de Sikasso, 1907, ANM, FA, 2M 144.

48. Natogoma v. Baba, 18 October 1907, "État des jugements rendus en matière civile et commerciale par le tribunal de province," Cercle de Sikasso, 1907, ANM, FA, 2M 144.

49. Soriba v. Fatimata, 6 October 1905, "État des jugements rendus en matière civile et commerciale par le tribunal," Cercle de Sikasso, October 1905, ANM, FA, 2M 144.

50. Mama v. Aoua, 13 September 1907, "État des jugements rendus en matière civile et commerciale par le tribunal de province," Cercle de Sikasso, September 1907, ANM, FA, 2M 144.

51. Moussa v. Nalle, 19 September 1905, "État des jugements rendus en matière civile et commerciale par le tribunal de province," Cercle de Sikasso, 1905, ANM, FA, 2M 144.

52. See, for example, Dem v. Oumarou, 2 June 1905, "État des jugements rendus en matière civile et commerciale par le tribunal de province," Cercle de Sikasso, June 1905, ANM, FA, 2M 144. The wife brought her husband to court seeking divorce on the grounds of abandonment and insufficient provisions, but she also asked for child custody. The court granted her a divorce but ruled in favor of the father on the matter of child custody.

53. See Camilla Toulmin, *Cattle, Women, and Wells: Managing Household Survival in the Sahel* (Oxford: Oxford University Press, 1992).

54. Martin Chanock, "A Peculiar Sharpness: An Essay on Property in the History of Customary Law in Colonial Law," *Journal of African History* 32, no. 1 (1991): 67.

55. Onofo v. Coulibaly, 1 March 1907, "État des jugements rendus en matière civile et commerciale par le tribunal de province," Cercle de Sikasso, 1907, ANM, FA, 2M 144.

56. Kounate v. Sidibé, 1 March 1907, "État des jugements rendus en matière civile et commerciale par le tribunal de province," Cercle de Sikasso, 1907, ANM, FA, 2M 144.

57. In 1906, Governor Ponty reminded his local administrators that paternity and marital authority were not to be conflated with slavery. Martin Klein highlights both 1903 and 1906 examples in his chapter titled "The Banamba Slave Exodus," in Martin Klein, *Slavery and Colonial Rule in French West Africa* (Cambridge: Cambridge University Press, 1998), 164.

58. Here the record is confusing on the relationship between Soungourou and Birama. In one instance it states that Birama is Soungourou's father, and in another it states that he is her brother. In either case, he is considered the patriarchal guardian of Soungourou.

59. Mory v. unnamed, 30 June 1905, "État mensuel des jugements rendus en matière civile et commerciale par le tribunal de province," Cercle de Sikasso, June 1905, ANM, FA, 2M 144.

60. Tenekoro v. Karidia, 19 September 1905, "États des jugements rendus en matière civile et commerciale par le tribunal de province," Cercle de Sikasso, September 1905, ANM, FA, 2M 144.

61. Meillassoux writes that manumission should be understood as another stage of slavery. Claude Meillassoux, *Anthropologie de l'esclavage: Le ventre de fer et d'argent* (Paris: Presses Universitaires de France, 1986); Trevor Getz, *Slavery and Reform in West Africa: Toward Emancipation in Nineteenth-Century Senegal and Gold Coast* (Athens: Ohio University Press, 2004).

62. Marcia Wright, *Strategies of Slaves and Women: Life Stories from East/Central Africa* (New York: Lilian Barber Press, 1993).

63. Martin Klein, "Women in Slavery in the Western Sudan," in *Women and Slavery in Africa*, ed. Claire C. Robertson and Martin A. Klein (Madison: University of Wisconsin Press, 1983), 69.

64. Klein, "Women in Slavery"; Suzanne Miers and Igor Kopytoff, eds., *Slavery in Africa: Historical and Anthropological Perspectives* (Madison: University of Wisconsin Press, 1977). Paul E. Lovejoy, "Concubinage and the Status of Women Slaves in Early Colonial Nineteenth-Century Northern Nigeria," *Journal of African History* 29, no. 2 (1988): 245–66; Richard Roberts and Martin Klein, "The Banamba Slave Exodus of 1905 and the Decline of Slavery in the Western Sudan," *Journal of African History* 21, no. 3 (1980): 375–94; Pamela Scully and Diana Paton, eds., *Gender and Slave Emancipation in the Atlantic World* (Durham, NC: Duke University Press, 2005).

65. Myron Echenberg, *Colonial Conscripts: The Tirailleurs Sénégalais in French West Africa* (Portsmouth, NH: Heinemann, 1991).

66. Joseph Gallieni, *Deux campagnes au Soudan Français, 1886–1888* (Paris: Librairie Hachette, 1891), 121–58.

67. Klein, "Women in Slavery," 67.

68. Richard L. Roberts, *Warriors, Merchants, and Slaves: The State and the Economy in the Middle Niger Valley, 1700–1914* (Stanford: Stanford University Press, 1987), 135–73; A. S. Kanya-Forstner, *The Conquest of the Western Sudan* (Cambridge: Cambridge University Press, 1969).

69. Kanya-Forstner, *Conquest*; Roberts, *Warriors*; Klein, *Slavery*.

70. Getz, *Slavery*, 69–84.

71. Other scholars have handily addressed this issue: Kanya-Forstner, *Conquest*; Klein, *Slavery*; Getz, *Slavery*. For similar arguments in different Atlantic World contexts, see Frederick Cooper, Thomas Holt, and Rebecca Scott, eds., *Beyond Slavery: Explorations of Race, Labor, and Citizenship in Post-Emancipation Societies* (Durham, NC: Duke University Press, 2000).

72. Roume, "Rapport au Ministre des Colonies," 1905, in *Slavery and Its Abolition in French West Africa*, ed. Paul E. Lovejoy and A. S. Kanya-Forstner (Madison: University of Wisconsin Press, 1994), 93–110.

73. Emily S. Burrill, "'Wives of Circumstance': Gender and Slave Emancipation in Late Nineteenth-Century Senegal," *Slavery and Abolition* 29, no. 1 (2008): 49–63.

74. Roume, "Rapport au Ministre des Colonies," 109.

75. Roberts and Klein, "Banamba"; Peterson, "Slave Emancipation."

76. RP, Cercle de Sikasso, May 1906, ANM, FA, 1E 73.

77. Scully, *Liberating the Family?*; Pamela Scully, "Gender, History, and Human Rights," in *Gender and Culture at the Limits of Rights*, ed. Dorothy Hodgson (Philadelphia: University of Pennsylvania Press, 2011), 17–31. The literature on this historical period in

the North American context is vast, but see, for example, Herbert Gutman, *The Black Family in Slavery and Freedom, 1750–1925* (New York: Vintage, 1977); Amy Dru Stanley, *From Bondage to Contract: Wage Labor, Marriage, and the Market in the Age of Slave Emancipation* (Cambridge: Cambridge University Press, 1998).

78. Conklin, *Mission*, 86–88.

79. RP, Cercle de Sikasso, June 1908, ANM, FA, 1E 73.

80. Correspondances, Affaires Administratives, Cercle de Sikasso, 1903–17, ANM, FA, 2D 103; Correspondances avec les cercles, Sikasso, 1905, ANM, FA, 4E 25.

81. This question "Which women?" stems from texts in US women's history on race and class in the debates that defined the historiography on women and gender in the 1980s. Much of this foundational work concerns women and slavery in the US South. See Deborah Gray White, *Ar'n't I A Woman? Female Slaves in the Plantation South* (New York: W. W. Norton, 1985); Jacqueline Jones, *Labor of Love, Labor of Sorrow: Black Women, Work, and Family from Slavery to the Present* (New York: Basic Books, 1985).

82. "Little marabout" in this context is a loaded expression. The French term, "*maraboutaillon*," likely coined by Paul Marty, gained currency in the administrative vernacular as a pejorative description of Muslim men of local authority and prestige whom the administrators believed to be of no consequence—usually because administrators could not discern if the men in question belonged to *turuq* that the French found to be significant. Dow is telling us here that his father was not a "little marabout," but rather, an important man. Thanks to Jeremy Berndt for a clarifying discussion on this expression in the French Soudan; see also Paul Marty, *Études sur l'Islam et les tribus du Soudan* (Paris: Editions Ernest Leroux, 1920).

83. Interview with Yaya Dow, Kaboïla, 22 March 2005. Yaya Dow was widely respected throughout the villages immediately surrounding Sikassoville for his extremely advanced age, his religious piety, and his professional success as a merchant and as an interpreter for the local administration during the later colonial years. Dow did not know his age, but he and others guessed that he was in his mid-90s at the time of the interview. Dow passed away in 2008.

84. I agree with Tamara Giles-Vernick that this type of historical representation should be understood as a "conversational hybrid" as opposed to Vansina's definition of oral history and its applicability. Tamara Giles-Vernick, "Lives, Histories, and Sites of Recollection," in *African Words, African Voices: Critical Practices in Oral History*, ed. Luise White, Stephan F. Miescher, and David William Cohen (Bloomington: Indiana University Press, 2001), 194–213. See also Susan Geiger, "Women's Life Histories: Method and Content," *Signs* 11, no. 2 (1986): 334–51; E. Ann McDougall, "A Sense of Self: The Life of Fatma Barka," *Canadian Journal of African Studies* 32, no. 2 (1998): 285–315.

CHAPTER 3: RETURNED SOLDIERS
AND RUNAWAY WIVES

1. Bintou Traoré v. Daouda Traoré, 10 April 1919, subdivision tribunal, Sikasso, Sikasso cercle archives, unclassified.

2. Richard Roberts sees this as a colony-wide decline in divorce claims brought by women after 1910 between the years 1905 and 1912, and Sikasso certainly fits within this trend. I argue that this decline seems to have extended into the 1920s. Richard L.

Roberts, *Litigants and Households: African Disputes and Colonial Courts in the French Soudan, 1895–1912* (Portsmouth, NH: Heinemann, 2005), particularly chap. 5, "Women Seeking Divorce, Men Seeking Control."

3. Ernest Roume, *Justice Indigène: Instructions aux administrateurs sur l'application du Décret de 10 novembre 1903 portant réorganisation du service de la justice dans les colonies relevant du général de l'AOF* (Gorée: l'Imprimerie du Gouvernement General, 1905).

4. Many scholars have examined William Ponty as a historical subject. See in particular Alice Conklin, *A Mission to Civilize: The Republican Idea of Empire in France and West Africa, 1895–1930* (Stanford: Stanford University Press, 1997); Roberts, *Litigants*; Christopher Harrison, *France and Islam in Africa, 1860–1960* (Cambridge: Cambridge University Press, 1988); G. Wesley Johnson, "William Ponty and Republican Paternalism in French West Africa, 1866–1915," in *African Proconsuls: European Governors in Africa*, ed. L. H. Gann and Peter Duignan (New York: Free Press, 1978), 127–56.

5. Like Ponty, Delafosse is a well-studied historical figure in French colonial history. He was also well published in his own right. See in particular Jean-Loup Amselle and Emmanuelle Sibeud, *Maurice Delafosse: Entre orientalisme et ethnographie: L'itinéraire d'un africaniste (1870–1926)* (Paris: Maisonneuve et Larose, 1998); Harrison, *France*.

6. E. Beurdeley, *La justice indigène en Afrique occidentale française: Mission d'études, 1913–1914* (Paris: Publication de la Comité de l'Afrique Française, 1916).

7. Conklin, *Mission*, 114–15.

8. Roberts, *Litigants*, 90–91; Conklin, *Mission*, 108–9; Harrison, *France*, 51.

9. Governor-General to Lieutenant Governor, Haut-Senegal-Niger, Dakar, 2 May 1910, ANM, 2M 459.

10. Conklin, *Mission*.

11. G. Wesley Johnson Jr., *The Emergence of Black Politics in Senegal: The Struggle for Power in the Four Communes, 1900–1920* (Stanford: Stanford University Press, 1971).

12. Conklin, *Mission*, 108; Johnson, "William Ponty," 128.

13. Conklin, *Mission*.

14. David Robinson, *Paths of Accommodation: Muslim Societies and French Colonial Authorities* (Athens: Ohio University Press, 2000); Harrison, *France*, 104–5.

15. Maurice Delafosse, "Étude préparatoire d'un programme de measures à prendre en vue d'améliorer la situation des indigènes au double point de administrative et social," May 1919, 317. Reprinted in Marc Michel, "Un programme réformiste en 1919: Maurice Delafosse et la 'politique indigène' in AOF," *Cahiers d' études africaines* 15, no. 58 (1975): 313–27.

16. Maurice Delafosse, *Les Noirs de l'Afrique* (Paris: Payot and Cie., 1922), 140.

17. Maurice Delafosse, *Les Nègres* (Paris: Éditions Rieder, 1927), 36.

18. ANM, FA, 1D 198.

19. Terence Ranger, "The Invention of Tradition in Colonial Africa," in *The Invention of Tradition*, ed. Eric J. Hobsbawm and Terence O. Ranger, 11th ed. (Cambridge: Cambridge University Press, 1983), 211–12.

20. Anita Glaze, *Art and Death in a Senufo Village* (Bloomington: Indiana University Press, 1981); Ferdinand Ouattara Tiona, *La mémoire Sénufo: Bois sacré, éducation, et chefferie* (Paris: Association pour la promotion de la recherche scientifique de l'Afrique noire, 1988).

21. "Fiches de renseignements des chefs des cantons, Kaboïla: Keletigui Berté, 1908–1955," ANM, FR, 2E 59.

22. Theodore André, "Le Droit Privé des Senefo du Kénédougou (Cercle de Sikasso)" (doctoral thesis, University of Bordeaux, 1913), 25; Bohumil Holas, *Les Sénoufo (y compris les Minianka)* (Paris: Presses Universitaires de France, 1966), 96–97.

23. Sall and Diarra v. Mohammed, 18 May 1922, subdivision tribunal, Sikasso, Sikasso cercle archives, unclassified.

24. Traoré v. Traoré, Traoré, Berté, 13 March 1919, subdivision tribunal, Sikasso, Sikasso cercle archives, unclassified.

25. André, "Le Droit Privé," 29.

26. Ibid.

27. RP, Cercle de Sikasso, 1911, ANM, FA, 1E 73.

28. "Fiches de renseignements des chefs de canton, Canton de Folona (Sikasso)," 1908–50, ANM, FR, 2E 59.

29. Rapports sur le fonctionnement des tribunaux cercle de Sikasso 1905–20, 1913, ANM, FA, 2M 93.

30. RP, September 1914, ANM, FA, 1E 73.

31. Raymond Betts, *Assimilation and Association in French Colonial Theory, 1890–1914* (Lincoln: University of Nebraska Press, 1960).

32. Sara Berry, *No Condition Is Permanent: The Social Dynamics of Agrarian Change in Sub-Saharan Africa* (Madison: University of Wisconsin Press, 1993).

33. Betts, *Assimilation*, 106.

34. RP, Cercle de Sikasso, August 1915, ANM, FA, 1E 73.

35. RP, Cercle de Sikasso, February 1916, ANM, FA, 1E 73.

36. Rapport trimestriel (RT), first trimester, 1918, ANM, FA, 1E 73.

37. Myron Echenberg, *Colonial Conscripts: The Tirailleurs Sénégalais in French West Africa, 1857–1960* (Portsmouth, NH: Heinemann, 1991), 25.

38. Ibid., 15. See also "Recensement statistique de la population," Cercle de Sikasso, 1905–14, ANM, FA, 5D 82.

39. Echenberg, *Colonial*, 57.

40. Ibid., 58; Joe Lunn, *Memoirs of the Maelstrom: A Senegalese Oral History of the First World War* (Portsmouth, NH: Heinemann, 1999), 34–39; Gregory Mann, *Native Sons: West African Veterans and France in the Twentieth Century* (Durham, NC: Duke University Press, 2006), 90–91.

41. Monica M. van Beusekom, *Negotiating Development: African Farmers and Colonial Experts at the Office du Niger, 1920–1960* (Portsmouth, NH: Heinemann, 2002).

42. Ibid.; Catherine Mornane Bogosian, "Forced Labor, Resistance, and Memory: The *deuxième portion* in the French Sudan, 1926–1950" (PhD diss., University of Pennsylvania, 2003).

43. Bengali v. Diarrassambo, 18 December 1919, subdivision tribunal, Sikasso, Sikasso cercle archives, unclassified.

44. Traoré v. Konaté, 12 June 1919, subdivision tribunal, Sikasso, Sikasso cercle archives, unclassified.

45. Touré v. Diallo, 16 April 1922, subdivision tribunal, Sikasso, Sikasso cercle archives, unclassified.

46. Berté v. Kondé, 20 June 1922, subdivision tribunal, Sikasso, Sikasso cercle archives, unclassified.

47. Adjoint des Services Civils à Governeur de Soudan, "Memoire sur le Divorce en Droit Coutumier," 31 March 1937, p. 5, ANM, FR, 2M 263.

48. Marjorie Mbilinyi, "Runaway Wives in Colonial Tanganyika: Forced Labour and Forced Marriage in Rungwe District, 1919–1961," *International Journal of the Sociology of Law* 16 (1988): 1–29.

49. Jean Allman and Victoria Tashjian, *"I Will Not Eat Stone": A Women's History of Colonial Asante* (Portsmouth, NH: Heinemann, 2000), 169–77.

50. Jane Parpart, "Where Is Your Mother? Gender, Urban Marriage, and Colonial Discourse on the Zambian Copperbelt, 1924–1945," *Canadian Journal of African Historical Studies* 27, no. 2 (1994): 241–71.

51. Brett Shadle, "Bridewealth and Female Consent: Marriage Disputes in African Courts, Gusiiland, Kenya," *Journal of African History* 44, no. 2 (2003): 241–62.

52. Marie Rodet, "Continuum of Gendered Violence: The Colonial Invention of Desertion as a Customary Criminal Offense, 1900–1949," in *Domestic Violence and the Law in Colonial and Postcolonial Africa*, ed. Emily S. Burrill, Richard L. Roberts, and Elizabeth Thornberry (Athens: Ohio University Press, 2009), 74–93.

53. Dorothy L. Hodgson and Sheryl A. McCurdy, "Introduction: 'Wicked' Women and the Reconfiguration of Gender in Africa," in *"Wicked" Women and the Reconfiguration of Gender in Africa*, ed. Dorothy L. Hodgson and Sheryl A. McCurdy (Portsmouth, NH: Heinemann, 2001), 1–24.

54. Shadle, "Bridewealth," 244.

55. The surname "Courobary" is probably a mistaken rendering of the more common surname "Coulibaly" or "Kulibali."

56. Courobary v. Diarra, 27 March 1927, subdivision tribunal, Sikasso, Sikasso cercle archives, unclassified.

57. Traoré v. Traoré, 16 June 1921, subdivision tribunal, Sikasso, Sikasso cercle archives, unclassified.

58. André, "Le Droit Privé," 53.

59. Holas, *Les Sénoufo.*

60. Gouverneur Général de l'Afrique Occidentale Française à Monsieur le Ministre des Colonies, Paris, "Projet de circulaire sur les mariages indigénes," 27 June 1936, Centre des archives de la France d'outre mer (CAOM), 1affpol541.

61. Ibid.

CHAPTER 4: WEALTH IN WOMEN, WEALTH IN MEN

1. "Rapport économique et agricole du 2e trimestre," Cercle de Sikasso, 1933, ANM, FR, 1Q 360.

2. "Extrait du procès-verbal, reunion des chefs," Cercle de Sikasso, 19 May 1933, ANM, FR, 1Q 360; "Monographies du cercle de Koutiala," n.d., Cercle de Koutiala, ANM, FA, 1D 45.

3. "Rapport économique et agricole du 2e trimestre," Cercle de Sikasso, 1933, ANM, FR, 1Q 360.

4. "Extrait du procès-verbal, réunion des chefs," Cercle de Sikasso, 12 October 1933, ANM, FR, 1Q 360.

5. "Rapport économique et agricole du 2e trimestre," Cercle de Sikasso, 1933, ANM, FR, 1Q 360.

6. Judith Carney, *Black Rice: The African Origins of Rice Cultivation in the Americas* (Cambridge, MA: Harvard University Press, 2002), 46–49.

7. Richard L. Roberts, *Two Worlds of Cotton: Colonialism and the Regional Economy in the French Soudan, 1800–1946* (Stanford: Stanford University Press, 1996), 206–10.

8. Roland Colin, "Comment les 'gens du mil' ont commencé d'être les 'gens du coton'—les raisons communautaire et raison marchande," chap. 13 in *Kènèdougou au crépuscule de l'Afrique coloniale: Mémoires des années cinquantes* (Paris: Présence Africaine, 2004), 303–24.

9. This period is based on observations by early administrators and ethnographers such as René Caillié, Gustave Binger, and Maurice Delafosse. See also "Étude sur la mise engage des personnes dans la coutume Senufo," 1937, ANM, FA, 1D 197.

10. In northern Côte d'Ivoire the field is called a *segnon* or *segbo*; in Supyire, which is more commonly spoken in the Sikasso area, the collective field is called a *forobakerege*, which literally translates as the "big family field." Thanks to Bob Carlson for Supyire language explanations.

11. These fields are called *tologo, kagon*, or *ferenkerege*.

12. This is also reflected in ethnographic writings on the Minyanka of Koutiala. "Enquête sur l'organisation de la famille les fiançailles et le mariage," Cercle de Koutiala, 1910, ANM, FA, 1D 198.

13. Thomas Bassett, *The Peasant Cotton Revolution in West Africa: Côte d'Ivoire, 1880–1995* (Cambridge: Cambridge University Press, 2001), 99; Sinali Coulibaly, *Le paysan Senoufo* (Abidjan-Dakar: Les Nouvelles Editions Africaines, 1978); Bohumil Holas, *Les Sénoufo (y compris les Minianka)* (Paris: Presses Universitaires de Paris, 1966.

14. Megan Vaughan, "Which Family? Problems in the Reconstruction of the History of the Family as an Economic and Cultural Unit," *Journal of African History* 24, no. 2 (1983): 278.

15. Catherine Mormane Bogosian, "Forced Labor, Resistance, and Memory: The *deuxième portion* in the French Soudan, 1926–1950" (PhD diss., University of Pennsylvania, 2002).

16. Frederick Cooper, *Decolonization and African Society: The Labor Question in French and British Africa* (Cambridge: Cambridge University Press, 1996), 38.

17. Bogosian, "Forced Labor"; Monica M. van Beusekom, *Negotiating Development: African Farmers and Colonial Experts at the Office du Niger, 1920–1960* (Portsmouth, NH: Heineman, 2002), 19. *Sativa* is an Asian rice with a higher yield than native, "red" rice, the latter of which more resilient.

18. Cékoura Berté, Kaboïla, 5 March 2005.

19. "Tournées," 1947, Cercle de Sikasso, administration générale, carton D 3D, Sikasso cercle archives.

20. Yacouba Koné, Sikasso, 3 May 2005. Koné estimated that he was fifteen years old when he left to work on the plantations in Côte d'Ivoire. As he was born in 1918, this indicates that he first went to Côte d'Ivoire for work in 1933, which would have been right at the time that the effects of the global depression were felt in the Sikasso region.

21. Bassett, *Peasant*, 99–100.

22. Holas, *Les Sénoufo*, 98.

23. Cékoura Berté, Kaboïla, 5 March 2005.

24. Yaya Dow, Kaboïla, 9 April 2005. It is worth noting that Dow used the general bamanankan term for hoe (*daba*) in reference to an act that is commonly associated with Senufo practices. There are many different types of Senufo hoes, most of which are gender-specific and associated with particular types of work. The one that Dow describes here is probably a *kamag'*, a small hand hoe suitable for tasks such as clearing small weeds and digging up root vegetables and used by men and women. A child who had reached the age where he or she could use a *kamag'* in the field, even as child's play, would have survived the perils of infancy and proved to be in good health. Sinali Coulibaly, *Le Paysan*, 162.

25. Holas, *Les Sénoufo*, 99.

26. "Mémoire sur le divorce," 1937, Cercle de Sikasso, ANM, FR, 1D 208.

27. Holas, *Les Sénoufo*, 100.

28. Aminata Kouyaté, Sikasso, 12 February 2005.

29. Myron Echenberg and Jean Filipovich, "African Military Labour and the Building of the *Office du Niger* Installations, 1920–1950," *Journal of African History* 27 (1986): 533–34. Von Beusekom, *Negotiating*; Roberts, *Two Worlds*.

30. Martin Klein and Richard Roberts, "The Resurgence of Pawning in French West Africa during the Depression of the 1930s," *African Economic History* 16 (1987): 23–37; Toyin Falola and Paul Lovejoy, eds., *Pawnship in Africa: Debt Bondage in Historical Perspective* (Boulder, CO: Westview Press, 1994); Paul E. Lovejoy and David Richardson, "The Business of Slaving: Pawnship in Western Africa, c. 1600–1810," *Journal of African History* 42 (2001): 67–89.

31. Klein and Roberts, "Resurgence," 23.

32. "Rapport sur la traite des femmes et des enfants," 1933, Bamako, ANM, FA, 1D 210.

33. Klein and Roberts, *Resurgence*, 27–28. The Sangalan Affair was scandalous in the eyes of the administration and made its way up to the files of the Minster of Colonies.

34. Yaya Dow, Kaboïla, 9 April 2005. See chap. 1 for more on the importance of Kélétigi Berté. Kélétigi Berté was a military leader under Tiéba and Babemba. Abderahamane was Kélétigi's oldest son and successor as canton chief of Kaboïla. The fact that Abderahamane Berté offered a "Traoré woman" to Dow as a wife indicates she was likely the descendant of slaves belonging to the Berté family. Kélétigi's *sofa* would have probably taken Tiéba and Babemba's family name. As one informant aptly stated, "You never know if a Traoré is a *real* Traoré around here [Sikasso]," meaning that so many who use the royal name in Sikasso were the descendants of Babemba's and Tiéba's slaves.

35. "Rapports économiques," 1936–37, Cercle de Sikasso, ANM, FR, 1Q 360.

36. Karen Offen, "Feminism, Antifeminism, and National Family Politics in Early Third Republic France," in *Connecting Spheres*, ed. Marilyn Boxer and Jean Quataert (New York: Oxford University Press, 2000), 212.

37. Soeur Marie-André du Sacré-Coeur, *La femme indigène en Afrique Noire* (Paris: Payot, 1939), 18.

38. Joseph-Roger de Benoist, *Eglise et pouvoir colonial au Soudan français: Administrateurs et missionaires dans la Boucle du Niger (1885–1945)* (Paris: Karthala, 1987), 289.

39. Soeur Marie-André du Sacré-Coeur, "Vers l'évolution de la femme indigène en A.O.F.," *Outre-Mer*, troisième trimestre, 1934, 1 affpol 541, dossier 2, ANSOM.

40. Ibid.

41. Ibid.

42. Ibid.

43. "Rapport sur la traite des femmes et des enfants (exécution des prescriptions du Télégramme Lettre circulaire no. 54 Janvier 1934)," January 1934, Cercle de Sikasso, ANM, FA, 1D 210.

44. Florence Rochefort, "Laïcisation des mœurs et équilibres de genre, le débat sur la capacité civile de la femme mariée (1918–1938)," *Vingtième Siècle. Revue d'histoire* 87 (July–September 2005): 129–41.

45. Judith Tucker, *In the House of the Law: Gender and Islamic Law in Ottoman Turkey and Syria* (Berkeley: University of California Press, 2000).

46. Brévié was not the governor-general in 1939, but his term as governor-general was arguably more influential than those of his immediate successors, de Coppet (1936–38) and Cayla (1939–40), who served very briefly. It was Brévié who wrote the first circulars that determined the language and the policy of the Mandel Decree.

47. Jules Brévié, *Islamisme contre "Naturisme" au Soudan Français. Essai de psychologie politique, coloniale* (Paris: Éditions Ernest Leroux, 1923), 297.

48. Ibid., 293.

49. Ibid., 304. Christopher Harrison, *France and Islam in West Africa, 1860–1960* (Cambridge: Cambridge University Press, 1988), 148. Louis Brenner, *Controlling Knowledge: Religion, Power, and Schooling in a West African Muslim Society* (Bloomington: Indiana University Press, 2001), 154–55.

50. Brévié, *Islamisme,* 257.

51. Jules Brévié, *La politique et l'administration indigène en Afrique Occidentale Française* (Gorée: Imprimerie du Gouvernement Général, 1935), 31.

52. Ibid.

53. James Genova, "Conflicted Missions: Power and Identity in French West Africa during the 1930s," *Historian* 66, no. 1 (March 2004): 5.

54. Maupoil, *Coutumiers juridiques de l'Afrique occidentale française* (Paris: Larose, 1939), 9.

55. Ibid, 6n1.

56. Gary Wilder, *The French Imperial Nation-State: Negritude and Colonial Humanism between the Two World Wars* (Chicago: University of Chicago Press, 2005), 4–5.

57. Jules Brévié, *La politique,* 60.

58. Ibid.

59. Le Gouverneur-Général de l'Afrique Occidentale Française à Monsieur le Ministre des Colonies, Direction des Affaires Politiques, "Projet de circulaire sur les mariages indigènes," 27 June 1936, CAOM AP/2/966, 1 Affpol 541.

60. See letter no. 893, Direction des Affaires Politiques et Administratives, "Mariage indigène, question posé par Monsieur Louis Marin," 8 June 1937, CAOM, 1 Affpol 541, dossier 2.

CHAPTER 5: DEFINING THE LIMITS AND
BARGAINS OF PATRIARCHY

1. This description is based on the testimony of Ouaraba Bayogo, Kadidya Traoré, and Salia Sangaré. Trial of Salia Sangaré, 19 January 1939, *tribunal criminel*, Cercle de Sikasso, Sikasso cercle archives, unclassified.

2. The fact of the autopsy is significant here. Scientific and medical examination of bodies, particularly in the form of autopsy, merits further research in the field of

African history. The records here do not provide information regarding the time that elapsed between death, autopsy, and burial, or the conditions under which Massara's body was turned over to the commandant's office and the colonial doctor. For more on autopsies and connections between law, medicine, and empire in a different context, see Khaled Fahmy, "The Anatomy of Justice: Forensic Medicine and Criminal Law in Nineteenth-Century Egypt," *Islamic Law and Society* 6, no. 2 (1999): 224–71.

3. All of the parties involved in this case spoke Jula, or Bamanankan, as a first language. Their testimony was translated into French by an interpreter and transcribed into French by the court clerk. Present at the hearing were three European court assessors (the commandant of Sikasso and president of the tribunal, the school headmaster, and the French owner of a local farm), two African assessors (one for Senufo custom and one for Jula/Bamana custom), the African secretary-clerk, and the African interpreter.

4. It should be noted here that co-wives also abused one another from time to time and still do today. In interviews, women often spoke of the role that poison and witchcraft played in conflicts between co-wives. This is another compelling aspect of domestic abuse that introduces a new component to gender violence to be explored elsewhere.

5. Deniz Kandiyoti, "Bargaining with Patriarchy," *Gender and Society* 2, no. 3 (1988): 274–90.

6. This historical dynamic is developed earlier in the dissertation. I agree with Richard Roberts that French colonial administrators were increasingly concerned with upsetting the patriarchal authority of the family, and this resulted in a decrease in successful divorce cases. However, I also suggest that once the authority of canton chiefs was regularized within the structure of the colonial state, this significantly changed the frequency of civil cases appearing at the *tribunaux de première instance*.

7. Emily S. Burrill, Richard L. Roberts, and Elizabeth Thornberry, eds., *Domestic Violence and the Law in Colonial and Postcolonial Africa* (Athens: Ohio University Press, 2010).

8. See, for example, Judith Byfield, "Women, Marriage, Divorce, and the Emerging Colonial State in Abeokuta (Nigeria), 1892–1904," in *"Wicked" Women and the Reconfiguration of Gender in Africa*, ed. Dorothy Hodgson and Sheryl McCurdy (Portsmouth, NH: Heinemann, 2001), 27–46; Sean Hawkins, "'The Woman in Question': Marriage and Identity in the Colonial Courts of Northern Ghana, 1907–1954," in *Women in African Colonial Histories*, ed. Jean Allman, Susan Geiger, and Nakanyike Musisi (Bloomington: Indiana University Press, 2002), 116–43; Victoria Tashjian and Jean Allman, "Marrying and Marriage on a Shifting Terrain: Reconfigurations of Power and Authority in Early Colonial Asante," in *Women*, ed. Allman, Geiger, and Musisi, 237–25; Richard Roberts, *Litigants and Households: African Disputes and Colonial Courts in the French Soudan, 1895–1912* (Portsmouth, NH: Heinemann, 2005).

9. Michael Crowder, *The Flogging of Phinehas McIntosh: A Tale of Colonial Folly and Injustice: Bechuanaland, 1933* (New Haven, CT: Yale University Press, 1998); Steven Pierce and Anupama Rao, eds., *Discipline and the Other Body: Correction, Corporeality, Colonialism* (Durham, NC: Duke University Press, 2006). Florence Bernault, ed., *Enfermement, prison et châtiments en Afrique du 19e siècle à nos jours* (Paris: Karthala, 1999). A study that incorporates both domestic violence and corporal

punishment at the hands of the colonial state is Stacey Hynd, "Imperial Gallows: Capital Punishment, Violence, and Colonial Rule in Britain's African Territories, c. 1908–68" (DPhil diss., Oxford University, 2007).

10. See Lata Mani, *Contentious Traditions: The Debate on Sati in Colonial India* (Berkeley: University of California Press, 1998) for a rich discussion that examines just this theme in the case of colonial India.

11. In the case of Salia Sangaré, for example, the president of the tribunal weighed Salia's remorse and the fact that the couple was on otherwise good terms against the fact that wife abuse leading to unintended death was "contrary to French civilization." See the trial of Salia Sangaré, 19 January 1939. See also Roberts, *Litigants*, 74.

12. Shahrzad Mojab, "'Honor Killing': Culture, Politics, Theory," *Middle East Women's Studies Review* 17, nos. 1–2 (2002): 1. See also Lynn Thomas, *Politics of the Womb: Women, Reproduction, and the State in Kenya* (Berkeley: University of California Press, 2003), and Dorothy Hodgson and Sheryl McCurdy, eds., *"Wicked" Women and the Reconfiguration of Gender in Africa* (Portsmouth, NH: Heinemann, 2001, for their discussions of the connections between gender relations at home and sociopolitical dynamics.

13. Banfora saying from the region of Sikasso, as quoted in Roland Colin, *Kènèdougou au crépuscule de l'Afrique colonial: Mémoires des années cinquante* (Paris: Présence Africaine, 2004), 184.

14. It is interesting to note that in Sikasso today, divorce cases and marriage reconciliation hearings are still conducted almost exclusively in Jula. However, I was present at court cases in late 2004 and 2005 where Senufo-speaking litigants required the assistance of a translator, and even very rural litigants who spoke Jula as their native language but could not understand the vocabulary of the northern "Bamako" or "Segu-style Bamanakan" spoken by the educated, female judge, required a local Bamana-speaking translator. There was a court clerk present (also female, in this particular instance) who recorded all testimony in French, though she herself spoke Jula.

15. Colin, *Kènèdougou*, 280.

16. Ibid., 279.

17. Haut Commissariat de l'Afrique Française, *La justice indigène en Afrique Occidentale Française* (Rufisque: Imprimerie du Haut Commissariat, 1948), 68.

18. Although there is not a lot of information on this process, I assume that the *chef de canton* had a role in determining appropriate witnesses and possibly coaching them on what they should say within certain parameters.

19. See Susan Berk-Seligson, *The Bilingual Courtroom: Court Interpreters in the Judicial Process* (Chicago: University of Chicago Press, 1990); Richard Roberts, "Text and Testimony in the Tribunal de Première Instance, Dakar, during the Early Twentieth Century," *Journal of African History* 31, no. 3 (1990): 447–63. For more on how intermediaries shaped colonial Africa and the view that historians have of Africa, see Benjamin Lawrance, Emily Osborn, and Richard Roberts, eds., *Intermediaries, Interpreters, and Clerks: African Employees and the Making of Colonial Africa* (Madison: University of Wisconsin Press, 2006).

20. Trial of Lamoussa Traoré, 26 July 1934, tribunal criminel, Sikasso, Sikasso cercle archives, unclassified.

21. Ibid. "I've been unhappy because of it" is my translation of the peculiar phrase written by the court clerk, *"J'ai eu des coups malheureux."* Although we do not know exactly what Lamoussa said in Jula, the word "coups" means blows or hits, and the use of the word in this context seems to indicate that he is talking about being unhappy as a result of his actions, rather than the physical blows that he inflicted upon his wife. In either case, the sense of bad luck or misfortune is invoked.

22. "Memoire sur le divorce," 1937, Cercle de Sikasso, ANM, FA, 1D 208.

23. A. Aubert, *Coutumière Juridique de l'Afrique Occidentale Française* (Paris: Larose, 1939), 2:86.

24. Ibid., 68.

25. Diakité v. Traoré, 20 January 1936, *tribunal de province*, Sikasso cercle archives, unclassified.

26. Coulibaly v. Coulibaly, 20 January 1936, *tribunal de province*, Sikasso cercle archives, unclassified.

27. N'Diaye v. N'Diaye, 24 July 1937, *tribunal de province*, Sikasso cercle archives, Sikasso, unclassified.

CHAPTER 6: GENDER JUSTICE AND THE MEANINGS OF MARRIAGE

1. Jacquinot served three different terms as Minister of Overseas France: 1951–52, 1953–54, and 1961–66. Jean Lacouture, *De Gaulle: The Ruler, 1945–1970*, trans. Alan Sheridan (New York: Norton, 1992). For the full text of the Jacquinot Decree, see "Décret no. 51–1100," *Journal officiel de l'Afrique Occidentale Française (JOAOF)*, no. 2558, 20 October 1951, p. 1609.

2. "Déclaration d'enregistrement en 1956 par les diverses centres d'état civil du Cercle de Sikasso, Enquêtes-concession rural, questions diverses," 1905–52, Sikasso cercle archives, carton 2C/4.

3. Frederick Cooper, "'Our Strike': Equality, Anti-Colonial Politics, and the 1947–48 Railway Strike in French West Africa," *Journal of African History* 37, no. 1 (1996): 81–118.

4. Gregory Mann, *Native Sons: West African Veterans and France in the Twentieth Century* (Durham, NC: Duke University Press, 2006), 110. For a counterperspective on organized resistance, see Elizabeth Schmidt, *Mobilizing the Masses: Gender, Ethnicity, and Class in the Nationalist Movement in Guinea, 1939–1958* (Portsmouth, NH: Heinemann, 2005). The foundational text on this period, which centers on organized movement but addresses local, small-scale innovation, is Frederick Cooper, *Decolonization and African Society: The Labor Question in French and British Africa* (Cambridge: Cambridge University Press, 1996).

5. Mann, *Native Sons*, 110.

6. James C. Scott, *Seeing Like a State: How Certain Schemes to Improve the Human Condition Have Failed* (New Haven, CT: Yale University Press, 1998).

7. Sean Hawkins, *Writing and Colonialism in Northern Ghana: The Encounter between the LoDagaa and the "World on Paper"* (Toronto: University of Toronto Press, 2002).

8. Meredith McKittrick, "Faithful Daughter, Murdering Mother: Transgression and Social Control in Colonial Namibia," *Journal of African History* 40, no. 2 (1999): 275.

9. All of the details included here regarding the contested marriage of Koniba and Daouda are included in the dossier, Commandant de Sikasso to Monsieur le Procureur de la République à Bamako, August 1948, Sikasso cercle archives, unclassified. The surnames of the main parties have been omitted to protect their privacy, with the exception of Abderamane Berté, who was a well-documented and public historical figure in Sikasso.

10. Dorothy Hodgson, "'My Daughter . . . Belongs to the Government Now': Marriage, Maasai, and the Tanzanian State," *Canadian Journal of African Studies* 30, no. 1 (1996): 107. This argument is further developed in Dorothy Hodgson and Sheryl McCurdy, eds., *"Wicked" Women and the Reconfiguration of Gender in Africa* (Portsmouth, NH: Heinemann, 2001).

11. Bohumil Holas, *Les Sénoufo (y compris les Minianka)* (Paris: Presses Universitaires de France, 1966), 93–94.

12. See, for example, Frederick Cooper, *Africa since 1940: The Past of the Present* (Cambridge: Cambridge University Press, 2002), 40–49; Mann, *Native Sons*, 116–34; Brian Peterson, *Islamization from Below: The Making of Muslim Communities in Rural French Sudan, 1880–1960* (New Haven, CT: Yale University Press, 2011), 186–87.

13. Cooper, *Africa since 1940*, 44.

14. Johannes Morsink, *The Universal Declaration of Human Rights: Origins, Drafting, and Intent* (Philadelphia: University of Pennsylvania Press, 2000). See in particular chap. 3, "Colonies, Minorities, and Women's Rights," 92–129.

15. The Universal Declaration of Human Rights, http://www.un.org/en/documents/udhr/.

16. Abd-el Kader Boye et al, "Marriage Law and Practice in the Sahel," *Studies in Family Planning* 22, no. 6 (1991): 343–49.

17. "Procès-Verbal (P-V) de réunion du Conseil des Notables," Sikasso, July 1955, premier carton, Fonds du Bureau Politique Nationale US-RDA (FBPN), ANM.

18. Ibid.

19. Governor of French Soudan to Local Offices of Political Affairs, Circulaire no. 28, 2 February 1952, APAS/4, premier carton, FBPN, ANM.

20. P-V, July 1955, Cercle de Sikasso, premier carton, FBPN, ANM.

21. Administrator of Sikasso to Governor of French Soudan, 17 July 1955, premier carton, FBPN, ANM.

22. Ibid.

23. Jeanne Maddox Toungara, "Inventing the African Family: Gender and Family Law Reform in Côte d'Ivoire," *Journal of Social History* 28, no. 1 (1994): 37–61.

24. Roland Colin, *Kènèdougou au crépuscule de l'Afrique coloniale: Mémoires des années cinquante* (Paris: Présence Africaine, 2004), 279.

25. Colin also worked as the chief of staff for Mamadou Dia, the first prime minister of Senegal. Roland Colin, *Sénégal notre pirogue: Au soleil de la liberté: Journal de bord 1955–1980* (Paris: Présence Africaine, 2007).

26. In the early twenty-first century the stone structure still stands at the top of the mamelon and is one of the most important monuments of collective memory in Sikasso. What it symbolizes is debatable, as most people in Sikasso seemed to associate it with Tiéba Traoré rather than the colonial tribunal.

27. Samba v. Konimba, 7 August 1950, *Tribunal de premier degré*, Sikasso cercle archives, unclassified.

28. Kouloutelou v. Koro, 18 September 1950, *Tribunal de premier degré*, Sikasso cercle archives, unclassified.

29. Koné v. Traoré, 21 July 1952, *Tribunal de premier degré*, 1950–53, Sikasso cercle archives, unclassified.

30. James Clifford, "Identity in Mashpee," in *The Predicament of Culture: Twentieth-Century Ethnography, Literature, and Art* (Cambridge, MA: Harvard University Press, 1988), 179–205.

31. Diarra v. Bengali, 21 July 1952, *Tribunal de premier degré*, Sikasso cercle archives, unclassified.

32. Fata v. Nampaga, 25 August 1952, *Tribunal de premier degré*, 1950–53, Sikasso cercle archives, unclassified.

CONCLUSION

1. Robert M. Cover, "Violence and the Word," *Yale Law Journal* 95, no. 8 (1986): 1604.

2. Mahmood Mamdani, *Citizen and Subject: Contemporary Africa and the Legacy of Late Colonialism* (Princeton, NJ: Princeton University Press, 1996).

3. Carole Pateman, "Women and Consent," *Political Theory* 8, no. 2 (1980): 149–68.

4. Philip Nord, *The Republican Moment: Struggles for Democracy in Nineteenth-Century France* (Cambridge, MA: Harvard University Press, 1995); Jeremy Popkin, *A History of Modern France*, 3rd ed. (Upper Sadle River, NJ: Prentice Hall, 2005).

5. Dorothy Hodgson, "'My Daughter . . . Belongs to the Government Now': Marriage, Maasai, and the Tanzanian State," *Canadian Journal of African Studies* 30, no. 1 (1996): 106–23.

Bibliography

ORAL INTERVIEWS — MALI

Note: Information is noted in the following order: name, place, date(s) of interview(s). All interviews were conducted and translated with the assistance of Oumou Sidibé.

Individual Interviews

Cékoura Berté, Kaboïla, 5 March 2005
Jata Coulibaly, Misirikoro, 9 February 2005; 26 February 2005
Coulibaly, Coumba Traoré, Sikasso, 12 February 2005
Salimata Dembélé, Sikasso, 5 February 2005
Drissa Dembélé, M'Pegnesso, 2 March 2005
Seydou Diamoutene, M'Pegnesso, 2 March 2005
Yaya Dow, Kaboïla, 22 March 2005; 30 March 2005; 9 April 2005; 12 April 2005; 16 April 2005; 2 May 2005
Zanga Koné, Kafoziela, 14 February 2005.
Bakary Koné, Sikasso, 1 May 2005
Yacouba Koné, Sikasso, 26 April 2005; 3 May 2005
Aminaya Kouyaté, Sikasso, 12 February 2005
Oumou Sangaré, Sikasso, 14 May 2005
Karissoulé Sanogo, Farakala, 8 April 2005; 15 April 2005
Abdoulaye Traoré, Sikasso, 1 May 2005
Adama Traoré, Madubugu, 21 March 2005
Fousseyni Traoré, Madubugu, 21 March 2005
Mamadou Traoré, Sikasso, 26 April 2005
Mariam Traoré, Sikasso, 1 May 2005
Tenimba, Sikasso, 2 March 2005

Discussion groups

Note: Discussion groups were composed of people who were willing to talk with Oumou Sidibé and me about the research project, but who felt uncomfortable doing so in a one-on-one setting and wished to remain anonymous. Most groups were divided along gender lines, though the youth discussion in Sikasso was composed of men and women in their twenties.

The Kafozela discussion group was a multigenerational group of men and women who lived in neighboring compounds of the same village.

Women's discussion group, Gongasso, 12 February 2005
Multigender discussion group, Kafozela, 14 February 2005
Women's discussion group, Madubugu, 21 March 2005
Women's discussion group, Misirikoro, 4 March 2005
Men's discussion group, M'Pegnesso, 2 March 2005
Women's discussion group, M'Pegnesso, 2 March 2005
Youth discussion group, Sikasso, 10 February 2005

ARCHIVAL SOURCES

Mali

ARCHIVES NATIONALES DU MALI (ANM), BAMAKO, MALI. FONDS ANCIENS (FA), FONDS RÉCENTS (FR)

Fonds Anciens

Series D
1D 2 Etude sur la captivité au Soudan par A. Grodet, 1894
1D 5 Notice Générale sur le Soudan—Notice sur la region Sud, 1895–99
1D 22 Notice sur la formation historique et la constitution administrative de la Colonie du Haut-Sénégal-Niger, 1905
1D 37 Monographies du cercle de Bougouni, 1907–55
1D 45 Monographies du cercle de Koutiala, no date (n.d.)
1D 58 Monographies du cercle de Sikasso, 1895 and 1916
1D 76 Note sur l'Organisation de la famille en Pays Bambara—Coutume Bambara-Musulman, n.d.
1D 77 Note sur les événements auxquels ont donné lieu les opérations contre Samory, 1898
1D 179 Notice sur la Côte d'Ivoire, 1908
1D 189 Coutoumier Bambara du cercle de Bougouni, 1932
1D 197 Etude sur la mise engage des personnes dans la coutume Senufo, 1937
1D 198 Enquête sur l'organisation de la famille les fiancailles et le mariage, cercle de Koutiala, 1910
1D 208 Memoire sur le divorce, Cercle de Sikasso, 1937
1D 210 Rapport sur la traite des femmes et des enfants, 1934
2D 103 Correspondances, Affaires Administratives, Cercle de Sikasso, 1903–17
2D 108 Correspondances avec le Côte d'Ivoire, 1907–10
2D 173 Rapport administratif, Cercle de Bougouni, 1907
2D 180 Rapport administratif, Cercle de Koutiala, 1905
2D 214 Procès Verbal de remise de Commandement, Cercle de Sikasso, 1905
2D 238 Statistiques de l'organisation, Administrative, Cercle de Sikasso, 1914
5D 82 Recensement statistique de la population, Cercle de Sikasso, 1905–14

Series E

1E 73 Rapports Politiques, Sikasso.
4E 25 Correspondances avec les cercles, Sikasso, 1905
1E 156 Rapports sur la pression de la Traite des Esclaves dans le Haute Sénégal Niger, 1894–1904

Series G

1G 322 Monographie du Cercle de Sikasso, n.d.

Series M

1M 10 Correspondances, Sikasso, 1913–17
2M 93 Rapport sur le fonctionnement de la justice indigène, Sikasso, 1905–20
2M 144 Etat des jugements et extraits des registres d'ecrou, Sikasso, 1902–20
2M 296 Justice Réclamations/Requêtes, Sikasso, 1909–20
2M 427 Statistique judiciaires, Sikasso, 1907–14

Series Q

1Q 84 Sikasso, Rapports commerciaux, 1899–1919

Fonds Récents

Series E

1E 41 Rapports politiques, Sikasso, 1923, 1941–23
2E 59 Fiches de renseignments, chefs de canton, Sikasso, 1908–55
2E 143 Correspondances générales au sujet des chefs de canton, Cercle de Sikasso, 1926–1959

Series M

2M 263 Notice des Jugements rendus, Sikasso, 1932–44

Series Q

1Q 360 Rapport économique cercle de Sikasso 1921–45

Fonds Bureau Politique Nationale

Premier Carton

1–4e Congrès de l'USRDA 1955

Sikasso cercle Archives, Office of the Prefecture, Sikasso.

Note: Some of the documents and files contained within the Sikasso archives were classified in labeled cartons and are thus noted below. However, some of the archives, such as court cases, were not classified.

D 2D/1 Notes sur les chefs du canton, divers, 1948–57
2C/4 Enquêtes-concession rural, questions diverses, 1905–52
Registre des jugements: matière civile et commerciale, 1919–27, unclassified

Registre des jugements: matière civile et commerciale, Tribunal de 1e degré de Sikasso, 1935–40, unclassified

Registre des jugements: matiers civile et commerciale, Trib. de 1e degré de Sikasso, June 1950–March 1953, unclassified

Dossier—Commandant de Sikasso to Monsieur le Procureur de la République à Bamako, August 1948, unclassified

Sénégal

Archives Nationales du Sénégal (ANS), Dakar, Sénégal. Archives de l'Afrique Occidentale Française (ANS-AOF)

1D 137 Archinard, Rapport de campagne, 1892–93
1G 146 Mission du Capitaine Quiquandon dans le Kénédougou, 1890
18G 2 Trentinian, L'organisation d'un gouvernment-général de l'AOF, 1899

Italy

Archives de la Société des Missionaires d'Afrique, Pères Blancs (APB), Rome, Italy

N 49/5 Anonyme, "Le probleme des chefs dans le cercle de Sikasso," 1950

France

Archives Nationales—Section d'Outre Mer (ANSOM), Aix-en-Provence, France

Fonds Ministérielles (FM)

FM/1affpol/540/1–4 Mariage indigène, affaire Sangalan, mise en gage, 1935–38
FM 61/1affpol/3349/8 Situation Politique de la Femme Africaine, 1939, 1951
FM/1affpol/3658 Mariage Coutumier, Survey on African Marriage and Family Life, 1949–52
AP/2/966

PUBLISHED AND UNPUBLISHED SOURCES

Allman, Jean, Susan Geiger, and Nakanyike Musisi, eds. *Women in African Colonial Histories.* Bloomington: Indiana University Press, 2002.

Allman, Jean, and Victoria Tashjian. *"I Will Not Eat Stone": A Women's History of Colonial Asante.* Portsmouth, NH: Heinemann, 2000.

Amselle, Jean-Loup. *Mestizo Logics: Anthropology of Identity in Africa and Elsewhere.* Stanford: Stanford University Press, 1998.

———. *Negoçiants de la Savanne: Histoire et organisation sociale des Kooroko (Mali).* Paris: Editions Anthropos, 1977.

Amselle, Jean-Loup, and Elikia M'Bokolo, eds. *Au coeur de l'ethnie.* Paris: Édition La Découverte, 1985.

Amselle, Jean-Loup, and Emmanuelle Sibeud, eds. *Maurice Delafosse: Entre oriental-isme et ethnographie: L'itinéraire d'un africaniste, 1870–1926*. Paris: Maisonneuve et Larose, 1998.

André, Théodore. "Le Droit Privé des Sénéfo du Kénédougou (Cercle de Sikasso)." Doctoral thesis, University of Bordeaux, 1913.

Aubert, A. *Coutumière Juridique de l'Afrique Occidentale Française*, vols. 1–2. Paris: Larose, 1939.

Austen, Ralph, ed. *In Search of Sunjata: The Mande Epic as History, Literature, and Performance*. Bloomington: Indiana University Press, 1999.

Bâ, Amadou Hampaté, and Jacques Daget. *L'Empire Peul de Macina*. Koulouba: Institut Français d'Afrique Noire, Centre du Soudan, 1955.

Barnett, Michael. *Empire of Humanity: A History of Humanitarianism*. Ithaca, NY: Cornell University Press, 2011.

Bassett, Thomas. *The Peasant Cotton Revolution in West Africa: Côte d'Ivoire, 1880–1995*. Cambridge: Cambridge University Press, 2001.

Bay, Edna. *Wives of the Leopard*. Charlottesville: University of Virginia Press, 1998.

Bay, Edna, ed. *Women and Work in Africa*. Boulder, CO: Westview, 1982.

Bayart, Jean-François. *L'état en Afrique: La politique du ventre*. Paris: Fayard, 1989.

Bazin, Jean. "À chacun son Bambara." In *Au coeur de l'ethnie*, edited by Jean-Loup Amselle and Elikia M'Bokolo, 87–127. Paris: Édition La Découverte, 1985.

———. "Guerre et servitude à Ségou." In *L'Esclavage en Afrique précoloniale*, edited by Claude Meillassoux, 135–81. Paris: François Maspero, 1975.

Benton, Lauren. *Law and Colonial Cultures: Legal Regimes in World History, 1400–1900*. Cambridge: Cambridge University Press, 2002.

Berger, Iris. *Threads of Solidarity: Women in South African Industry, 1900–1980*. Bloomington: Indiana University Press, 1992.

Berk-Seligson, Susan. *The Bilingual Courtroom: Court Interpreters in the Judicial Process*. Chicago: University of Chicago Press, 1990.

Bernault, Florence, ed. *Enfermement, prison et châtiment en Afrique du XIXe siècle à nos jours*. Paris: Karthala, 1999.

Berry, Sara. *No Condition Is Permanent: The Social Dynamics of Agrarian Change in Sub-Saharan Africa*. Madison: University of Wisconsin Press, 1993.

Berté, Oumar. "Memorial de Kélétigui Berté." In Roland Colin, *Kènèdougou au crépuscule de l'Afrique coloniale: Mémoires des années cinquantes*, 359–83. Paris: Présence Africaine, 2004.

Betts, Raymond. *Assimilation and Association in French Colonial Theory, 1890–1914*. Lincoln: University of Nebraska Press, 1960.

Beurdeley, E. *La justice indigène en Afrique occidentale française: Mission d'études, 1913–1914*. Paris: Publication de la Comité de l'Afrique Française, 1916.

Binger, Louis Gustave. *Du Niger au Golfe de Guinée par le pays de Kong et le Mossi*. 2 vols. (1887–89). Paris: Hachette, 1892.

———. *Une vie d'explorateur: Souvenirs extraits des carnets de route*. Paris: F. Sorlot, 1938.

Bledsoe, Caroline. *Women and Marriage in Kpelle Society* (Stanford: Stanford University Press, 1980.

Bledsoe, Caroline, and Gilles Pison, eds. *Nuptiality in Sub-Saharan Africa: Contemporary Anthropological and Demographic Perspectives*. Oxford: Clarendon Press, 1994.

Boddy, Janice. "Clash of Selves: Gender, Personhood, and Human Rights Discourse in Modern Sudan." *Canadian Journal of African Studies* 41, no. 3 (2007): 402–26.

Bogosian, Catherine Mornane. "Forced Labor, Resistance, and Memory: The *deuxième portion* in the French Soudan, 1926–1950." PhD diss., University of Pennsylvania, 2002.

Bohannan, Paul. "Some Principles of Exchange and Investment among the Tiv." *American Anthropologist* 57, no. 1 (1955): 60–70.

Boserup, Ester. *Woman's Role in Economic Development*. London: George Allen and Unwin, 1970.

Boxer, Marilyn, and Jean Quataert, eds. *Connecting Spheres: European Women in a Globalizing World, 1500 to the Present*. 2nd ed. New York: Oxford University Press, 2000.

Boye, Abd-el Kadr, Kathleen Hill, Stephen Isaacs, and Deborah Gordis. "Marriage Law and Practice in the Sahel." *Studies in Family Planning* 22, no. 6 (1991): 343–49.

Brenner, Louis. *Controlling Knowledge: Religion, Power, and Schooling in a West African Muslim Society*. Bloomington: Indiana University Press, 2001.

Brévié, Jules. *Islamisme contre "Naturisme"au Soudan Français. Essai de psychologie politique, coloniale*. Paris: Éditions Ernest Leroux, 1923.

———. *La politique et l'administration indigène en Afrique Occidentale Française*. Gorée: Imprimerie du Gouvernement Général, 1935.

Brooks, George. *Landlords and Strangers: Ecology, Society, and Trade in Western Africa, 1000–1630*. Boulder, CO: Westview Press, 1993.

Bruijn, Mirjam de. "The Hearthhold in Pastoral Fulbe Society, Central Mali: Social Relations, Milk, and Drought." *Africa: Journal of the International African Institute* 67, no. 4 (1997): 625–51.

Bumiller, Kristin. "Fallen Angels: The Representation of Violence against Women in Legal Culture." In *At the Boundaries of the Law: Feminism and the Legal Theory*, edited by Martha Fineman and Nancy Thomadsen, 95–112. New York: Routledge, 1991.

Burrill, Emily S. "Disputing Wife Abuse: Tribunal Narratives of the Corporal Punishment of Wives in Colonial Sikasso, 1930s." *Cahiers d'études africaines* 187–88 (2007): 603–22.

———. "'Wives of Circumstance': Gender and Slave Emancipation in Late Nineteenth-Century Senegal." *Slavery and Abolition* 29, no. 1 (2008): 49–63.

Burrill, Emily S., Richard L. Roberts, and Elizabeth Thornberry, eds. *Domestic Violence and the Law in Colonial and Postcolonial Africa*. Athens: Ohio University Press, 2010.

Byfield, Judith. "Women, Marriage, Divorce, and the Emerging Colonial State in Abeokuta (Nigeria), 1892–1904." *Canadian Journal of African Studies* 30 (1996): 32–51. Reprinted in *"Wicked" Women and the Reconfiguration of Gender in Africa*, edited by Dorothy Hodgson and Sheryl McCurdy, 27–46. Portsmouth, NH: Heinemann, 2001.

Caillié, René. *Travels through Central Africa to Timbuktoo*, vol. 2. London: Colburn and Bentley, 1830.

———. *Voyage à Tombouctou*. 2 vols. Paris: François Maspero, 1979. Reprint edition of *Journal d'un voyage à Temboctou et à Djenné dans l'Afrique centrale*. Paris: L'Imprimerie Royale, 1830.

Carney, Judith. *Black Rice: The African Origins of Rice Cultivation in the Americas*. Cambridge, MA: Harvard University Press, 2002.

Chanock, Martin. *Law, Custom, and Social Order: The Colonial Experience in Malawi and Zambia.* Cambridge: Cambridge University Press, 1985.

———. "A Peculiar Sharpness: An Essay on Property in the History of Customary Law in Colonial Law." *Journal of African History* 32, no. 1 (1991): 65–88.

Christelow, Allen. *Muslim Law Courts and the French Colonial State in Algeria.* Princeton, NJ: Princeton University Press, 1985.

Clancy-Smith, Julia. *Rebel and Saint: Muslim Notables, Populist Protest, Colonial Encounters (Algeria and Tunisia, 1800–1914).* Berkeley: University of California Press, 1997.

Clifford, James. *The Predicament of Culture: Twentieth-Century Ethnography, Literature, and Art.* Cambridge, MA: Harvard University, 1988.

Cmiel, Kenneth. "The Recent History of Human Rights." *American Historical Review* 109, no. 1 (2004): 117–35.

Cohen, David William. "Doing Social History from Pim's Doorway." In *Reliving the Past: The Worlds of Social History,* edited by Olivier Zunz and David William Cohen, 191–236. Chapel Hill: University of North Carolina Press, 1985.

Cohen, David William, Stephan F. Miescher, and Luise White. "Introduction: Voices, Words, and African History." In *African Words, African Voices: Critical Practices in Oral History,* edited by Luise White, Stephan F. Miescher, and David William Cohen, 1–27. Bloomington: Indiana University Press, 2001.

Cohen, William. *Rulers of Empire: The French Colonial Service in Africa.* Stanford: Hoover Institution Press, 1971.

Cole, Catherine M., Takyiwaa Manuh, and Stephan F. Miescher, eds. *Africa after Gender?* Bloomington: Indiana University Press, 2007.

Colin, Roland. *Kènèdougou au crépuscule de l'Afrique coloniale: Mémoires des années cinquantes.* Paris: Présence Africaine, 2004.

———. *Sénégal notre pirogue: Au soleil de la liberté: Journal de bord 1955–1980.* Paris: Présence Africaine, 2007.

Colleyn, Jean-Paul, and Danielle Jonckers. "Ceux qui refusent le maître: La conception du pouvoir chez les Minyanka du Mali." *Africa: Journal of the International African Institute* 53, no. 4 (1983): 43–58.

Comaroff, John, ed. *The Meaning of Marriage Payments.* London: Academic Press, 1980.

Conklin, Alice. "Colonialism and Human Rights: A Contradiction in Terms? The Case of France and West Africa, 1895–1914." *American Historical Review* 103, no. 2 (1998): 419–42.

———. *A Mission to Civilize: The Republican Idea of Empire in France and West Africa, 1895–1930.* Stanford: Stanford University Press, 1997.

Conrad, David C., ed. *A State of Intrigue: The Epic of Bamana Segu according to Tayiru Banbera.* Transcribed and translated with the assistance of Soumaila Diakité. Oxford: British Academy, 1990.

Cooper, Barbara. *Marriage in Maradi: Gender and Culture in a Hausa Society in Niger.* Portsmouth, NH: Heinemann, 1997.

———. "Reflections on Slavery, Seclusion, and Female Labor in the Maradi Region of Niger in the Nineteenth and Twentieth Centuries." *Journal of African History* 35, no. 1 (1994): 61–78.

———. "Women's Worth and Wedding Gift Exchange in Maradi, Niger: 1907–1989." *Journal of African History* 36, no. 1 (1995): 121–40.

Cooper, Frederick. *Africa since 1940: The Past of the Present.* Cambridge: Cambridge University Press, 2002.

———. "Conflict and Connection: Rethinking Colonial African History." *American Historical Review* 99, no. 5 (December 1994): 1516–45.

———. *Decolonization and African Society: The Labor Question in French and British Africa.* Cambridge: Cambridge University Press, 2002.

———. "'Our Strike': Equality, Anti-Colonial Politics, and the 1947–48 Railway Strike in French West Africa." *Journal of African History* 37, no. 1 (1996): 81–118.

Cooper, Frederick, Thomas Holt, and Rebecca Scott, eds. *Beyond Slavery: Explorations of Race, Labor, and Citizenship in Post-Emancipation Societies.* Durham, NC: Duke University Press, 2000.

Cooper, Frederick, and Ann Stoler, eds. *Tensions of Empire: Colonial Cultures in a Bourgeois World.* Berkeley: University of California Press, 1997.

Cott, Nancy. *Public Vows: A History of Marriage and the Nation.* Cambridge, MA: Harvard University Press, 2002.

Crowder, Michael. *The Flogging of Phinehas McIntosh: A Tale of Colonial Folly and Injustice: Bechuanaland, 1933.* New Haven, CT: Yale University Press, 1988.

Coulibaly, Sinali. *Le paysan Sénoufo.* Abidjan-Dakar: Nouvelles Éditions Africaines, 1978.

de Benoist, Joseph-Roger. *Eglise et pouvoir colonial au Soudan français: Administrateurs et missionaires dans la Boucle du Niger (1885–1945).* Paris: Karthala, 1987.

Delafosse, Maurice. "Étude préparatoire d'un programme de measures à prendre en vue d'améliorer la situation des indigènes au double point de administrative et social." May 1919. Reprinted in Marc Michel, "Un programme réformiste en 1919: Maurice Delafosse et la 'politique indigène' in AOF." *Cahiers d' études africaines* 15, no. 58 (1975): 313–27.

———. *Haut-Sénégal-Niger,* vols. 1–3. Paris: Maisonneuve, 1972.

———. *Les Nègres.* Paris: Editions Rieder, 1927.

———. *Les Noirs de l'Afrique.* Paris: Payot and Cie., 1922.

de l'Afrique. Paris: Payot and Cie., 1922.

Desan, Suzanne. *The Family on Trial in Revolutionary France.* Berkeley: University of California Press, 2004.

Dobkin, Marlene. "Colonialism and the Legal Status of Women in Francophonic Africa." *Cahiers d'études africaines* 8, no. 3 (1968): 390–405.

Duran, Lucy. "Ngaraya: Women and Musical Mastery in Mali." *Bulletin of the School of Oriental and African Studies, University of London* 70, no. 3 (2007): 569–602.

Echenberg, Myron. *Colonial Conscripts: The Tirailleurs Sénégalais in French West Africa.* Portsmouth, NH: Heinemann, 1991.

Echenberg, Myron, and Jean Filipovich. "African Military Labour and the Building of the *Office du Niger* Installations, 1920–1950." *Journal of African History* 27, no. 3 (1986): 533–51.

Englund, Harri. *Prisoners of Freedom: Human Rights and the African Poor.* Berkeley: University of California Press, 2006.

Fahmy, Khaled. "The Anatomy of Justice: Forensic Medicine and Criminal Law in Nineteenth-Century Egypt." *Islamic Law and Society* 6, no. 2 (1999): 224–71.

Fallers, Lloyd. *Law without Precedent: Legal Ideas in Action in the Courts of Colonial Basoga.* Chicago: University of Chicago Press, 1969.

Falola, Toyin, and Paul Lovejoy, eds. *Pawnship in Africa: Debt Bondage in Historical Perspective.* Boulder, CO: Westview Press, 1994.

Ferme, Mariane. *The Underneath of Things: Violence, History, and the Everyday in Sierra Leone*. Berkeley: University of California Press, 2001.

Fineman, Martha, and Nancy Thomadsen, eds. *At the Boundaries of the Law: Feminism and Legal Theory*. New York: Routledge, 1991.

Finnis, John. *Natural Law and Natural Rights*. New York: Oxford University Press, 1980.

Gallieni, Joseph. *Deux campagnes au Soudan Français, 1886–1888*. Paris: Librairie Hachette, 1891.

Gann, L. H., and Peter Duignan, eds. *African Proconsuls: European Governors in Africa*. New York: Free Press, 1978.

Geiger, Susan. "Women's Life Histories: Method and Content." *Signs* 11, no. 2 (1986): 334–51.

Genova, James. "Conflicted Missions: Power and Identity in French West Africa during the 1930s." *Historian* 66, no. 1 (March 2004): 45–66.

Getz, Trevor. *Slavery and Reform in West Africa: Toward Emancipation in Nineteenth-Century Senegal and Gold Coast*. Athens: Ohio University Press, 2004.

Giles-Vernick, Tamara. "Lives, Histories, and Sites of Recollection." In *African Words, African Voices: Critical Practices in Oral History*, edited by Luise White, Stephan F. Miescher, and David William Cohen, 194–213. Bloomington: Indiana University Press, 2001.

Glassman, Jonathon. *Feasts and Riot: Revelry, Rebellion, and Popular Consciousness on the Swahili Coast, 1856–1888*. Portsmouth, NH: Heinemann, 1995.

Glaze, Anita. *Art and Death in a Senufo Village*. Bloomington: Indiana University Press, 1981.

———. "Dialectics of Gender in Senufo Masquerades." *African Arts* 19, no. 3 (1986): 30–39, 82.

———. "Women and Power in a Senufo Village." *African Arts* 8, no. 3 (1975): 24–29, 64–68, 90.

Grosz-Ngaté, Maria. "Monetization of Bridewealth and the Abandonment of 'Kin Roads' to Marriage in Sana, Mali." *American Ethnologist* 15, no. 3 (1988): 501–14.

Grosz-Ngaté, Maria, and Omari H. Kokole, eds. *Gendered Encounters: Challenging Cultural Boundaries and Social Hierarchies in Africa*. New York: Routledge, 1997.

Gutman, Herbert. *The Black Family in Slavery and Freedom, 1750–1925*. New York: Vintage, 1977.

Guyer, Jane. "Household and Community in African Studies." *African Studies Review* 24, no. 2/3 (1981): 87–137.

———. "Lineal Identities and Lateral Networks: The Logic of Polyandrous Motherhood." In *Nuptiality in Sub-Saharan Africa: Contemporary Anthropological and Demographic Perspectives*, edited by Caroline Bledsoe and Gilles Pison, 231–52. Oxford: Clarendon Press, 1994.

———, ed. *Money Matters: Instability, Values, and Social Payments in the Modern History of West African Communities*. Portsmouth, NH: Heinemann, 1995.

———. "Wealth in People and Self-Realization in Equatorial Africa." *Man* 28, no. 2 (1993): 243–65.

Guyer, Jane, and Samuel Eno Belinga. "Wealth in People as Wealth in Knowledge: Accumulation and Composition in Equatorial Africa." *Journal of African History* 36, no. 1 (1995): 91–120.

Hale, Thomas. "Griottes: Female Voices from West Africa." *Research in African Literatures* 25, no. 3 (1994): 71–91.

Hall, Bruce S. *A History of Race in Muslim West Africa, 1600–1960.* Cambridge: Cambridge University Press, 2011.

Hanretta, Sean. *Islam and Social Change in French West Africa: History of an Emancipatory Community.* Cambridge: Cambridge University Press, 2009.

Hanson, John. *Migration, Jihad, and Muslim Authority in West Africa: The Futanke Colonies in Karta.* Bloomington: Indiana University Press, 1996.

Harrison, Christopher. *France and Islam in Africa, 1860–1960.* Cambridge: Cambridge University Press, 1988.

Haut Commisariat de l'Afrique Française. *La justice indigène en Afrique Occidentale Française.* Rufisque: Imprimerie du Haut Commissariat, 1941.

Hawkins, Sean. "'The Woman in Question': Marriage and Identity in the Colonial Courts of Northern Ghana, 1907–1954." In *Women in African Colonial Histories,* edited by Jean Allman, Susan Geiger, and Nakanyike Musisi, 116–43. Bloomington: Indiana University Press, 2002.

———. *Writing and Colonialism in Northern Ghana: The Encounter between the LoDagaa and the "World on Paper."* Toronto: University of Toronto Press, 2002.

Hay, Margaret Jean. "Queens, Prostitutes, and Peasants: Historical Perspectives on African Women, 1971–1986." *Canadian Journal of African Studies* 22 (1988): 431–47.

Hay, Margaret Jean, and Marcia Wright, eds. *African Women and the Law: Historical Perspectives.* Boston: Boston University African Studies Center, 1982.

Henige, David. *The Chronology of Oral Tradition.* Oxford: Oxford University Press, 1974.

Hirsch, Susan. *Pronouncing and Persevering: Gender and Discourses of Disputing in an African Islamic Court.* Chicago: University of Chicago Press, 1998.

Hodgson, Dorothy, ed. *Gender and Culture at the Limit of Rights.* Philadelphia: University of Pennsylvania Press, 2011.

———, ed. *Gendered Modernities: Ethnographic Perspectives.* New York: Palgrave, 2001.

———. "'My Daughter . . . Belongs to the Government Now': Marriage, Maasai, and the Tanzanian State." *Canadian Journal of African Studies* 30, no. 1 (1996): 106–23.

Hodgson, Dorothy, and Sheryl McCurdy, eds. *"Wicked" Women and the Reconfiguration of Gender in Africa.* Portsmouth, NH: Heinemann, 2001.

Holas, Bohumil. *Les Sénoufo (y compris les Minianka).* Paris: Presses Universitaires de France, 1966.

Holmes, LeVell. "Tieba Traore, Fama of Kenedougou: Two Decades of Political Development, 1873–1893." PhD diss., University of California, Berkeley, 1972.

Hunt, Lynn. *Inventing Human Rights: A History.* New York: W. W. Norton, 2008.

Hunt, Nancy Rose. Introduction to *Gendered Colonialisms in African History,* edited by Nancy Rose Hunt, Tessie P. Liu, and Jean Quataert, 1–10. Malden, MA: Blackwell, 1997.

Hunwick, John. *Shari'a in Songhay: The Replies of al-Maghili to the Questions of Askia al-Hajj Muhammad.* Oxford: Oxford University Press, 1985.

———. *Timbuktu and the Songhay Empire: Al-Sadi's "Tarikh al-Sudan" down to 1613 and Other Contemporary Documents.* Leiden: Brill, 1999.

Hynd, Stacey. "Imperial Gallows: Capital Punishment, Violence, and Colonial Rule in Britain's African Territories, c. 1908–68." DPhil diss., Oxford University, 2007.

Integrated Regional Information Networks (IRIN). *Mali: Back to the Drawing Board for New Family Code*, 1 September 2009. http://www.unhcr.org/refworld/docid/4aa0c1941a.html.

Jeppie, Shamil, Ebrahim Moosa, and Richard Roberts, eds. *Muslim Family Law in Sub-Saharan Africa: Colonial Legacies and Post-Colonial Challenges.* Amsterdam: Amsterdam University Press, 2010.

Johnson, G. Wesley, Jr. *The Emergence of Black Politics in Senegal: The Struggle for Power in the Four Communes, 1900–1920.* Stanford: Stanford University Press, 1971.

———. "William Ponty and Republican Paternalism in French West Africa, 1866–1915." In *African Proconsuls: European Governors in Africa*, edited by L. H. Gann and Peter Duignan, 127–56. New York: Free Press, 1978.

Jones, Jacqueline. *Labor of Love, Labor of Sorrow: Black Women, Work, and Family from Slavery to the Present.* New York: Basic Books, 1985.

Kandiyoti, Deniz. "Bargaining with Patriarchy." *Gender and Society* 2, no. 3 (1988): 274–90.

Kanya-Forstner, A. S. *The Conquest of the Western Sudan: A Study in French Military Imperialism.* Cambridge: Cambridge University Press, 1969.

Karma, Weybi. "Stop Crying Bride." In *Women's Voices from West Africa*, edited and translated by Aissata G. Sidikou and Thomas A. Hale, 47. Bloomington: Indiana University Press, 2012.

Khalil ibn Ishaq al-Jundi. *Maliki Law: Being a Summary from French Translations of the Mukhtasar of Sidi Khalil: With Notes and Bibliography.* Westport, CT: Hyperion Press, 1980.

Kimble, Sara. "Emancipation through Secularization: French Feminist Views of Muslim Women's Conditions in Interwar Algeria." *French Colonial History* 7 (2006): 109–28.

Klein, Martin. "Defensive Strategies: Wasulu, Masina, and the Slave Trade." In *Fighting the Slave Trade: West African Strategies*, edited by Sylviane Diouf, 62–78. Athens: Ohio University Press, 2003.

———. *Slavery and Colonial Rule in French West Africa.* Cambridge: Cambridge University Press, 1998.

———. "Women in Slavery in the Western Sudan." In *Women and Slavery in Africa*, edited by Claire C. Robertson and Martin A. Klein, 67–94. Madison: University of Wisconsin Press, 1983.

Klein, Martin, and Richard Roberts. "The Resurgence of Pawning in French West Africa during the Depression of the 1930s." *African Economic History* 16 (1987): 23–37.

Kodjo, Georges Niamkey. *Le Royaume de Kong, Côte d'Ivoire: Des origines à la fin du XIXème siècle.* Paris: Harmattan, 2006.

Konaré, Alpha Oumar. *Sikasso Tata.* Bamako: Editions Jamana, 1983.

Lacouture, Jean. *De Gaulle: The Ruler, 1945–1970.* Translated by Alan Sheridan. New York: Norton, 1992.

Launay, Robert. *Beyond the Stream: Islam and Society in a West African Town.* Berkeley: University of California Press, 1992.

———. "Landlords, Hosts, and Strangers among the Dyula." *Ethnology* 18, no. 1 (1979): 71–83.

———. "Stereotypic Vision: The 'Moral Character' of the Senufo in Colonial and Post-Colonial Discourse." *Cahiers d'études africaines* 54, no. 154 (1999): 271–92.

————. *Traders without Trade: Responses to Change in Two Dyula Communities.* Cambridge: Cambridge University Press, 1982.

————. "Tying the Cola: Dyula Marriage and Social Change." PhD diss., Cambridge University, 1975.

Lawrance, Benjamin, Emily Osborn, and Richard Roberts, eds. *Intermediaries, Interpreters, and Clerks: African Employees and the Making of Colonial Africa.* Madison: University of Wisconsin Press, 2006.

Lévi-Strauss, Claude. *The Savage Mind.* Chicago: University of Chicago Press, 1968.

Levtzion, Nehemia. *Ancient Ghana and Mali.* New York: Africana, 1980.

Lindsay, Lisa, and Stephan Miescher, eds. *Men and Masculinities in Modern Africa.* Portsmouth, NH: Heinemann, 2003.

Lovejoy, Paul E. *Transformations in Slavery: A History of Slavery in Africa.* 2nd ed. Cambridge: Cambridge University Press, 2000.

————. "Concubinage and the Status of Women Slaves in Early Colonial Nineteenth-Century Northern Nigeria." *Journal of African History* 29, no. 2 (1988): 245–66.

Lovejoy, Paul E., and A. S. Kanya-Forstner, eds. *Slavery and Its Abolition in French West Africa.* Madison: University of Wisconsin Press, 1994.

Lovejoy, Paul, and David Richardson. "The Business of Slaving: Pawnship in Western Africa, c. 1600–1810." *Journal of African History* 42, no. 1 (2001): 67–89.

Lunn, Joe. *Memoirs of the Maelstrom: A Senegalese Oral History of the First World War.* Portsmouth, NH: Heinemann, 1999.

Lydon, Ghislaine. "Obtaining Freedom at the Muslims' Tribunal: Colonial Kadijustiz and Women's Divorce Litigation in Ndar (Senegal)." In *Muslim Family Law in Sub-Saharan Africa: Colonial Legacies and Post-Colonial Challenges,* edited by Shamil Jeppie, Ibrahim Moosa, and Richard Roberts, 135–64. Amsterdam: Amsterdam University Press, 2010.

————. *On Trans-Saharan Trails: Islamic Law, Trade Networks, and Cross-Cultural Exchange in Nineteenth-Century Western Africa.* Cambridge: Cambridge University Press, 2010.

————. "Writing Trans-Saharan History: Methods, Sources, and Interpretations across the African Divide." *Journal of North African Studies* 10, no. 3–4 (2005): 293–324.

Mahmood, Saba. *The Politics of Piety: The Islamic Revival and the Feminist Subject.* Princeton, NJ: Princeton University Press, 2005.

Majumdar, Rochona. *Marriage and Modernity: Family Values in Colonial Bengal.* Durham, NC: Duke University Press, 2009.

Mali, Joseph. *Mythistory: The Making of a Modern Historiography.* Chicago: University of Chicago Press, 2003.

Malkki, Liisa. *Purity and Exile.* Chicago: University of Chicago Press, 1995.

Mamdani, Mahmood. *Citizen and Subject: Contemporary Africa and the Legacy of Late Colonialism.* Princeton, NJ: Princeton University Press, 1996.

Mani, Lata. *Contentious Traditions: The Debate on Sati in Colonial India.* Berkeley: University of California Press, 1998.

Mann, Gregory. *Native Sons: West African Veterans and France in the Twentieth Century.* Durham, NC: Duke University Press, 2006.

————. "What Was the *Indigénat?* The 'Empire of Law' in French West Africa." *Journal of African History* 50 (2009): 331–53.

Mann, Kristin. *Marrying Well: Marriage, Status, and Social Change among the Educated Elite in Colonial Lagos.* Cambridge: Cambridge University Press, 1985.

Mann, Kristin, and Richard Roberts, eds. *Law in Colonial Africa*. Portsmouth, NH: Heinemann, 1991.

Marty, Paul. *Études sur l'Islam et les tribus du Soudan*. Paris: Editions Ernest Leroux, 1920.

Mauss, Marcel. *The Gift: The Form and Reason for Exchange in Archaic Societies*. London: Cohen and West, 1954.

Mbilinyi, Marjorie. "Runaway Wives in Colonial Tanganyika: Forced Labour and Forced Marriage in Rungwe District, 1919–1961." *International Journal of the Sociology of Law* 16 (1988): 1–29.

McClendon, Thomas. *Genders and Generations Apart: Labor Tenants and Customary Law in Segregation Era South Africa, 1920s–1940s*. Portsmouth, NH: Heinemann, 2002.

McDougall, E. Ann. "A Sense of Self: The Life of Fatma Barka." *Canadian Journal of African Studies* 32, no. 2 (1998): 285–315.

McGovern, Mike. *Making War in Côte d'Ivoire*. Chicago: University of Chicago Press, 2011.

McIntosh, Roderick. *Ancient Middle Niger: Urbanism and the Self-Organizing Landscape*. Cambridge: Cambridge University Press, 2005.

McKittrick, Meredith. "Faithful Daughter, Murdering Mother: Transgression and Social Control in Colonial Namibia." *Journal of African History* 40, no. 2 (1999): 265–83.

McNaughton, Patrick R. *The Mande Blacksmiths: Knowledge, Power, and Art in West Africa*. Bloomington: Indiana University Press, 1988.

McNeill, William H. *Mythistory and Other Essays*. Chicago: University of Chicago Press, 1986.

Meillassoux, Claude. *Anthropologie de l'esclavage: Le ventre de fer et d'argent*. Paris: Presses Universitaires de France, 1986.

———. "État et conditions des esclaves à Gumbu (Mali) au XIXe siècle," *Journal of African History* 14, no. 3 (1973): 429–52.

Meillassoux, Claude, ed. *L'Esclavage en Afrique précoloniale*. Paris: François Maspero, 1975.

Méniaud, Jacques. *Les pionniers du Soudan, avant, avec, et après Archinard, 1879–1894*. Paris: Société des publications modernes, 1931.

———. *Sikasso, ou, l'histoire dramatique d'un royaume noir au XIXe siècle*. Paris: Bouchy, 1935.

Merle, Isabelle. "Retourdans sur le régime de l'indigénat: Genèse et contradictions des principes répressifs dans l'empire français." *French Politics, Culture, and Society* 20, no. 2 (2002): 77–97.

Michel, Marc. "Un programme réformiste en 1919: Maurice Delafosse et la 'politique indigène' en AOF." *Cahiers d'études africaines* 15, no. 58 (1975): 313–27.

Miers, Suzanne, and Igor Kopytoff, eds. *Slavery in Africa: Historical and Anthropological Perspectives*. Madison: University of Wisconsin Press, 1977.

Miescher, Stephan. *Making Men in Ghana*. Bloomington: Indiana University Press, 2005.

Mikell, Gwendolyn, ed. *African Feminism: The Politics of Survival in Sub-Saharan Africa*. Philadelphia: University of Pennsylvania Press, 1997.

Miller, Joseph. *Way of Death: Merchant Capitalism and the Angolan Slave Trade, 1730–1830*. Madison: University of Wisconsin Press, 1988.

Mojab, Shahrzad. "'Honor Killing': Culture, Politics, Theory." *Middle East Women's Studies Review* 17, nos. 1–2 (2002): 1–7.

Monteil, Charles. *Les Bambaras de Ségou et du Kaarta.* Paris: Maisonneuve, 1924.

Moore, Donald, and Richard Roberts. "Listening for the Silences." *History in Africa* 17 (1990): 319–25.

Morris, H. F. "Native Courts: A Corner-Stone of Indirect Rule." In *Indirect Rule and the Search for Justice: Essays in East African Legal History,* edited by H. F. Morris and James Read, 131–66. Oxford: Oxford University Press, 1972.

Morsink, Johannes. *The Universal Declaration of Human Rights: Origins, Drafting, and Intent.* Philadelphia: University of Pennsylvania Press, 2000.

Moyn, Samuel. *The Last Utopia: Human Rights in History.* Cambridge, MA: Harvard University Press, 2010.

Nader, Laura. *Harmony Ideology: Justice and Control in a Zapotec Mountain Village.* Stanford: Stanford University Press, 1991.

Newbury, C. W. "The Formation of the Government General in French West Africa." *Journal of African History* 1, no. 1 (1960): 111–28.

Niakate, Moussa. "Quatre Royaume au Soudan Français." Unpublished manuscript, 1982.

Nord, Philip. *The Republican Moment: Struggles for Democracy in Nineteenth-Century France.* Cambridge, MA: Harvard University Press, 1995.

Offen, Karen. "Feminism, Antifeminism, and National Family Politics in Early Third Republic France." In *Connecting Spheres: European Women in a Globalizing World, 1500 to the Present,* edited by Marilyn Boxer and Jean Quataert. New York: Oxford University Press, 2000.

Osborn, Emily Lynn. *Our New Husbands Are Here: Households, Gender, and Politics in a West African State from the Slave Trade to Colonial Rule.* Athens: Ohio University Press, 2011.

O'Sullivan, John. "Slavery in the Malinke Kingdom of Kabadougou (Ivory Coast)." *International Journal of African Studies* 13, no. 4 (1980): 633–50.

Oxfam International. http://www.oxfam.org/en/about/issues/gender.

Oyéwùmí, Oyèrónké. *The Invention of African Women: Making an African Sense of Western Gender Discourse.* Minneapolis: University of Minnesota Press, 1997.

———, ed. *African Gender Studies: A Reader.* New York: Palgrave, 2005.

Paques, Viviana. "Bouffons Sacres du Cercle de Bougouni (Soudan Français)." *Journal de la Société des Africanistes* 24, no. 1 (1954): 63–110.

Parpart, Jane. "Where Is Your Mother? Gender, Urban Marriage, and Colonial Discourse on the Zambian Copperbelt, 1924–1945." *Canadian Journal of African Historical Studies* 27, no. 2 (1994): 241–47.

Pateman, Carole. "Women and Consent." *Political Theory* 8, no. 2 (1980): 149–68.

Paton, Diana, and Pamela Scully. "Introduction: Gender and Slave Emancipation in Comparative Perspective." In *Gender and Slave Emancipation in the Atlantic World,* edited by Pamela Scully and Diana Paton, 1–34. Durham, NC: Duke University Press, 2005.

Perinbam, B. Marie. *Family Identity and the State in the Bamako Kafu, c. 1800–c. 1900.* Boulder, CO: Westview Press, 1997.

Person, Yves. *Samori: Une révolution dyula.* Vols. 1–3. Paris: IFAN, 1970.

Peterson, Brian. *Islamization from Below: The Making of Muslim Communities in Rural French Sudan, 1880–1960.* New Haven, CT: Yale University Press, 2011.

————. "Slave Emancipation, Trans-Local Social Processes and the Spread of Islam in French Colonial Buguni (Southern Mali), 1893–1914." *Journal of African History* 45, no. 3 (2004): 421–24.

Pierce, Steven, and Anapuma Rao, eds. *Discipline and the Other Body: Correction, Corporeality, Colonialism.* Durham, NC: Duke University Press, 2006.

Piot, Charles. *Remotely Global: Village Modernity in West Africa.* Chicago: University of Chicago Press, 1999.

Pratt, Mary Louise. *Imperial Eyes: Travel Writing and Transculturation.* 2nd ed. New York: Routledge, 2008.

Quiquandon. "Histoire de la puissance Mandinque d'après la legende et la tradition." *Bulletin de la Société de géographie commerciale de Bordeaux* 15 (1892): 305–18.

————. *Renseignements sur la situation des colonies: Rapport adressé à M. Le Lieutenant-Colonel Commandant Supérieur de Sudan Française sur la Mission Auprès de Tíeba, Roi Du Kénédougou.* Paris: s.n., 1891.

Rabinow, Paul. *French Modern: Norms and Forms of the Social Environment.* Cambridge, MA: MIT Press, 1989.

Ranger, Terence. "The Invention of Tradition in Colonial Africa." In *The Invention of Tradition*, edited by Eric Hobsbawm and Terence Ranger, 211–62. Cambridge: Cambridge University Press, 1983.

Rawls, John. *A Theory of Justice.* Cambridge, MA: Belknap Press of Harvard University Press, 1971.

Renault, François. *L'abolition de l'esclavage au Sénégal: L'attitude de l'administration française, 1848–1905.* Paris: Société française d'histoire d'outre-mer, P. Geuthner, 1972.

Roberts, Richard L. "The Case of Faama Mademba Sy and the Ambiguities of Legal Jurisdiction in Early Colonial French Soudan." In *Law in Colonial Africa*, edited by Kristin Mann and Richard Roberts, 185–201. Portsmouth, NH: Heinemann, 1991.

————. "The End of Slavery in French Soudan, 1905–1914." In *The End of Slavery in Africa*, edited by Suzanne Miers and Richard Roberts. Madison: University of Wisconsin Press, 1988.

————. *Litigants and Households: African Disputes and Colonial Courts in the French Soudan, 1895–1912.* Portsmouth, NH: Heinemann, 2005.

————. "Representation, Structure, and Agency: Divorce in the French Soudan during the Early Twentieth Century." *Journal of African History* 40, no. 3 (1999): 389–410.

————. "Text and Testimony in the Tribunal de Première Instance, Dakar, during the Early Twentieth Century." *Journal of African History* 31, no. 3 (1990): 447–63.

————. *Two Worlds of Cotton: Colonialism and the Regional Economy in the French Soudan, 1800–1946.* Stanford: Stanford University Press, 1996.

————. *Warriors, Merchants, and Slaves: The State and the Economy in the Middle Niger Valley, 1700–1914.* Stanford: Stanford University Press, 1987.

Roberts, Richard, and Martin Klein. "The Banamba Slave Exodus of 1905 and the Decline of Slavery in the Western Sudan." *Journal of African History* 21, no. 3 (1980): 375–94.

Roberts, Richard, and Kristin Mann. "Law in Colonial Africa." In *Law in Colonial Africa*, edited by Kristin Mann and Richard Roberts, 3–58. Portsmouth, NH: Heinemann, 1991.

Roberts, Richard, and Donald Moore. "Listening for the Silences." *History in Africa* 17 (1990): 319–32.

Robertson, Claire. "Developing Economic Awareness: Changing Perspectives in Studies of African Women, 1976–1985." *Feminist Studies* 13, no. 1 (1987): 97–135.

———. *Sharing the Same Bowl? A Socioeconomic History of Women and Class in Accra, Ghana.* Bloomington: Indiana University Press, 1984.

Robertson, Claire C., and Martin A. Klein, eds. *Women and Slavery in Africa.* Madison: University of Wisconsin Press, 1983.

Robinson, David. *The Holy War of Umar Tal: The Western Sudan in the Mid-Nineteenth Century.* Oxford: Clarendon Press, 1985.

———. *Paths of Accommodation: Muslim Societies and French Colonial Authorities.* Athens: Ohio University Press, 2000.

Rochefort, Florence. "Laïcisation des mœurs et équilibres de genre, le débat sur la capacité civile de la femme mariée (1918–1938)." *Vingtième Siècle. Revue d'histoire*, no. 87 (July–September 2005): 129–41.

Rodet, Marie. "Continuum of Gendered Violence: The Colonial Invention of Desertion as a Customary Criminal Offense, 1900–1949." In *Domestic Violence and the Law in Colonial and Postcolonial Africa*, edited by Emily S. Burrill, Richard L. Roberts, and Elizabeth Thornberry, 74–93. Athens: Ohio University Press, 2009.

———. *Les migrantes ignorées du Haut-Sénégal, 1900–1946.* Paris: Karthala, 2009.

Roume, Ernest. *Justice Indigène: Instructions aux administrateurs sur l'application du Décret de 10 novembre 1903 portant réorganisation du service de la justice dans les colonies relevant du gouvernement général de l'AOF.* Gorée: l'Imprimerie du Gouvernement General, 1905.

Saada, Emmanuelle. "The Empire of Law: Dignity, Prestige, and Domination in the 'Colonial Situation.'" *French Politics, Culture, and Society* 20, no. 2 (2002): 98–120.

Sacré-Coeur, Marie-André du. *La femme indigène en Afrique Noire.* Paris: Payot, 1939.

Salacuse, Jeswald. *An Introduction to Law in French-Speaking Africa.* Charlottesville, VA: Michie, 1969.

Schmidt, Elizabeth. *Mobilizing the Masses: Gender, Ethnicity, and Class in the Nationalist Movement in Guinea, 1939–1958.* Portsmouth, NH: Heinemann, 2005.

———. *Peasants, Traders, and Wives: Shona Women in the History of Zimbabwe, 1870–1939.* Portsmouth, NH: Heinemann, 1992.

Schultz, Dorothea. "Political Factions, Ideological Fictions: The Controversy over Family Law Reform in Democratic Mali." *Islamic Law and Society* 10, no. 1 (2003): 132–64.

Scott, James C. *Seeing Like a State: How Certain Schemes to Improve the Human Condition Have Failed.* New Haven, CT: Yale University Press, 1998.

Scott, Joan. "Gender: A Useful Category of Historical Analysis," *American Historical Review* 91, no. 5 (1986): 1053–75.

Scully, Pamela. "Gender, History, and Human Rights." In *Gender and Culture at the Limit of Rights*, edited by Dorothy Hodgson, 17–31. Philadelphia: University of Pennsylvania Press, 2011.

———. *Liberating the Family?: Gender and British Slave Emancipation in the Rural Western Cape, South Africa, 1823–1853.* Portsmouth, NH: Heinemann, 1997.

————. "Should We Give Up on the State? Feminist Theory, African Gender History, and Transitional Justice." *African Journal on Conflict Resolution* 9, no. 2 (2009): 29–43.

Scully, Pamela, and Diana Paton, eds. *Gender and Slave Emancipation in the Atlantic World*. Durham, NC: Duke University Press, 2005.

Semley, Lorelle D. *Mother Is Gold, Father Is Glass: Gender and Colonialism in a Yoruba Town*. Bloomington: Indiana University Press, 2011.

Shadle, Brett. "Bridewealth and Female Consent: Marriage Disputes in African Courts, Gusiiland, Kenya." *Journal of African History* 44, no. 2 (2003): 241–62.

Shetler, Jan Bender. "Restriction of Women's Networks and the Rise of Domestic Violence in Interior Areas of Colonial Mara Region, Tanzania, 1930s–40s." Unpublished conference paper, African Studies Association Conference, Philadelphia, 30 November 2012.

Silla, Eric. *People Are Not the Same: Leprosy and Identity in Twentieth-Century Mali*. Portsmouth, NH: Heinemann, 1998.

Soares, Benjamin. *Islam and the Prayer Economy: History and Authority in a Malian Town*. Ann Arbor: University of Michigan Press, 2005.

————. "Islam in Mali in the Neoliberal Era." *African Affairs* 105, no. 418 (2005): 77–95.

Spear, Thomas. "Neo-Traditionalism and the Limits of Invention in British Colonial Africa." *Journal of African History* 44, no. 1 (2003): 3–27.

Spivak, Gayatri Chakravorty. "Can the Subaltern Speak?" In *Marxism and the Interpretation of Culture*, edited by Cary Nelson and Lawrence Grossberg, 271–313. Urbana: University of Illinois Press, 1988.

Stanley, Amy Dru. *From Bondage to Contract: Wage Labor, Marriage, and the Market in the Age of Slave Emancipation*. Cambridge: Cambridge University Press, 1998.

Strathern, Marilyn. *The Gender of the Gift: Problems with Women and Problems with Society in Melanesia*. Berkeley: University of California Press, 1990.

Strobel, Margaret. *Muslim Women in Mombasa: 1890–1975*. New Haven, CT: Yale University Press, 1979.

Tashjian, Victoria, and Jean Allman. "Marrying and Marriage on a Shifting Terrain: Reconfigurations of Power and Authority in Early Colonial Asante." In *Women in African Colonial Histories*, edited by Jean Allman, Susan Geiger, and Nakanyike Musisi, 282–304. Bloomington: Indiana University Press, 2002.

Tautain, L. "Le Dioula-dougou et le Sénéfo." *Revue d'ethnographie* 6 (1887): 395–99.

Tauxier, Louis. *Les Etats du Kong (Côte d'Ivoire)*. Paris: Karthala, 2003.

Thomas, Lynn. *Politics of the Womb: Women, Reproduction, and the State in Kenya*. Berkeley: University of California Press, 2003.

Tiona, Ferdinand Ouattara. *La mémoire Sénufo: Bois sacré, éducation, et chefferie*. Paris: Association pour la promotion de la recherche scientifique de l'Afrique noire, 1988.

Toulmin, Camilla. *Cattle, Women, and Wells: Managing Household Survival in the Sahel*. Oxford: Oxford University Press, 1992.

Toungara, Jeanne Maddox. "Changing the Meaning of Marriage: Women and Family Law in Côte d'Ivoire." In *African Feminism: The Politics of Survival in Sub-Saharan Africa*, edited by Gwendolyn Mikell, 53–76. Philadelphia: University of Pennsylvania Press, 1997.

———. "Inventing the African Family: Gender and Family Law Reform in Côte d'Ivoire." *Journal of Social History* 28, no. 1 (1994): 37–61.

Tsing, Anna Loenhaupt. *In the Realm of the Diamond Queen: Marginality in an Out-of-the-Way Place*. Princeton, NJ: Princeton University Press, 1993.

Tucker, Judith. *In the House of the Law: Gender and Islamic Law in Ottoman Turkey and Syria*. Berkeley: University of California Press, 2000.

Van Allen, Judith. "'Sitting on a Man': Colonialism and the Lost Political Institutions of Igbo Women." *Canadian Journal of African Studies* 6, no. 2 (1972): 165–81.

Van Beusekom, Monica M. *Negotiating Development: African Farmers and Colonial Experts at the Office du Niger, 1920–1960*. Portsmouth, NH: Heinemann, 2002.

Vansina, Jan. *How Societies Are Born: Governance in West Central Africa before 1600*. Charlottesville: University of Virginia Press, 2004.

———. *Oral Tradition: A Study in Historical Methodology*. Translated by H. M. Wright. London: James Currey, 1985.

———. *Oral Tradition as History*. Madison: University of Wisconsin Press, 1985.

———. *Paths in the Rainforest: Toward a History of Political Tradition in Equatorial Africa*. Madison: University of Wisconsin Press, 1990.

Vaughan, Megan. "Which Family? Problems in the Reconstruction of the History of the Family as an Economic and Cultural Unit." *Journal of African History* 24, no. 2 (1983): 275–83.

Vendeix, Marie-Joseph. "Nouvel essai de monographie du pays Senoufo." *Bulletin du Comité d'études historiques et scientifiques de l'Afrique occidentale française* 17 (1934): 578–652.

Vogl, Martin. "Mali Women's Rights Bill Blocked." http://news.bbc.co.uk/2/hi/8223736.stm.

Vydrine, Valentin. "Who Speaks 'Mandekan'?: A Note on Current Use of Mande Ethnonyms and Linguonyms." *Mande Studies Newsletter* 29 (Winter 1995–96): 6–9.

Warms, Richard. "Continuity and Change in Patterns of Trade in Southern Mali." PhD diss., Syracuse University, 1987.

White, Deborah Gray. *Ar'n't I A Woman? Female Slaves in the Plantation South*. New York: W. W. Norton, 1985.

White, Luise. *The Comforts of Home: Prostitution in Colonial Nairobi*. Chicago: University of Chicago Press, 1990.

White, Luise, Stephan F. Miescher, and David William Cohen, eds. *African Words, African Voices: Critical Practices in Oral History*. Bloomington: Indiana University Press, 2001.

Wilder, Gary. *The French Imperial Nation-State: Negritude and Colonial Humanism between the Two World Wars*. Chicago: University of Chicago Press, 2005.

———. *H-France Forum* 1, 3 (2006).

Wright, Gwendolyn. *The Politics of Design in French Colonial Urbanism*. Chicago: University of Chicago Press, 1991.

Wright, Marcia. *Strategies of Slaves and Women: Life Stories from East/Central Africa*. New York: Lilian Barber, 1993.

Zunz, Olivier, ed. *Reliving the Past: The Worlds of Social History*. Chapel Hill: University of North Carolina Press, 1985.

Index

marriage certificates: and abandonment, 171–75; and bridewealth, 74, 154, 155–56, 159; and child custody, 22, 156; false, 159–63

marriage legibility project, 4, 108, 157–58, 181; and consent, 182–83; increased participation in, 185; and structural violence, 10–11. *See also* consent in marriage

marriage reform: gender justice in, 5, 12–13, 108, 180, 181, 184; state enforcement, 158; and women's rights, 123–26. *See also* Jacquinot Decree (1951); Mandel Decree (1939)

Marty, Paul, 85, 128, 202n82

maternalism and violence, 10

matrilineage, 28, 36–37, 81, 87–89, 112–14, 117, 118–19, 180–81

McKittrick, Meredith, 158

migration. *See under* labor obligations

military conscription, 80, 81, 83, 95–96, 108, 114, 119

Minianka people, 36

Ministry of the Colonies (France), 58, 108

mise en garantie practice, 126

mise en valeur agenda, 72, 96, 108

mission civilisatrice. See civilizing mission

Mohammed, Sidi, 88, 89

"Monagraphie du Sikasso," 50

Morrison (French captain), 47

Mory, 69

M'Pegnesso/M'Pegnegue, 39–40

Muslim identity, 36, 39–40, 60–61, 79–80, 107, 128, 147

mythhistories, 27–30, 32–33

Nampaya, 176

Napoleonic Code (France, 1804), 3

National Archives of Mali (ANM), 17, 91

National Assembly (Mali), 1

National Union of Muslim Women's Associations, 1

native customary law practices, 9, 20, 51; in civilizing mission, 49, 50, 77; colonial court system on, 59–70, 130–31; court testimony, 140–42; definition vs. application in, 64–65; formation of native justice, 52; individual rights,

102–4, 176; vs. Islamic law, 61, 80; patriarchal, 82, 85–86, 104, 164; reform in, 83–99, 130; tribunal composition, 141–42

natural law, 128–30, 132

N'Diaye, Fanta, 148–51

N'Diaye, Oumar, 148–51

Niger River as lifeline, 14

Nyerere, Julius, 4, 157

obligations. *See* community obligations; gendered obligations; labor obligations

Oeil de Kénédougou, L' (journal), 13–14

Offen, Karen, 123

Office du Niger project, 119, 157

oral traditions, 9, 18; on bridewealth, 61; on end of slavery, 77; Kenedugu, 47–48, 50; Mande, 192n53; M'Pegnegue, 38–43; Senufo, 36, 38, 44, 109, 112–13

Osborn, Emily, 27, 189n21

Outre Mer (journal), 124

Parti Progressiste Soudanais (PSP), 157, 169

Pateman, Carole, 183

paternalism, 6, 10, 59, 73, 84

patriarchy: challenges to, 169, 181; local authority, 12, 47–52, 72–73, 80, 81, 84–87, 89–91, 94–99, 102–5, 152, 180; patriarchal bargain, 137, 142–43, 146, 181–82; rights of, 59; and violence, 135

pawning, 108, 120–27, 154–55

Person, Yves, 38

Personal Status and Family Code (Mali, 2009), 1

Peterson, Brian, 195n57

politique des races, 83–84, 90, 92, 94, 104, 180

polygyny, 32, 73–74, 88, 124, 144, 154

Ponty, William: on African family, 80–81; on canton chiefs, 82–83, 84, 104; colonial development programs, 96–97; on conscription, 95–96; marriage law reform, 180; native court reform, 83–85, 92; on patriarchal authority, 82, 84–85, 90, 103–4; *politique des races*, 83–84, 90, 92, 94, 104, 180

poro, 28